Psychosocial Spaces

Psychosocial Spaces

VERBAL AND
VISUAL READINGS
OF BRITISH CULTURE
1750–1820

Steven J. Gores

WAYNE STATE UNIVERSITY PRESS
DETROIT

Copyright © 2000 by Wayne State University Press,
Detroit, Michigan 48201. All rights are reserved.
No part of this book may be reproduced without formal permission.
Manufactured in the United States of America.
04 03 02 01 00   5 4 3 2 1

Library of Congress Cataloging-in-Publication Data

Gores, Steven J.
Psychosocial spaces : verbal and visual readings of British culture, 1750–1820 / Steven J. Gores.
p.   cm.
Includes bibliographical references and index.
ISBN 0-8143-2663-3 (alk. paper)
1. English fiction—18th century—History and criticism. 2. Social psychology and literature—Great Britain—History—18th century.   3. Social psychology and literature—Great Britain—History—19th century.   4. English fiction—19th century—History and criticism.   5. Great Britain—Social life and customs—18th century.   6. Great Britain—Social life and customs—19th century.   7. Identity (Psychology) in literature.   8. Subjectivity in literature.   9. Social psychology in art   10. Self in literature.   11. Art, British.   I. Title.
PR858.S615G67   2000
823'.609353—dc21   99-41382

An early version of chapter 4, "Erotic Space," was previously published. Reprinted by permission of *SEL Studies in English Literature 1500–1900* 37, 3 (Summer 1997).

To Paige,
Hal,
Jasper,
Hugh, and Simon

Contents

List of Illustrations
9

Acknowledgments
11

Introduction
13

1. The Historical Context:
Subjectivity and Circulation in
Eighteenth-Century England
23

2. Circulation and Specularity in Social Space
65

3. The Ruin as Object of Desire:
The Recess, Visual Art, and Historical Space
95

4. Erotic Space:
Amelia and the Miniature
141

CONTENTS

Afterword
175

Notes
179

Works Cited
207

Index
221

List of Illustrations

1. *Roslin Castle, Midlothian,* Paul Sandby   39
2. *The Macaroni Printshop* (1772), E. Topham   46
3. *Very Slippy-Weather* (1808), James Gillray   47
4. *A View of the Rotunda House and Gardens at Ranelagh,* Nathaniel Parr after Antonio Canaletto   52
5. *Vauxhall Gardens,* Thomas Rowlandson   55
6. *The Inside of the Elegant Music Room in Vauxhall Gardens,* H. Roberts after Samuel Wale   57
7. *Royal Crescent, Bath*   74
8. *An Inside View of the Rotundo in Ranelagh Gardens,* Nathaniel Parr after Antonio Canaletto   77
9. *The City of Bath*   83
10. *Plan of the Assembly Rooms*   86
11. *Temple of Venus, Rome,* William Pars   105
12. *The Grotto of Posilippo,* Francis Towne   106
13. *The Warwick Vase, Warwick Castle*   112
14. *The Bank of England in Ruins,* Joseph Gandy   116
15. *The Grande Galerie of the Louvre in Ruins—a Fantasy,* Hubert Robert   117
16. *Hadleigh Castle* (1829), John Constable   119
17. *The Chapel of the Greyfriars Monastery,* Michael Angelo Rooker   120

18. *West End of Netley Abbey,* Thomas Walmsley   121
19. Plan of the Cathedral of Rouen   125
20. Frontispiece to Sophia Lee's *The Recess* (1783–85)   130
21. *Sir Sampson Gideon and an unidentified companion* (1767), Pompeo Girolamo Batoni   149
22. *Sir Edward Dering,* Pompeo Girolamo Batoni   150
23. *Georgiana, Duchess of Devonshire,* Richard Cosway   152
24. *Georgiana, Duchess of Devonshire,* Richard Cosway   153
25. *Miniature of a Lady's Eye Set in a Brooch,* Anonymous   154
26. Portrait miniature back: *Woman in a White Dress* (ca. 1790), Thomas Hull   156
27. Portrait miniature back: *Mrs. H.* (ca. 1790), George Place   157
28. Portrait miniature back: *P. P.* (1790), Richard Cosway   158
29. "Prison Scene from *Amelia,*" Harrison ed. of *The Novelist's Magazine* (1780)   160
30. *An Academy by Lamplight* (ca. 1768–69), Joseph Wright of Derby   168
31. *Strolling Actresses Dressing in a Barn,* William Hogarth   170

Acknowledgments

This book has been profoundly shaped by many hands other than my own. I would like to thank my first readers, Eric Rothstein and John O. Lyons, whose insightfulness and frankness forced me to rethink many ideas and assumptions. Thanks also go to the Northern Kentucky University Writing Group, especially to Bob Wallace and to my wife, Paige Byam, who read large portions of the manuscript at various stages in its revision.

Institutional support for this project has been extensive. My thanks in this regard go first to the Northern Kentucky University Faculty, who granted me a fellowship to complete initial revisions on this manuscript. Among the many individuals in the university community who have supported my work I am especially grateful to Paul Reichardt, Rogers Redding, Cliff Shisler, Sharon Taylor, and Beth Merten.

I would also like to thank the readers and my editors, Arthur Evans, Janet Witalec, and Sandra Judd, whose wisdom and advice have been invaluable in helping me prepare my final text.

Finally, I owe a great debt of gratitude to my family, without whose understanding and input I could not have succeeded.

Introduction

This study explores some of the options that late eighteenth- and early nineteenth-century Britons had in attempting to construct an identity. My choice of historical "frame" for this study is prompted by its particular ability to demonstrate the necessity of constructing individual identity, something I will explain further in the following. Rather than focusing on contemporary eighteenth-century philosophical investigations of subjectivity, which would emphasize learned, abstract structures of selfhood, I have chosen to study practical modes of establishing subjectivity that were provided through two popular media: visual representations and novels. Together, the literary and visual arts during this time constituted forms of emergent mass media that created cultural spaces; in turn, these cultural spaces were used as vehicles for both cultural and individual self-representations.

I have organized each of the three analytical chapters (2, 3, and 4) around a representative mode or psychosocial "space" in which an eighteenth-century subject could choose to situate him- or herself, thus establishing a practical, lived sense of identity. The notion of *space* here refers to a number of both physical and abstract phenomena. On the most physical level, space designates the concrete materiality of books, canvases, ivory miniatures, buildings, and other aesthetic objects. However, space may also denote a kind of experience that these objects provide: for example, the microcosmic world of a novel, the vision of place created by a painting, or the shape of living space created through domestic architecture. Finally, space may describe the psychosocial realm in which the individual situates him- or herself in relation to culture and specific communities within it. Psychosocial space is manifold and is constructed imaginatively by each individual, both consciously and unconsciously. The representative spaces dealt with here—the social, the historical, and the erotic (the realm of desire)—correspond roughly to the temporal categories of present, past, and future.

In the sense that these spaces are positional and internalizable for individual subjects within culture, they are part of "ideology" as it is described by John B. Thompson: "a practical consciousness rooted in social collectivities and animated by secular systems of belief."[1] This form of ideology operates on a popular level, in the media of mass communication and the public sphere that were activated in the second half of the eighteenth century. Chapter 1 of this study attempts to give a résumé of what Thompson calls the "mass production and mass distribution of symbolic goods."[2] The spaces constructed out of the "symbolic goods" made available by the visual/verbal complex were enlisted not only in the disciplinary structure of society, but also in the individual subject's personal, practical construction of identity.

As my perspective in this project is essentially archaeological, I feel the need to confess, first of all, my uneasiness with confident assertions of historical "truth" as the basis for literary arguments and to announce my sympathy with those who have sought to revise critical assumptions about history. At the root of the modern critique of traditional historical practice is Jacques Lacan's formulation of history as an inaccessible "real" that is external to all human efforts to conceptualize it. Lacan postulated the inaccessibility of history in accord with his model of the self, in which subjectivity is caught up in "imaginary" and/or "symbolic" relations to culture. Thus, no subject can write a detached, objective history; the structure of the self necessarily produces historical narratives that are imbricated in that self's culture, reflecting its biases and priorities concerning what is judged to be important enough to be considered "history."[3]

To a certain extent, the delineation of psychosocial spaces that I am attempting here grows out of my uneasiness with the assumptions of traditional historical practice and my interest in the tendency of recent social historians and anthropologists such as Michel Foucault, E. P. Thompson, Pierre Bourdieu, and Lawrence Stone to "spatialize" history.

Rather than presenting history as a linear chain of cause-and-effect events, they "thicken" it by including popular or social phenomena. This spatialization occurs, for example, in Bourdieu's *La Noblesse d'état,* where he develops the idea of a "field of power," in which all members are both dominated and dominators. Within this field, it is not populations that matter, but rather positions, since one individual can occupy the most powerful position. What is important is the system of relations between positions, and the fact that the distribution of power is constantly shifting. This vision of culture and history as a system, field, or network in which power circulates replaces the traditional, vertical metaphors for socioeconomic reality—the hierarchy of upper, middle, and lower classes, the superstructure, the infrastructure, and so on—in which power is imposed from above.[4] For the individual, this revised notion of power implies that there is far more latitude and freedom available in the processes of self-creation.

Moreover, not only do social historians like Thompson and Bourdieu spatialize culture and history as "equilibrium," field, system, and so on, they also recognize more than one form of power and reject the notion that any class could effectively monopolize all forms of domination. For Bourdieu, this means that power can be symbolic, social, or financial; for Thompson, this means that there is a semicoherent popular culture that acts as a counterpoise to polite culture. By acknowledging a multiplicity of forms of power, or "cultural capital," as Bourdieu calls it, social history assumes that causality in history cannot be linear and direct. Instead, it is a complex, spatial phenomenon, the result of a number of different factors that operate as a "field" of influence.

Within this field, individual acts constitute the realm of "practice." Reacting against an anthropological/sociological context that was dominated by the structuralist approach of Claude Lévi-Strauss, Bourdieu argues that "practice"—the everyday manipulation of cultural rules and customs—is more important than the overarching structure of cultural organization: "The rule is never . . . more than a second-best intended to make good the occasional misfirings of the collective enterprise of inculcation tending to produce habitus that are capable of generating practices regulated without express regulation or any institutionalized call to order."[5] For historical and cultural analysis, the implication is that a more accurate assessment of the past may be attained by displacing the broad structures and patterns that historians have so long sought in order to organize history into a causal narrative sequence. Foucault's later writings—including *Discipline and Punish* and *The History of Sexuality*—

demonstrate a sophisticated, practice-oriented revision of traditional historical assumptions. For instance, in tracing the birth of the prison, Foucault argues that the British laws that codified prison reform reflect not the beginning of reform, but rather its normalization and, perhaps, morbidity. In other words, practice—reform, in this case—always precedes structure—in this case, the entry of reform into the penal code. Therefore, Foucault suggests that the traditional importance history has granted to dates of treaties, laws, wars, and so on, is misplaced: instead of recording momentous events that provoked change, traditional history pays homage to chronological "dead spots," in which the real workings of practice are hidden by the illusion of structure and order.[6]

These innovations in social historical theory—the concept of culture as a space or field of circulating power relations, the recognition of the multiplicity of forms that power or "cultural capital" may take, and the emphasis on microscopic practice over macroscopic structure—suggest the need to reexamine assumptions about the ways in which individuals have interacted with the field of verbal and visual representations that has come to be known as "mass media." In late-eighteenth-century Britain, this field was just emerging.

However, for centuries before—and to this day—conjunctions of and connections between verbal and visual art forms had been discussed not as representational or communications media, but as "sister arts." Thus, drawing together these two fields of representation—the literary and visual arts—may be seen, from this point of view, as constituting another entry in the long tradition of interart dialogue that includes theoretical discussions of the "sister arts," ekphrastic poetry, illustration, and "spatial" theories of literature.[7] The field of the sister arts is perhaps the oldest form of interdisciplinary study in Western culture, as Rensselaer Lee has pointed out in his *Ut Pictura Poesis*. While Lee discusses how the idea of the sister arts was passed down from Aristotle, Plato, and Horace to the Renaissance humanists, Jean Hagstrum's *The Sister Arts* traces this theory as it developed more specifically in the eighteenth century. Rather than attempting to emulate either of these scholars in tracing the history of the sister arts as a concept, my purpose here is to recast the sister arts as representational media that were available to late-eighteenth-century and early-nineteenth-century Britons.

Examining why so much has been written about these "sisters"—literature and the visual arts—is a necessary prelude to achieving this goal, especially since, as Hagstrum has shown, sister arts theory and criticism were particularly strong during the eighteenth century, and this has understandably colored modern critical approaches to the visual and verbal productions of this historical field. Ironically, the tradition of sister arts writing has been shaped by the assumption that the critic must side with one art or the other in order to maintain an objective perspective on the (supposedly) limited formal contacts between literature and the visual arts. Thus Leonardo da Vinci's polemical attempt to raise painting to superiority over literature; thus Hagstrum's more subtle prioritizing of literature in narrowing his field to "literary pictorialism" as "a phenomenon that often *did* bear direct relation to particular paintings and particular schools of painting but that does not necessarily bear those relations."[8] Counter to this tradition of sister arts criticism, my position is that too much has been made of the differences between the arts and of their supposed rivalry. Seen from the perspective of the reader or viewer, literature and the visual arts are simply two forms of representation whose content is far more important than their formal dimensions.[9] Modern delineators of the tradition of the sister arts argue that they are simply reporting historical distinctions between the arts that were made by artists and theoreticians of the Renaissance and eighteenth century, and with respect to theoretical discourse their approach is justified; however, they neglect to historicize these distinctions by comparing them to practice and by questioning the cultural value of maintaining the perception of division and hierarchy within the field of the representational arts.

Moreover, sister arts scholars themselves have perpetuated divisions and hierarchy among the arts by reinscribing them as objective "truths" when in fact the boundaries between the arts and attempts to place them within a hierarchy are each subjective and ideologically motivated. A fear of "Going Too Far with the Sister Arts"—the title of W. J. T. Mitchell's analysis of sister arts writing—has resulted in critical anxiety about maintaining "proper" boundaries between the arts. In other words, there is a critical imperative to avoid the "promiscuity" of leveling differences between visual and verbal sign systems. On the one hand, the implicit analogy between the breaking of artistic boundaries and sexual promiscuity is one that is embedded in the very commonplace term "sister arts," which suggests that (male) scholars and artists must maintain deference to the female arts they court, and that, in all propriety, they must not allow themselves to partake of the charms of more than one of the sisters. On the other hand, the division between visual and verbal arts has to do with another, different gender distinction: because the visual arts are associated with space and objectified spectacle, they are traditionally seen as "female"; in contrast, literature is traditionally seen as "male."[10]

INTRODUCTION

The degree to which the sister arts tradition is connected to gender codes, which are of major importance in determining power relations between the sexes, illustrates how the "sister" arts is an ideological field, not an ahistorical, objective "fact."[11] As such, disposing of the traditional, restrictive sister arts concept, with its stress on boundaries between various forms of representation, may open up a history of artistic and representational practice that has been masked by ideological discourse.

Instead of considering the visual and verbal sister arts from the point of view of eighteenth-century theorists, artists, and writers, I want to approach them from the point of view of the viewer or reader, who would have experienced them as media forms rather than critical abstractions. Seen from this perspective, the differences in form and appropriate function of the "sister arts" are relatively unimportant when compared to their potentially common effects on the readers and viewers that they share. In practice, eighteenth-century audiences could treat the arts as various representational "discourses" among which difference was largely a matter of translation. By "discourse," I mean a group of signs—whether aural, textual, visual, or the like—that are united by a certain social practice and that tend to produce a culturally approved meaning. "Discourse" can be literal and readily quantifiable, as in the specific linguistic field of a novel, or it can be more figural and culturally dispersed, as in the discourse of the modern state, which is composed of leaks to the press, TV images, speeches, the practice of governmental agencies, and so on.[12]

I will assume both of these complementary definitions, which can be associated with, respectively, the work of Mikhail Bakhtin and Michel Foucault. Indeed, although the Bakhtinian and Foucauldian notions of discourse may initially seem to be very different, with the former rooted in verbal or linguistic practice and the latter invested in a visual or spatial approach to total cultural structure, they share a common ground in their emphasis on the plural, dynamic quality of discursive systems. This is evident in Bakhtin's heteroglossia—the tendency of the text to record a network of varied "voices" that are in contention and work against the novel's attempt to systematize and unify its language and meaning—and in Foucault's description of discourse as a "system of dispersion."[13] Thus, both Foucault and Bakhtin assume that, rather than being rigid, unified structures, discourses are loose orders that are in dialogue with each other, and, as a result, are in constant flux. Applying the concept of discourse to the field of eighteenth-century verbal and visual arts helps to remove the ideological biases of "sister arts" criticism against interart similarities and against the perspective of the reader or viewer while contextualizing the basics: each art is a discourse unto itself, but at the same time is part of the larger discourse of "art" and the cultural function of that entity in culture. Thus the discourse of "art" or representation can be viewed simultaneously as a communicative practice and as a spatial field in which a variety of representational forms are intertextually linked in a network of interrelationships.

This theoretical discussion provides the framework for a macroscopic, spatial analysis of culture that is necessary in order to reveal how, on a microscopic level, the spatio-visual is a means for individual subjects to achieve access to cultural representations. For my purpose—reclaiming the spatio-visual both as a field of cultural investigation and as a conduit to external reality for the subject—Jacques Lacan's definitions of the gaze and vision are useful because they allow for resistance to domination; they do not assume any position of subjectivity to be automatically dominant because of gender or social class; and because, as a result, they seem to rely on a model of culture in which power is circulating and shifting rather than fixed.[14] A comparison between feminist and Lacanian definitions of the gaze indicates how different the two approaches are: whereas for feminist critics the gaze is an instrument of male power (the Same), for Lacan it is what disturbs the subject by eluding vision and pointing to something outside the subject's normal "way of seeing" (the Other). In this way, for Lacan, "the gaze is that underside of consciousness" to which the subject would like to remain blind.[15] In contrast, "vision" or "the eye" signify conventional visual consciousness, which the subject creates by seizing upon a set of representations of the external world and normalizing them as "reality." The discrepancy or "scandal" between vision and the gaze, Lacan maintains, results in the "scopic drive," which consists of the subject's desire to conquer this threat to the integrity of his or her consciousness.[16] For Lacan, then, the spatio-visual is a field in which power is quite tentative in that the subject's sense of identity depends upon conventional ways of seeing, which are constantly vulnerable to disruption by the gaze.

The Lacanian view of the relation between the subject and the visual serves as one of the foundations for my inquiry into the process of constructing subjectivity in the late eighteenth and early nineteenth centuries. I assume, like Lacan and like a host of eighteenth-century scholars, that individual identity and sense of self *does* need to be constructed. The process of self-construction in the late eighteenth and early nineteenth centuries was both an opportunity and a necessity for an increasing number of individuals. During this period, the previously centralized cultural control of identity and meaning production was undermined by a decentralized flow of representation, a phenomenon reflected in particular by the destabilization of individual identity, the splintering of aesthetics from moral ideals, and the increase in all kinds of cultural circulation: money, social rank, travel, images, the printed word, and so on. As literacy and access to visual art increased, representational space was democratized, giving voice not only to traditional, aristocratic values, but also to those deemed more popular. Furthermore, not only were new voices heard, but the breadth of the public exposed to these voices in the print and visual media was greatly expanded. This is the topic of chapter 1.

Each of the three representative psychosocial "spaces" that I have selected—social space, historical space, and erotic space—is a normalized, conventional way of seeing in which an individual subject may choose to construct his or her sense of identity. These spaces overlap and intersect in the novelistic and visual representations on which I focus: no representation is a pure example of the social, historical, or erotic alone. Similarly, for most subjects, the spaces are intertwined in the process of constructing identity. In fact, unidimensional subjects—those who are excessively dependent on one space or another for their sense of identity—are widely ridiculed in novels, plays, and the visual arts; they become objects of satire or are labeled as grotesques.

The ways in which individuals reflect their commitments to social, historical, or erotic identities may be described within the broad concept of theatricality. Like a theatrical performer, an individual will visualize him- or herself in a certain role provided by a representational space. My work here has much in common with that of the sociologist Erving Goffman, who has suggested that all social interactions may be described as theatrical performances: "a 'performance' may be defined as all the activity of a given participant on a given occasion which serves to influence in any way any of the other participants. . . . we may refer to those who contribute the other performances as the audience, observers, or co-participants."[17] Goffman's emphasis on the observers or the audience makes it clear that the "participant's" or individual's self-visualization is not the only visual element in the construction of identity: for identity to be solidified, this internal self-visualization must be projected through display and exhibition of appropriate signs, recognized by the audience, and reflected back to the individual. Moreover, Goffman's sociological analysis reinforces my contention that identity is constructed out of cultural representations of selfhood: "the pre-established pattern of action which is unfolded during a performance and which may be presented or

Introduction

played through on other occasions may be called a 'part' or 'routine.' "[18] Elsewhere, Goffman refers to these patterns and roles as a "frame"; although he is less concerned with the internal, psychological ramifications of the frame than with external behavior, I take this term to be a rough synonym for my representational "spaces."[19]

The concept of theatricality in the subject's efforts to construct identity through these spaces also furthers the sense of tentativeness and relative instability, or perhaps fluidity, in these efforts. Goffman's theory implies that identity is socially and visually staged within a certain "frame" of codified roles, covering a discrepancy between the actor or subject and the role that he or she projects. However, I do not see this discrepancy or "scandal" as debilitating: actor-subjects are not determined by these roles unless they are unaware of them, and those who are aware may be capable of playing with them. In other words, the necessity of manipulating one's self-image is potentially both a crisis and an opportunity, both a confining "frame" and a freeing "space." It indicates the necessary resourcefulness of the subject in using a variety of "spaces" to anchor his or her sense of identity, and in continually modifying his or her way of seeing. Finally, in terms of cultural analysis, it points to the importance of accessibility to a variety of representations of selfhood in determining the subject's freedom of self-definition, as well as the degree to which a culture may be perceived as either dynamic or static.

I have already indicated that chapter 1 explores the historical conditions associated with the rise of mass media; chapters 2 to 4 offer verbal and visual readings of three cultural spaces: the social, the historical, and the erotic. Chapter 2 explores social space, the space of the present. Examining Tobias Smollett's *Humphry Clinker* (1771), Jane Austen's *Persuasion* (1818), and visual evidence of the social settings they contain, including the London pleasure gardens of Ranelagh and Vauxhall and the city of Bath, this chapter describes an expansion of the social realm and corresponding complications in asserting identity and rank. In it, I contend that social space was shaped not only by economic changes, but also by the architectural articulation of space in social sites and the codification of rules of etiquette.

Chapter 3 treats Sophia Lee's gothic/historical novel *The Recess* (1783–85) and the late-eighteenth-century British fascination with ruins as evidence of probings into the historical space, or the past. The explosion of interest in native ruins is explored through an analysis of selected picturesque prints and sketches, which then leads to several hypotheses on the desires—both cultural and individual—that coalesced in the ruin image. Using the construction of artificial ruins (follies) as further evidence of this fascination, this chapter emphasizes the Catholic, monastic ruin as the site of a desire to repress discontinuity and alterity in the past, and to construct a stable identity based on genealogy.

Chapter 4 discusses erotic space, the space of deferral and the future. Glancing at the use of the miniature portrait in Mary Shelley's *Frankenstein* (1816) as an example, this chapter discusses how the miniature or silhouette was used to fetishize and objectify erotic ties. As a relatively affordable visual form, the portrait miniature played an important role in representing the erotic interests of the same class of citizens who were novel readers. The miniaturization of erotic space is traced further in a study of Henry Fielding's *Amelia* (1751), in which Captain Booth's relations with Amelia exemplify erotic deferral to the extent that she becomes a mere pendant to the primary, male action of the novel, even though she is the title character. The circumscribing or miniaturization of Amelia herself is represented not only through the appearance of her portrait miniature near both the beginning and ending of the novel, but also through the narrative use of visual techniques like the *tableau vivant* and the circle of expression. In essence, this chapter shows how the miniature was used, in narrative and visual forms, to supply an image of the beloved "other" to be used as a secure basis for the construction of individual identity.

Finally, a brief afterword draws together the three psychosocial spaces that I have considered, concluding that, despite the presence of disciplinary structures in each "space," they were at least potentially liberating for individual subjects. The connection that I have delineated between the increased availability of psychosocial means of establishing identity and the rise of visual and print media suggests that the influence of the psychosocial on the formation of our impressions of the self may only have grown more important and complex with the continued expansion of mass communication media in the nineteenth and twentieth centuries.

1
The Historical Context

Subjectivity and
Circulation in
Eighteenth-Century
England

British culture of the late eighteenth and early nineteenth centuries offers a particular, though not unique, avenue toward demonstrating the necessity of constructing identity through psychosocial means.[1] This is true first of all because of challenges to the existing cultural order in terms of increased social tensions, the multiplication of new ideologies, and socioeconomic change. Structures of increasing circulation that were associated with these challenges effectively decentered and disrupted traditional means of fixing individual subjects' identities. In my attempts to describe the disruption of cultural stability and the corresponding structures of circulation that arose from it, I will specify the types of socioeconomic subjects who were affected most by cultural circulation. I will also suggest why this specific period is particularly revealing of both circulative and identity-solidifying processes.[2]

One can extend to the end of the eighteenth century Michael McKeon's assertion that "the reigning analysis of early eighteenth-century social structure presents a disarmingly settled picture," as the rest of the century has also been caricatured as a placid period of unequaled social stability and prosperity.[3] However, more recent historians have pointed to the political, economic, and social instability indicated in the second half of the eighteenth century by the Wilkes affair, the Gordon riots, and the controversy surrounding the American and French Revolutions. H. T. Dickinson notes, for example, that

> [h]istorians concerned with political structure and action at the national level have generally . . . recognized a period from the 1760s to the 1790s when political agents became increasingly polarized between those who wished to reform the political and social order, sometimes quite radically, and those who were determined to defend the *status quo*.[4]

If the stability of Hanoverian England was put into question on the level of political discourse by "political agents" on both sides, however, it was also imperiled by uproar from the lower ranks:

> The 1749 Strand riots marked a turning point in the history of popular disturbance in the eighteenth century. The combination of social stop-go between warfare and painful peacetime readjustment plus the quickening pace of social change meant that rioting now became more frequent, more enduring in its peaks and more violent. . . . [In the 1760s,] agitation by weavers fearful of foreign competition coalesced with provincial food riots. Soon coalheavers, sailors, and others were locked in conflict with their employers. By the end of the decade English society was in turmoil.[5]

In view of the polarizations that existed in the eighteenth-century social order, it is no wonder that social categories first became codified as "class" differences at this time, although the word "did not entertain the notion of class conflict, at any rate in its modern sense."[6]

These socioeconomic and political changes clearly illustrate the ways in which British culture was rapidly becoming fractured by social tensions, but there are also indications that one of the dominant characteristics of British culture at this time was "circulation." This included a rapidly enlarged money supply and an increase in what economists call *money velocity*—receiving and spending—which accompanied a blurring of social rank; an increase in movement of people and goods, both within England, on new turnpikes and canals, and to and from other parts of the world; an increase in the number of new inventions; and a proliferation of printed images and written materials.[7] Circulation thus entailed a decentered or multicentered flow of people, things, and representations that eroded any single-normed control of identity and meaning production—such as traditional notions of rank or class—while it expanded the range of cultural materials available to individuals.

The dispersal or decentralization of power reflected in the erosion of rank distinctions, the fracturing of English society into new class solidarities, and the relative successes of challenges to the social order is described theoretically in Michel Foucault's notion of a "micro-physics of power." In contrast to conventional Marxist social analysis, in which power is imposed hierarchically, from top to bottom, Foucault argues that "power is exercised rather than possessed; it is not the 'privilege,' acquired or preserved, of the dominant class, but the overall effect of its strategic positions—an effect that is manifested and sometimes extended by the position of those who are dominated."[8] By claiming that "power is exercised rather than possessed," Foucault suggests that it circulates from position to position within a social structure, and cannot be captured and retained. He repeatedly denies that power stems from a centralized source: "in spite of the coherence of its results, it is generally no more than a multiform instrumentation . . . [that] cannot be localized in a particular type of institution or state apparatus."[9] Because power is "multiform," fragmented, and dispersed throughout culture rather than centrally held by a specific class or institution, the efforts of cultural critics to localize it are fruitless. The general form of the "instrumentation" that Foucault delineates is discipline—the observation and regulation of minute, discrete elements of behavior, which Foucault finds operative in the military, educational, hospital, and penal systems, beginning in the late eighteenth century.

However, I would disagree with Foucault's insistence that the system of circulative, disciplinary power he describes is exclusively repressive in its effects.[10] He argues that the dispersal and anonymization of power led to an unwitting internalization of disciplinary structures by the dominated as well as the dominant in society; the subtlety of this form of power resulted in the amplification of repressive force simultaneously with the illusion of individual freedom.

Foucault's emphasis on the repressive force of social power stems from his reliance on a deterministic model of individual subjectivity. While Foucault diverges considerably from Marxist assumptions about how power is exerted, he still envisions the subject in modern, capitalist society as being dominated by forces that are either directly or indirectly economic: the system of discipline that he describes is the result of the drive for greater efficiency in human use of time and space so as to maximize cultural (re)production. Similarly, in conventional Marxist analysis, the subject is identified primarily according to a single norm—his or her economic circumstances, or class status. This unidimensional subject can be associated with a linear vision of history and with a hierarchical conception of power relations within society, both of which serve as the grounds of the type of political history that has spawned the "Neoclassic norm." Such a history takes as its object the "public sphere," which, as Jürgen Habermas has pointed out, disintegrates "when considered within the boundaries of a particular social-scientific discipline," illustrating the need for an approach broader than either politics or economics alone.[11]

What I propose here instead is an approach that restores the multiplicitous identity of the subject by investigating other forms of what Pierre Bourdieu calls "cultural capital."[12] Such an approach assumes that class distinctions are not determined by a single factor like wealth or birth, but rather by the convergence and forging together of a number of factors, in which the individual subject has a degree of freedom. By thus spatializing the basis of power, this approach encourages a view of history as a network or text ("tissu") of diverse, interdisciplinary connections. Within this spatial field of power, the individual shifts and circulates, rather than remaining fixed in relation to a central authority.

The multiplication, and therefore the widespread dispersion and circulation, of cultural capital should complicate even the picture of elite eighteenth-century society drawn by historians who rely on traditional notions of status. Lawrence Stone, for example, who has consistently argued for a history of practice and of popular culture, claims in *An Open Elite? England 1540–1880,* co-authored by Jeanne C. Fawtier Stone, that social mobility into the elite class was extremely limited during the eighteenth century.[13] By their focus on the elite and by their use of family longevity as landholders as a criterion for "true" entry into the political elite, however, the Stones bias their conclusions toward lineal power and against more circulative and fluctuating power.

In contrast, in *Family Fortunes: Men and Women of the English Middle Class, 1780–1850,* Leonore Davidoff and Catherine Hall argue that landholding and lineal, dynastic succession are inadequate measures of family success for those outside of the elite. Instead, they claim that the middle classes preferred "the increasing liquidity of capital freed from land," so that wealth could be divided among inheritors rather than concentrated in a single successor.[14] It was here, on the margins of the elite class and in the middle classes, that "the centrifugal effects of individualistic multiplication of wealth threatened individual order" by enabling social mobility.[15] In contrast to the value placed on the concentration of tangible, landed capital by the Stones' elite, the mobile segments of society clearly valued distribution or circulation of a more abstract form of capital—money—that is but one of the intangibles that make up cultural capital.

Although the Stones' seeming embrace of the elite perspective limits the usefulness of their study for cultural historians, the evidence that they present concerning name changes and marriages with heiresses is quite useful in documenting the continuing instability of the elite in the late eighteenth century. This instability was apparently more severe in the late seventeenth and early eighteenth centuries, due to a demographic crisis that resulted in a lack of male heirs, but it is also apparent through the end of the century. To conceal indirect patterns of descent, name changes were used to "perpetuate through surrogate heirs the impression of unbroken descent in the male line. The appearance of patrilineal descent was thus preserved by the adoption of fictive kin."[16] The Stones note that the incidence of name changes rose from 5 percent of the owners studied in the early eighteenth century to 10 percent from 1760 onward.[17] Moreover, their overall analysis of inheritance patterns shows that the percentage of indirect inheritances was much higher throughout the eighteenth century—about 40 percent—than that of the preceding century—about 20 percent. They admit that "the persistence of this relatively low proportion of direct inheritances long after the demographic crisis was passed is hard to explain," testifying by default to the continuing disruption of direct, patrilineal inheritance among the elite.[18]

Besides name changes made in order to establish fictive direct lineage, another type of name changes that are significant indicators of instability are those made to accommodate marriages to heiresses: "by the mid-eighteenth century men of great new wealth but low birth were insisting that if their daughters and heiresses were to marry a nobleman, the occasion should be marked in perpetuity by the addition of their names as prefixes."[19] Both types of name changes indicate that, even within the very restricted elite with which the Stones concern themselves, there was a degree of permeability to interlopers, who would quite possibly have a different type of cultural capital than their new peers. The very fact that name changes occurred indicates a high degree of cultural anxiety over the representation of direct, patrilinear descent. In covering a larger kinship structure with the veneer of linear descent, the concept of fictive direct lineage supports the accuracy of attempts to explore the eighteenth century without presupposing its history and culture to be a continuous whole.

Although the elite group described by Lawrence Stone and Jeanne C. Fawtier Stone may have been to some degree exempted from the effects of circulation, their research nonetheless indicates that the most privileged quarters of British society in the late eighteenth century were not quite as placid as some political historians might suggest. Because of the ongoing instability of the traditional, aristocratic social order, awareness of social space was intensified at this time, even among the elite. For instance, new architectural plans for country homes stressed the obsolescence of the single, centralized, grand manor house and suggested, instead, that men of means build several "villas" that could be visited seasonally. In this way, the social presence of the gentry, as well as their investment in land, could be prudently dispersed and decentralized, spread over a variety of social and financial locales.[20]

A Verbal Culture: Circulation of Words

If even an apparently settled group, the landed elite, were affected by continuing change and circulation, one would expect circulation to affect the broader public still more, since their status was decidedly more uncertain. This public demanded—and received—a flurry of verbal and visual representations, which increasingly surrounded the eighteenth-century subject in everyday life. This phenomenon has been particularly well documented with respect to the printing of books, magazines, and newspapers, which both caused and corresponded to a rise in literacy levels.[21] The evidence concerning the rise in British literacy is so strong that perhaps the most astute recent commentator on the eighteenth-century novel, J. Paul Hunter, concludes that "we can now say with confidence what intuition and nineteenth-century social history only guessed: that literacy in the English-speaking world grew rapidly between 1600 and 1800 so that by the latter date a vast majority of adult males could read and write, whereas two centuries earlier only a select minority could do so."[22]

Over the course of the eighteenth century, the increase in readership was marked by the tripling of average publication of new book titles and by the popularity of lending libraries, which made books available to those who could not afford to buy them.[23] Moreover, the growing national importance of the printing industry was marked by the fact that the book trade was becoming increasingly institutionalized, as reflected in the publication of the first directory of the English book trade in 1785.[24] This institutionalization was matched by greater social prominence for booksellers, with some being elected as MPs and others actually being knighted.[25] Their customers were the newly literate masses, whose numbers "reached perhaps 75 percent among urban men by the end of the century."[26]

Readership of books later in the century was influenced by two events: the rise of book prices after 1780, due to inflation, and the 1774 enforcement of the Copyright Act.[27] Despite inflation, prices for older books actually went down after 1774, thanks to the Copyright Act, which had been passed in 1709, but had never been successfully inaugurated because of booksellers who had obtained injunctions to keep their rights to certain texts exclusive. When Alexander Donaldson won his battle to break a bookseller's exclusive right to Thomson's *The Seasons* in 1774, this revolutionized the book trade, making texts that had been in print for more than twenty-eight years part of the public domain.[28] This court decision opened the way for cheap reprints and serialization, making reading materials more accessible to a greater audience. Among those who took advantage of this publishing opportunity was John Bell, who printed cheap number series like the *Poets of Great Britain, Complete from Chaucer to Churchill* (109 vols., 1776–92), *Bell's British Theatre* (21 vols., 1777–78), and *Bell's Shakespeare* (1774). John Cooke's weekly serialization of *Tom Jones* was one of William Hazlitt's first exposures to popular novels, while James Harrison published weekly numbers of other novels in *The Novelist's Magazine* of the 1780s.[29] The great volume of books sold in serial or number form is indicated by the fact that Smollett's serialized *History of England* sold over ten thousand copies.[30]

Whereas early in the century books had been sold exclusively by booksellers and by private subscription in coffeehouses and other random locations, they now moved more firmly into the public domain as merchandisable commodities. Although Richard Altick claims that "except in London, Edinburgh, and a few other towns, there were no shops devoted exclusively to books," and uses this claim as evidence of the eighteenth-century market for books not being truly "popular," it seems to me that this really illustrates the beginning of modern marketing of books.[31] At first, no distinction was made between printed "goods," medicines, and other merchandise; then merchants began to specialize in books. One radical example of such specialization is mentioned by Altick in *The English Common Reader*: in James Lackington's London bookshop called the "Temple of the Muses," Lackington violated bookselling conventions by offering bargains and buying in huge quantities in order to reduce price. This resulted in vast sales: "in 1791 and 1792 . . . he had an annual turnover of 100,000 volumes and a profit of £4,000 and £5,000."[32] This new, mass-marketing approach to book sales definitely increased their accessibility to the public and foreshadowed the full-blown development of the bookshop in the nineteenth century.

Besides books, the eighteenth century saw a huge increase in a variety of more ephemeral printed matter as well. As John Feather has observed, "it was in the eighteenth century that the advertisement, the ticket, the printed form, and dozens of other varieties of ephemeral printing became a part of everyday life."[33] This increase was stimulated in part by the 1695 expiration of the Licensing Act, which had restricted printing to London, the Universities of Oxford and Cambridge, and York. One index of the great volume of eighteenth-century printing is the growth of a national paper-making industry: whereas at the beginning of the century most paper for printing was imported from the continent, by mid-century most English books were printed on domestic paper and by the end of the century English paper makers were exporting high-quality paper.[34] The development of newspaper and magazine circulations accounts for a great deal of this expanded paper consumption. While there was no London daily newspaper in the early 1700s, by the 1780s there were several dailies in London and other cities, and there was even a Sunday edition.[35] Outside London, "there were nine newspapers in seven different towns" by 1712 and thirty-seven by 1780.[36] This growth in the most inexpensive form of printed reading material indicates, on the most basic level, both an increasing accessibility of printed matter and an increasing readership.

As far as magazines are concerned, the *Gentleman's Magazine,* founded in 1731, is a paradigm of the formula that readers found most engaging: in contrast to the more limited, intellectualized fare provided by Joseph Addison in the *Spectator,* the *Gentleman's Magazine* offered a "highly miscellaneous fare that ranged from cooking recipes to conundrums," combined with political journalism, poetry, and critical reviews.[37] The *Gentleman's Magazine* had successors in the *Universal Magazine* (founded in 1747) and the *Monthly Magazine* (founded in 1796), among others.[38] It has been estimated that the *Gentleman's,* and magazines like it, reached circulations of at least ten thousand copies per month, with each issue most likely perused by several readers.[39] As Richard Altick has noted, newspaper and magazine subscription rates are deceptive because they do not reflect the number of readers who were able to peruse periodicals in places of social gathering such as coffeehouses. This kind of informal, unpaid access to written materials constitutes a much broader phenomenon, which is perhaps best illustrated by Terry Belanger's description of what kind of printed ephemera were *not* available to the people of late seventeenth-century, rural England: "There were no printed posters advertising estate or agriculture sales; there were no theatre bills or programmes, no newspapers, no printed handbills, bill headings, labels, tickets, or other commercial pieces. There were no printed forms meant to be completed by hand: no marriage certificates, printed indentures, or receipts."[40] By the end of the eighteenth century, such an absence of the printed word would seem unimaginable.

For the subject surrounded by such ephemera, magazines, newspapers, and books, the standardization of the printed word would seem to trumpet the necessity of reading and writing as everyday skills. But who actually were the literate in late eighteenth-century society? One clear boundary for literacy was economic: not everyone had the education or the leisure time to read and write. Despite acknowledging the rise of circulating libraries, which made books affordable to a broader readership and popularized the novel form, Richard Altick concludes that income and social ties were key to the acquisition of literacy throughout the century: "the class of tradesmen and artisans formed the dividing line, in this period, between the reading and the non-reading public."[41] Altick's "dividing line" is more blurred than he suggests here, however, because some servants, for example, had greater access to reading materials and education than their economic status alone would indicate.[42] Still, for the most part Altick's conclusion for the late eighteenth century seems justified: in socioeconomic terms, literacy was confined primarily to those of upper to lower-middle incomes.[43]

Geography is another potential literacy boundary, in that one might expect a greater literate population in urban rather than rural areas. To some extent this boundary holds true: "the acquisition of basic reading and writing skills by those on the margin of middle- and lower-class life, for whom they were coming to be an essential working asset, was a notable feature of urban society."[44] However, Roy McKeen Wiles's "The Relish for Reading in Provincial England Two Centuries Ago" has shown that literacy was by no means uncommon outside of London, England's only major urban center in the eighteenth century. As mentioned earlier, local newspapers were found in many provincial areas, and London papers were also available.[45] Magazines, too, had a rural clientele; in fact, this audience was so important to the *Monthly Magazine* that they adjusted their monthly date of issue to accommodate country subscribers.[46] Moreover, as Wiles has pointed out, "that vast quantities of substantial reading matter were to be found in the country is clear from the numerous advertisements for sales of used books, either at prices marked in catalogues or by auction."[47] As further evidence of widespread provincial literacy, Wiles cites the work of Paul Kaufman, who has compiled a list of 117

English towns (excluding London) that had circulating libraries.[48] The range of books in circulation in these libraries ranged from the six hundred volumes boasted of in the *Leeds Mercury* to the three thousand volumes announced in a 1773 issue of the *Hampshire Chronicle*.[49] Wiles concludes that there must have been a literate consumer demand for these libraries—most of them private ventures—in order for them to have encouraged investors: "the presence of a commercial lending library can be taken as evidence that a demand for reading matter was recognized by men who were ready to invest hundreds of pounds in expectation of substantial returns in the form of fees paid by borrowers."[50] Thus, although the evidence cannot indicate the precise proportion of readers among the country populace, the weight of it suggests that they were many and active in pursuing all sorts of reading materials.

The increase in production of printed texts and the accompanying rise in literacy that I have described here can only have made the individual subject more aware of different ways of seeing him- or herself, or of different ways of representing the individual's relation to culture. The importance of literacy to many religious sects, especially Wesleyanism,[51] indicates the degree to which the narrative "spaces" opened for the reader were seen as key to the formation of those readers' identities. The association between religion—one of the strongest means of fixing one's identity—and reading is also demonstrated by the popularity of didactic literature, including Bunyan's *Pilgrim's Progress,* throughout the century but especially during the first half.[52] The popularity of religious publications throughout the century is indicated by the fact that "on average three sermons were published in every week of the eighteenth century."[53]

However, even in the early part of the century, from 1700–40, analysis of the titles of published prose fiction shows that the largest proportion, more than 40 percent, were "romances"—that is, they were love stories.[54] Such secular themes predominated in the popular novels that proliferated toward the end of the century in subgenres such as the historical tale, the Oriental tale, the Gothic novel, domestic fiction, and so on, implying that this trend only continued more emphatically rather than abating to any degree. I would also argue that the splitting of the novel into various subgenres represents a multiplication of the "ways of seeing" the self that were not available when writing was closely associated with religion, and was supposed to convey the "one truth" of Christianity. Throughout the century, more traditional, spiritual ways of envisioning selfhood that involved communalism, a strong moral code, and sometimes even a belief in predestination (the ultimate assurance of identity) were progressively overwhelmed by the presentation of other, more secular and materialist models of selfhood in the novel.

In addition to offering religious and novelistic models of selfhood, the bulk of printed materials represented readers as independent, discriminating subjects. Jürgen Habermas traces this to the fact that, as art was increasingly removed from the control of private patronage, it was "released from its functions in the service of social representation, . . . [and] became an object of free choice and of changing preference."[55] The discourse that sprang up about art and aesthetics in the early eighteenth century was governed by two institutions—the critical journal and the coffeehouse. However, these institutions were not centers of authority, but rather the channels through which a heterogeneous discourse flowed between individuals who invited the free response of other writers and speakers. This model of free discourse in aesthetic matters was soon transferred to the domain of political discourse: official censorship ended with the Licensing Act of 1695, and strictures against reporting on Parliamentary debates were effectively nullified in 1771, permitting free discussion of political ideas and personages.[56] This dialogization of both political and aesthetic discourses suggests that the individual subject was increasingly invited to participate in the circulation of ideas and representations, and to situate him- or herself within a decentralized, democratized social space in which a variety of forms of cultural capital could be deployed in order to establish status.

In the magazines there was also an emphasis on how engagement in reading could shape the individual subject. As Robert Mayo has pointed out, the eighteenth-century reading audience was

> monolithic in size but not in character. The various types of magazines are themselves testimony to the heterogeneity of the public taste, and the appeals to reader interests and prejudices, sometimes within the same periodical, were extremely diversified, if not contradictory.[57]

The potential contradictions in intended audience that Mayo mentions mark both the growth and the fracturing of the reading public: no longer could a writer or editor assume that readers would be of a specific socioeconomic class. Instead, given the flood of readers from all different backgrounds, audiences had to be created or discovered by trial and error in miscellanies like the *Gentleman's Magazine*. I would also suggest that the miscellanies both created and reflected a certain degree of openness and variability in their readers. Being set upon an equal footing, at least in their shared status as readers, the audience felt freer to experiment with their own self-conceptions. In part, as Jon Klancher has shown, the magazines sponsored this sense of equality through their own self-representation as an interactive forum for readers—they often included a great number of letters that were supposedly written by subscribers. Hence the self-promoting arguments of James Anderson, editor of the Edinburgh *Bee,* (writing in 1790), as summarized by Klancher: "freedom of access to writing gives periodical writing the aura of the democratic and communal—the very opposite . . . of clerical language, that dictatorial discourse cast down from the pulpit."[58] By evading the monologic discourse of the pulpit, which would channel identity through the ultimate authority, God, the individual subject was urged to seek his or her own identity in a new community of equals united by discursive dialogue. Furthermore, Anderson employed a theatrical metaphor in referring to the readers' act of writing to the magazine as "periodical performance," highlighting the degree to which the readers' activities were conceived of as placing them in "roles" and thus, at least momentarily, helping to define their identities.[59]

These newly dialogized modes of defining individual identity—taste (aesthetics), political allegiance, and reader/writership, among others—caused a historical awareness of the inadequacy of social categories, or ranks. Although McKeon traces the decay of social rank to the late seventeenth century, which coincides well with Habermas's use of the Licensing Act of 1695 as a mark of increasing public circulation, I would argue, along with Habermas, that this was just the beginning of a trend that resulted in the decentralization and dialogization of meaning and identity production. In his study of late eighteenth- and early nineteenth-century reading audiences, Klancher shows the periodical press' awareness of this trend in their responses to a social structure that was undergoing change due to the increasing circulation of power and knowledge. He claims that social order was not static, but rather was formed through the circulations of monthly magazines, among other things: "readerships were no longer waiting to be discovered and acculturated; they could not be colonized. They must . . . be produced."[60] These readerships reflected "a new kind of ideologically cohesive discursive community" that replaced the notion of a social rank corresponding to vocation.[61] Moreover, these discursive communities defined their readers outside of the traditional, hierarchical vision of social order:

> The definition of readers sought by these journals was unavoidably imprecise by contrast to eighteenth-century journals, which mapped their audi-

ences by targeting specific ranks. Nineteenth-century periodicals often deliberately smudged social differences among their readers. . . . The intended audience must be defined by its ethos, its framework of educational capacity, ideological stance, economic ability, and cultural dispositions. But the readership must not be assigned a specific rank, nor be localized in a social order.[62]

Although Klancher's dichotomization of eighteenth- and nineteenth-century journals shows an overeagerness to differentiate between historical "periods" (in fact, the journals he refers to here range only from the *Edinburgh Review,* founded in 1802, to the *Metropolitan,* 1831), his description of the magazine's criteria for potential readers is constructive in that it reveals social status to be composed of a variety of factors that amount to "cultural capital." This variety of defining factors explains why it is difficult, in the circulative social space of the late eighteenth century, to clearly identify and separate specific, unified "classes."

At least in so far as the magazines are concerned, this situation did not remain static throughout the period with which I am concerned. Mayo and Klancher are in agreement that Anderson's vision of the periodical as democratic, discursive space was more elegiac than prophetic in 1790. For instance, Mayo sees a new social order being created in the periodical press toward the end of the century: "In the very years when the critics of mass culture celebrate the union of *popular* and *cultivated* taste, new magazines, addressed to the sentimental tastes and *genteel* aspirations of a numerous class of readers, were already circulating on a large scale" [emphasis added].[63] The separating-out of readerships along social ranks that Mayo sees in the magazines is confirmed by Klancher, who adds that, in the early nineteenth century, these readerships and ranks no longer existed "naturally," but were necessarily cultivated. The new periodicals "would not simply 'represent' a given social group or reflect it back to itself; now they would embody a principle, become actively ideological, and reshape the very contours and self-definitions of the readerships they addressed."[64]

Although Klancher's claim points to a reshaping of the entire social order that is beyond the range of the discussion that I want to pursue here,[65] his specific argument about the changing role of magazines in shaping readers' self-conceptions is very relevant. In sympathy with Klancher's argument that magazines became more "actively ideological," and thus more selective in their audiences, it is tempting to view the early nineteenth century as a period in which there was increasingly less freedom in constructing individual identity as subjects were constrained by a new solidifying of social space. Whereas the eighteenth-century miscellanies suggested a suspension of rank and categorization, the early nineteenth-century periodicals forced the reader into specific alignments, often with a single interest group. Therefore, in the nineteenth century the opportunity to participate in the kind of playful, theatrical re-visioning of self suggested by the *Bee*'s Anderson was displaced, at least from the pages of the magazines. Still, although the magazines may indicate a partial foreclosure of the spaces in which subjects were invited to envision themselves, I would argue that even in this foreclosure there was greater freedom and circulation than in the traditional means of fixing meaning and identity that dominated pre–1700 England.

Thus far, I have only hypothesized about the effect of the proliferation of *verbal* representations—books, magazines, newspapers, and other printed ephemera—on the eighteenth-century subject; now I want to consider the effect of *visual* representations as well. Other studies have emphasized the influence of ancient and Renaissance models on eighteenth-century art, calling this the age of "Neoclassicism."[66] Though the influence of these models was undoubtedly great, and though they were surely not always used in a conservative fashion, these models remain part of an older, traditional apparatus of meaning formation that was embodied in Greek and Latin texts for the literary arts and codified in Cesare Ripa's *Iconologia* for the visual arts.[67] The fixity of this system was disrupted by the new visual and narrative "spaces" that developed throughout the century, but particularly in the latter part. In addition to the explicitly visual medium of pictorial representation, I will also treat the phenomena of "shows," social spectacles, and museums or collections. For some of these visual phenomena, Frances Burney's novel *Evelina* will provide an introduction.

A Visual Culture: The Dissemination of Pictorial Representations

In part, the disruption of traditional forms of identity and meaning production was due to the increasing reproducibility of visual images, which led, in turn, to their removal from traditional, stable interpretive contexts and their dissemination across cultural ranks. In other words, visual images progressively became more commonplace in print shops, exhibitions, and the homes of even the lower middle ranks, whereas before these images had been restricted to the wealthy.[68] The increasing accessibility of visual forms of representation was the result of three factors: the vogue of the "picturesque" taste for sketches and watercolors, which were more often than not created by artists and amateurs at will rather than by commission; the marketing of the visual in exhibitions; and the increased availability of prints and engravings. It is these new, popular encounters with visual forms that I find interesting because they demonstrate the multiple, discontinuous character of representation in a rapidly evolving, circulatory culture. For the individual subject, the proliferation and accessibility of these new forms of visual representation presented a multiplicity of ways of seeing.

The rise of the picturesque mode and the art of sketches and watercolors is a well-documented phenomenon in eighteenth-century Britain.[69] Although there were landscape painters in seventeenth-century England, they painted in oil and their work was generally "of poor quality and . . . unrelated to the English scene."[70] In the eighteenth century, George Lambert (1700–65) and Richard Wilson (1713–82) were pioneers in their efforts to popularize the English landscape in oil, but their work remained isolated. Instead, the popularity of picturesque English landscapes is associated inextricably with the "rise" of painting with watercolors at the end of the eighteenth century. The growth in English watercolor painting and of the taste for watercolors was so remarkably evident that, as Martin Hardie has noted, it "gave birth later to the widely held patriotic idea that the art had its origin in" England, rather than in Northern Europe.[71] Still, the technique was so well suited to the English predilection for "open-air life and its accompaniments . . . and the observation of living people engaged in the normal activities of everyday life" that it was adopted as *the* English national art form.[72]

In fact, the patriotic flavor of English picturesque sketches and watercolors is undeniable: although rooted stylistically in the Italian landscapes of Salvator Rosa and Claude Lorrain,[73] the English vogue for the picturesque emphasized English landscapes. For the viewer, this had the effect of raising the aesthetic value of "common" English landscape and validating the local and particular. The various tour books of William Gilpin, which reproduce both his sketches and the narrative of his journeys, exemplify this elevation of the local in their focus on the River Wye, the Lake region, Wales, and so on. Gilpin's books were so popular that they inspired Thomas Rowlandson's parodic *The Tours of Doctor Syntax in Search of the Picturesque* (1809–11), which was accompanied by William Combe's verses.[74] While Gilpin was first a clergyman and only second an amateur artist and theorist of visual aesthetics, professional artists such as Paul Sandby also published collections of regional prints.

The fact that such native scenery was readily available to nearly any

English observer—and not rendered exclusive, like the ruined Roman Colosseum, by geographical and financial concerns—both nationalized and democratized what was conceived of as artistic "beauty." Gilpin's writings, as well as the more general proliferation of local scenes in watercolors and sketches, suggested to the individual viewer that any part of his or her surroundings might be worthy of representation, thus unsettling old aesthetic hierarchies and implying the validity of a range of tastes.

In this way, picturesque representations served as a model for viewers of both natural beauty and the visual arts because of these representations' emphasis on the power and unique value of the individual eye. As John Lyons notes, the kind of highly individualized, privatized narrative and "eye" that Gilpin cultivates in his tour books provides marked contrast with earlier "objective" and impersonal travel journals:

> travelers who wrote before the end of the eighteenth century seemed to assume that they were transparent.... Then, and quite suddenly, the narrator's transparency becomes clouded with the concern in the process of perception, his own feelings, his private ruminations, and chills and fevers. It is not that the narrator felt that he was telling us something less true, but rather that his tale was more true because truth had moved from the generality of the world of phenomena to the specificity of uniquely personal experience.[75]

For writers and viewers of natural scenery, descriptive narratives and sketches confirmed their subjectivity; similarly, for readers and viewers of prints and sketches, the process of identification or disagreement with the "eye" of the tour book also confirmed *their* subjectivity.

The more active, authoritative stance of the reader or viewer was rendered possible by the choice of local, native setting as subject matter: in this way, the writer and reader were placed on more or less equal, dialogic terms—as in the discourse of the magazines—because the subject matter was so accessible and so free of contextual allusions. Even those readers and viewers who had not visited the countryside that Gilpin described at least could potentially do so, and thus could become "authorities," in contrast to the general impossibility of doing so with distant spectacles of foreign lands or imaginary landscapes created by artists who were less rooted in the local, native scenery. Writer and reader, sketcher and viewer were thus united in the picturesque on more or less equal terms by their status as observers.

Such equality, stimulated both by the availability of "picturesque" scenery and by the open subjectivity of picturesque aesthetics, promoted the deprofessionalization of visual representation. Like the late-century magazines that depicted themselves as dialogues between writers and readers, encouraging the interchangeability of these roles, the vogue for picturesque sketches and watercolors encouraged every viewer to become a painter or sketcher. Within sketches and watercolors themselves, the act of creative perception was often thematized. Paul Sandby's (1730–1807) watercolor of "Roslin Castle, North Berwick" portrays a woman who is drawing the castle with the aid of a camera obscura. Such thematizations of visual perception draw the viewer's attention to his or her own act of perceiving the sketch, helping to erase distinctions between the (professional) artist and the (amateur) viewer (see figure 1).

One of the most radical erasures of the distinction between professional and amateur viewers is implied by the theory of blot art developed by Alexander Cozens (c. 1717–86). Beginning with a simple, random ink blot on paper, Cozens would envision a landscape from it and would

1. Roslin Castle, Midlothian, *Paul Sandby. Courtesy of Yale Center for British Art, Paul Mellon Collection.*

elaborate by using his brush both to distort the shape of the still-wet blot and to add new ink to it. This new technique effectively vanquished the subject—nature—in favor of the viewer's subjectivity. The late date of Cozens's publication of a treatise on the blot, entitled *A New Method of Assisting the Invention in Drawing Original Compositions of Landscape* (1786), should not obscure the fact that he was teaching this method for a good part of his career, both in private lessons and in his capacity as drawing master at Eton. As a teacher, he hoped that his blot method would encourage students "to see and work in masses instead of niggling with line," and "to stimulate their curiosity and interest."[76] Cozens's theory implies a certain equality between professional and amateur viewer, both of whom impose their own "way of seeing" on their subjects.[77]

Visual perception was also the subject of numerous eighteenth-century scientific treatises, which may have contributed to general awareness of the individual subject's involvement in the process of sight, visualization, and how scenes are "pictured." These treatises range from Robert Smith's *Compleat System of Optics* (1738) and Benjamin Martin's *A New and Compendious System of Optics* (1740) to Joseph Priestley's *History and Present State of Discoveries Relating to Vision, Light and Colours* (1772) and Joseph Harris's *Treatise of Optics* (1775). Although none of these works were as popular, surely, as Gilpin's tour books, the interest they reflect in the process of visual perception is also expressed in more popular media such as the magazine. An illustration of a room-sized camera obscura appeared in a 1752 issue of the *Universal Magazine* along with a written description of it that explained its "great use in explaining the nature of vision."[78] Moreover, the public—at least in London— was made aware of technical work on the subject of vision by window displays in opticians' shops.[79] I would argue that, much as the vogue for the picturesque defamiliarized English landscape and made it an aesthetic object, the interest in visual perception as an object of scientific inquiry defamiliarized it and—through the popularization of devices like the camera obscura that mechanically framed and re-presented "reality" in a fashion analogous to the workings of the human eye—increased the public's awareness of the importance of vision in constructing ways of seeing the self, the nation, and nature.

The camera obscura can serve both as a figure for this role of vision and as evidence of popular involvement in picturing nature. The camera obscura's status as a cultural figure is revealed by the fact that the preferred model of camera obscura was made to appear as a book until it was folded out for use. In fact, the commonness of such models is indicated by the 1794 edition of the *Encyclopaedia Britannica,* which portrays a book-form camera obscura as exemplary of the device.[80] The physical analogy thus constructed between the book and the viewing device reflects a conceptual analogy: the acts of reading and viewing are similar in that they are "ways of seeing." Both the camera obscura and the text are "descriptive" instruments, especially if we restore the eighteenth-century mathematical connotations of description as the drawing of a defining line or circle, which suggests both the framing of picture limits in the camera and the supposed scientific, mathematical accuracy of its field of view.[81] Moreover, although the camera obscura is nominally a scientific, objective instrument, the analogy with the potentially subjective structure of the book renders its objectivity suspect, at the very least.[82]

In addition to its significance as a cultural figure, the camera obscura is one of a number of late eighteenth- and early nineteenth-century technical aids for sketching and watercolor painting that indicate a growing popular involvement in the act of visual representation, or picturing. The woman portrayed using a camera obscura in Paul Sandby's "Roslin Castle," mentioned above, is most certainly an amateur, although the camera obscura was not disparaged by professionals—Thomas Sandby, Paul's brother, pioneered its use in topographical and architectural drawing. These instruments were available to even the lower middle ranks in their cheapest form, pocket-sized for nine shillings, and ranged in price up to £10 for the finest book-form models.[83] Less expensive were "Claude" glasses, which literally transformed natural landscapes into the subdued, picturesque tones of a Claude Lorrain landscape: the Claude glass "was a little convex mirror in which the traveller, placing his back to the view, could see a small-framed, tinted picture of the prospect. Claude Glasses could be obtained in various tints so that, whatever the natural state of the light, a suitably mellow glow could be imparted to the picture."[84] The existence of an instrument like the Claude glass shows the degree to which the act of "picturing" had become a rage. No longer were viewers satisfied with natural light and coloring and the wide-angle perspective of their own vision; instead, upon seeing a pleasing view, they translated nature into the conventions of painterly representation, including more controlled light and color tones and a selective, framed field of view. Besides the camera obscura, the Claude glass, and camera lucida (another early form of camera, patented in 1807), portable color boxes were added to the list of materials that were readily available to the average, nonprofessional watercolorist. These boxes—made especially to carry artists' watercolors and brushes—were first described in *The Art of Drawing, and Painting in Water-Colours* (1732) in a manner that suggested the necessity of making them for one's self; by 1801, Rudolf Ackermann was advertising a variety of such boxes, the smallest costing six shillings.[85] The development of a manufacture and trade in the apparatus necessary for sketching and watercolor painting illustrates the degree to which production of the visual had become an industry that thrived on the activity of amateurs.

Up to this point I have concentrated on the general public's awareness of the visual and its role in adding to the increasing flow of visual representations; now I would like to consider the issue from the professional artist's perspective. Although I have stated that the visual arts were deprofessionalized during the eighteenth century, this is only to say that they were no longer the *exclusive* province of professionals. In fact, the eighteenth century saw the rise of a truly national pool of professional artists such as William Hogarth, Thomas Gainsborough, and Sir Joshua Reynolds who displaced imported French, Dutch, and Italian artists from their position of favor in England. The broadening of the public's taste and awareness created a new market for visual representations that was cultivated and exploited by professional artists as a partial replacement for the financial support that patronage had formerly offered.[86]

One way in which visual representations were introduced to the public was through the exhibition. A benchmark for the growing accessibility of visual representations to the "common" public is Hogarth's 1740 staging of what amounted to the first public art exhibition in England at Captain Coram's Foundling Hospital.[87] Before more formal exhibitions could be held, however, the professional artists needed to organize themselves in a guild or union, which they accomplished only by fits and starts. The first formal art exhibition of this new organization was held in 1760, in the Society of Arts' rooms. Attendance at the first year's show was estimated to be about 20,000, while the next year's show—due to more restrictive admission policies—drew only 13,000 but made more money in entrance fees.[88] Beginning in 1765 and continuing until 1783, the Incorporated Society of Artists was rivalled in putting on art shows by the Free Society of Artists. In 1769, the Incorporated Society of Artists became the Royal Academy, eventually driving their rival society out of business.[89] Taking advantage of the relatively inexpensive admission charge—a shilling catalog—for one of these shows, a young army officer recorded his reactions in letters to his father:

When I entered the room, I was at a loss where first to fix my eyes, seeing so glaring a sight; but as, Dear Sir, my turn is military, you'll excuse me not keeping to the order of the catalogue, which has served me as ticket for six or seven days. Mr. Scott's piece of the taking of Quebec gave me great pleasure: the French ships on fire are finely expressed. . . . These pieces by Mr. Reynolds give me great satisfaction. I hope that gentleman will oblige the world with a print of them, which if he does he will have military subscribers enough.[90]

The strangeness of this exhibition to the officer is marked by his initial bewilderment and impression of "so glaring a sight," because of which he ultimately decides to limit himself to paintings that reflect his taste in military subject matter. In like fashion, the rest of the more common public was also introduced to this new "glaring" phenomenon. The effect was at least double: the common viewer's authority as discriminating subject was enhanced by the sight of such a variety of images offered for his or her appreciation, and the artist's potential market for his work was greatly expanded.[91]

Despite the novelty of his experience, the officer was familiar enough with visual representations in the form of prints, through which paintings could reach a much larger audience than that of the exhibition. Outside of the sales of original paintings, artists also garnered profits from prints and engravings of paintings they exhibited. This development was particularly important for watercolorists, who had never received the patronage or prices for their work that oil painters had, due to the lesser prestige of their medium among the elite. As Martin Hardie points out, before the exhibitions, most watercolorists were distanced from the buying public by the fact that

> the draughtsman had worked for the engraver; his commissions came from the publishers of prints; and it was through the engraving that his work was presented to the public eye. The advent of the public exhibition meant that the position was reversed. The artist, instead of working in simple tints, could enlarge his scope and give himself complete freedom of colour. . . . The engraving now became the accessory to the drawing, instead of being the principal end. . . . The artist as exhibitor, as producer for the publisher of prints, and as teacher, had three markets for his work, and from this time forward we find the water-colour painter firmly established as a prosperous professional man.[92]

In fact, the artist's interest in the marketing of prints had already received impetus through the efforts of Hogarth and others to restrict piracy through the 1735 passage of the Engraver's Act.[93] Hogarth's pioneering arrogation of artistic and financial control over the prints of his famous series paintings, beginning with the *Harlot's Progress* (1731), provided a precedent for later artists.[94] Until the era of the public exhibition, however, Hogarth's success with engravings and prints was unmatched.

The financial importance of prints and engravings to artists in watercolor and other "lesser" media shows how this means of mass circulation increased the variety of visual representations and effectively disrupted the cultural authority of the oil painting. Although there were many watercolorists active in the Royal Academy, including Paul Sandby and Joseph Farington, by 1804 specialists in watercolor had organized themselves professionally in the "Old Watercolour Society." In contrast to the Royal Academy, whose members, led by Sir Joshua Reynolds, were interested largely in emulating the French Academy and in establishing the "rules" of painterly discourse, the Old Watercolour Society and its later incarnations were occupied primarily with promoting watercolor painting and with holding exhibitions to encourage sales. Indeed, the difference between the watercolorists' practice and that of the Academy, with its emphasis on oil painting and abstract principle, has been recognized as part of "a strong desire in the British to overcome the restrictions of academic custom," and as a visual equivalent of the novel's revolutionary status among literary genres.[95] Watercolors were also like the novel in that they flooded the visual and verbal markets of the late eighteenth century.

Although the landscape prints made from watercolors and sketches are quite dissimilar in content from other popular prints with historical or political subject matter, together they compose part of the visual "ephemera" of eighteenth-century culture that was marketed at printsellers' shops, which served as the visual equivalent of the magazine. Printsellers had occupied the powerful place in the art world that booksellers occupied in the book trade until Hogarth's efforts resulted in the protection of the artist's visual property. By the end of the century, printsellers' shops were simply retailing centers for the visual, where the viewer could satisfy his or her taste for the picturesque—a democratizing aesthetic, as I have noted—or seek out "the most democratic form of art in eighteenth-century Britain," political or social satire.[96] Richard Altick notes that the political events of the end of the century, along with the talents of James Gillray and Thomas Rowlandson, "resulted in an unprecedented torrent of [satiric] prints."[97] Both satiric and picturesque prints were affordably priced—most cost several shillings, some only a matter of pence. Moreover, even those who did not or could not buy prints had the chance to view them in shop window displays,[98] as is seen in the background of Topham's "The Macaroni Printshop" or in Gillray's "Very Slippy-Weather." Some shops, like the Royal Academy shows, even charged a shilling admission fee, enticing customers through their bold and gaudy window displays (see figures 2 and 3).

Like picturesque prints, satiric or political prints required only a knowledge of the present in order to appreciate them. M. Dorothy George notes the democratic, antiemblematic tendencies of the satiric print:

> Only in the last three decades of the century was the transformation of the emblematical print to the political caricature complete. The engraving, complicated and sometimes cryptic, seldom comic, conceived in black and white and heavily cross-hatched, had been succeeded by a bold design, immediately striking to the eye, intended (usually) to amuse, and sold plain or coloured but commonly coloured.[99]

In this way, the printsellers' shops not only prompted the growth of the visual as a field of trade and increased public access to a broader range of circulating visual images, but also offered visions of the political present as a realm in which individual subjects were invited to listen to and witness, if not actively participate in, public dialogue on values and ideology. Therefore, like the picturesque images of home landscapes, political prints were an empowering medium for the individual subject.

The Show

The windows of the printsellers' shops are exemplary of the development of a "visual culture" in late eighteenth-century Britain, something along the lines of what Richard Altick describes in *The Shows of London*. This visual culture was not limited to the circulation of prints and engravings and the "fine" arts shows that I have described here; rather, as Altick's title indicates, it promoted the notion of the spectacular and of spectatorship in a variety of types of "show." These shows ranged from semitheatrical productions that staged recent events as spectacles, to explicitly social arenas where the audience was encouraged to view itself as spectacle, to museum collections that presented history, nature, and science as visual images to be consumed. Although there is clearly a long history of "shows" in Britain, the visual productions of the late eighteenth century go beyond traditional British spectacles such as the theater and fairs like St. Bartholomew's Fair in their volume, diversity, and accessibility to all ranks.

2. The Macaroni Printshop (1772), E. Topham. ©The British Museum.

    One of the first manifestations of this "show" phenomenon was the separation of stage scenery from the theater in spectacles that dramatized recent events or contemporary vistas. As traced by Altick, these shows were based—like modern cinema—on the use of light to create the illusion of movement and spatial depth. The magic lantern, which projected a scene painted on glass to a wall or screen, was the simplest device used to create such shows. Although magic lanterns were known and used in the Restoration, they underwent a boom in popularity from the mid-1770s into the first decade of the nineteenth century, due, perhaps, to their use in portraying caricatures.[100] Whereas the portability of the magic lantern and its simple design enabled it to be shown in private rooms by request, more complicated shows such as Philippe de Loutherbourg's "Eidophusikon," which combined light, sound, and elaborate scenery and mechanical devices, were housed semipermanently in larger

3. Very Slippy-Weather (1808), James Gillray. ©The British Museum.

rooms and advertised heavily in order to attract their audience. The fare offered in the program of the Eidophusikon ranged from dawn over London to sunset near Naples, sometimes drawing on literature, as in the portrayal of Milton's Pandemonium, sometimes drawing on contemporary events, as in the dramatization of "The Bringing of French and Dutch Prizes into the Port of Plymouth."[101] When de Loutherbourg first created the Eidophusikon in 1781, he charged five shillings admission; as the novelty of the show wore off, it became progressively more affordable—in 1786, admission was three shillings for the best seats, two for others. Because of the complexity of its workings, the Eidophusikon was not easily imitated. Thus, although it undoubtedly had an effect in stimulating the development of a visual culture, its effects were limited.

While the Eidophusikon last appeared in 1793 (and finally in 1800, in altered form), the panorama, another form of spectacle that attempted to improve on the "simple" visual image, had a longer run. In 1787, Robert Barker, a Scots artist, patented a building-sized apparatus for showing pictures in the round, so that the observer would have the illusion of being surrounded by whatever scene was depicted.[102] Barker opened his Leicester Square panorama in 1794 with a view of London; other views and imitators soon followed, focusing on cityscapes and historical and contemporary events. Increasingly, the images presented were of great battles from contemporary wars on the European continent and in India, of historical battles such as Agincourt, the siege of Acre, and so on, or of exotic and historic cities such as Jerusalem, Alexandria, and Rome. In this way, the panorama and its imitators opened new visual fields for their audiences, allowing them to see the exotic "Other" of ancient Middle Eastern cities, dramatizing the contemporary battlefield maneuvers of soldiers and generals, and providing access to visions of the past. In contrast to newspaper accounts of events or printed descriptions of exotic locales, the panoramas' size overwhelmed the viewer and offered a kind of immediacy that writing could not offer.[103] None of Barker's competitors, except for Thomas Hornor's later "Colosseum" (opened in 1832), matched his efforts in size and ability to surround the viewer. What was most important for commercial success, apparently, was size and sensational content.

Even before the advent of the panorama, in the 1770s and 1780s, well-respected artists such as Benjamin West and John Singleton Copley had actively marketed viewings of their massive paintings of contemporary events; similarly, de Loutherbourg, the creator of the Eidophusikon, charged a shilling to see his epic-sized paintings of "The Battle of Valenciennes" and "Lord Howe's Victory" in the 1790s.[104] In particular, Copley's efforts to merchandise the view of his paintings stretched the boundaries of what was considered appropriate to the "highest" genre of painting, history painting. Like de Loutherbourg, Copley charged a shilling admission to see his depictions of Pitt's stroke in Parliament, entitled "The Death of the Earl of Chatham" (1778), for which "most of the fifty-five noblemen included in the scene sat to him;" he enraged the Royal Academy by eschewing their show, subletting their old rooms, and drawing a huge crowd of 20,000 spectators.[105] The treasurer of the Academy accused him of putting on a "raree show." In essence, Copley was taking advantage of the marketing opportunities inherent in his subject, in the process violating the distinction between high and low art, exploiting the public's sensationalistic interest in the death of a powerful man, and exposing the personages of his noble sitters to the scrutiny of anyone who had a shilling for entry. Not only was Copley *not* put off by the scandal he had created, he continued it by setting up tents in 1791 and 1799 to market the view of other paintings. The self-interested activities of Copley, de Loutherbourg, West, Barker, and others helped to counteract the restriction of the visual to the wealthy, to disrupt the attempted control over visual images exerted by the Royal Academy, and to spread access to the visual across social boundaries.

Outside of London, "shows" of this sort were not often available, yet this is not necessarily an indication of a restricted audience for the visual. For instance, it has been estimated that one out of every six eighteenth-century Britons visited London during their lifetime, and thus may have been exposed to London shows. Moreover, if they were literate, they would have seen advertisements for shows in the London newspapers, which circulated nationally.

The Self as Show

I want to turn now from the explicitly visual, semitheatrical "shows" that were offered to the public to the increasing sense in which social relations were staged as spectacles. Much of what I say here is developed more specifically in chapter 2, on social space; this section serves to introduce as context for my entire work the concept of the self as spectacle. Because Frances Burney's *Evelina* (1778) traces the debut of a young gentlewoman from the country into late eighteenth-century London society, it is particularly relevant to my concern for illustrating the spectacularity of social experience: as the protagonist, Evelina, encounters for the first time various spectacles in which identity is at stake, they are exposed as such for the reading audience.[106] Moreover, by muddling Evelina's familial background, Burney defamiliarizes the notion of fixing identity through birth, placing Evelina in an unstable social position in which she must continually prove her worth. As an orphan and ingenue of no inherent social status, Evelina is particularly vulnerable to having her identity accidentally or deliberately misread.[107] Although the novel predates Copley's shows, panoramas, and the Eidophusikon, during its course Evelina enters a series of social sites that on the one hand promote the visual as a way of envisioning the self and one's place in social ranks, and on the other hand, show the inevitability of interaction with visual culture. The social sites visited by Evelina vary from the "high" or aristocratic, which she encounters through her friend Maria Mirvan and Maria's mother, Mrs. Mirvan, to the "low" or popular, which she encounters through her grandmother Mme. Duval and her cousins the Branghtons. This mixture in Evelina's experiences shows not only the penetration of the visual element into social entertainments for all ranks, but the fact that these entertainments are parts of the same phenomenon and are thus in dialogue with each other. In essence, *Evelina* illustrates how "display was the most consistent and most disapproved element in the recreations of an age of extravagance."[108] Ultimately, I would argue, *Evelina* shows how identity is produced through the individual subject's interaction with these spectacles and his or her demonstrated ability to negotiate them, both in terms of personal display and of the exercise of discriminatory power.

Evelina's introduction to London begins at the theater (where she sees Garrick's rendition of Hoadley's "Ranger"), then moves to the promenade at St. James's Park, where she remarks that "every body looked gay, and seemed pleased, and the ladies were so much dressed, that Miss Mirvan and I could do nothing but look at them."[109] We readers move with Evelina from the foregrounded spectacle of the stage to the social spectacle of St. James's Park, in which "seeming," "looking," and "dressing" are just as important as in the theater. This impression of the self as spectacle is reinforced in Evelina's visits to the opera, where she compares the explicitly staged show to that offered by the audience: "every body was dressed in so high a style, that, if I had been less delighted with the performance, my eyes would have found me sufficient entertainment from looking at the ladies" (38). Here the notion of self-presentation as performance anticipates Erving Goffman's theorizing, though not Goffman's morally neutral tone. *Evelina* equates performance with artifice and deception, with "seeming" as opposed to "being," and yet recognizes its necessity. The potential for treachery inherent to performance is instanced in Sir Clement Willoughby's gentlemanly exterior, which belies his rakish code of sexual behavior; nonetheless, performance is a cultural skill that the novel's logic suggests Evelina must acquire.[110]

Evelina goes well beyond simply developing an analogy between the stage and social life—it concretizes the spectacularity of social relations by describing Evelina's entry into eighteenth-century social arenas such as Ranelagh, the Pantheon, and Vauxhall. As the weight of critical and historical material on these attractions might suggest, eighteenth-century England was noted for its development of pleasure gardens and distinctive social gathering places. These were some of the best-known of London's attractions, Ranelagh and the Pantheon catering to a more exclusive crowd than Vauxhall. Evelina enjoys her first visit to the Ranelagh Rotunda: "the brilliancy of the lights . . . made me almost think I was in some *inchanted castle,* or *fairy palace,* for all looked like magic to me" (37). The brilliant, magical appearance of the buildings is matched by the press of fine people walking around the circular parade grounds; among them, in her second visit, Evelina encounters her friend and model nobleman, Lord Orville (58). In fact, although Ranelagh was sometimes frequented by the lower ranks, it was associated with the aristocracy and upper ranks. One reason for this was the rather high price of admission for its special evenings, which ranged from three shillings for fireworks night to two guineas for masquerade nights.[111]

Ranelagh's importance as a center for social display among the upper ranks is marked by events such as the 1759 "Jubilee Ball" to commemorate the birthday of the Prince of Wales (see figure 4), or the 1775 "Ranelagh Regatta," which consisted of a boat race and a procession of over two thousand pleasure boats down the Thames to Ranelagh. At this regatta all the ladies wore white, and the crowd was quite aristocratic, including the Dukes of Gloucester and Northumberland, the Duchess of Devonshire, and Lord North. At the Rotunda, dinner was served to music; after dinner a dance was held in a temporary, octagonal structure called "The Temple of Neptune." Not only was this an occasion for the upper ranks to view themselves, it was an opportunity for the London populace to see them:

> scaffold erections were to be seen on the banks, and even on the top of Westminster Hall. Gambling tables lined the approaches to Westminster Bridge; men went about selling indifferent liquor, Regatta songs and Regatta cards. The river banks now resembled a great fair, and the Thames itself a

4. A View of the Rotunda House and Gardens at Ranelagh,
*Nathaniel Parr after Antonio Canaletto. Courtesy of Yale Center for
British Art, Paul Mellon Collection.*

floating town. Wild calculations fixed the number of the spectators at 200,000, or "at least" three millions.[112]

The general populace's appropriation of this event, as well as the theatrical self-display practiced by the upper ranks, illustrates the theatrical relation between the ranks that E. P. Thompson postulates in eighteenth-century English society.[113] Moreover, the Regatta's extreme status as mass spectacle clarifies the importance of the visual and self-display as everyday practice at Ranelagh.

Before Ranelagh was heated, the Pantheon (1772–1862) was known as the "winter" Ranelagh, and attracted a similar crowd.[114] On Evelina's visit to the Pantheon, which is on a concert night, the admission fee is half a guinea (107). At the Pantheon, too, Evelina enjoys herself and appreciates the "magnificence of the room" and the "great deal of company" that fill it (104–5). She wonders at the audience's neglect of the music, a neglect that only emphasizes the primarily social role of the place. Although Evelina fails to make detailed reports on the decorations of the Pantheon, Horace Walpole described it as having panels "painted like Raphael's loggia in the Vatican" and enthused that "all the friezes and niches were edged with alternated lamps of green and purple glass that shed a most heathen light, and the dome was illuminated by a heaven of oiled paper well painted with gods and goddesses."[115] From this description, it is clear that the Pantheon was itself an ornate spectacle, unlike the Rotunda, whose vastness would have been uninteresting without its crowd. Both the ornateness of the Pantheon, which foregrounds its status as "sight," and its use as a site for self-display indicate its participation in the visual culture that I have described.

At the Pantheon, and in almost every public social arena depicted in *Evelina,* the visual arises as a mode of asserting identity and personal will. This occurs most frequently when male characters like Willoughby gaze or stare at Evelina, subjecting her to their discriminating scrutiny. For instance, when, following his attempted rape of Evelina, Willoughby meets her at the Pantheon, she describes their encounter as a visual conflict: "I could not look at him . . . without recollecting the chariot adventure; but, to my great amazement, I observed that he looked at me without the least apparent discomposure" (105). Although Evelina is frightened by these stares, others apparently found them flattering, as is evidenced by Mrs. Robinson's contention that "she had been corrupted by the Pantheon itself, that circle of enchantment where young women underwent 'the gaze of impertinent high breeding.' "[116] In contrast to the male stare—exhibited even by Lord Orville, whose eyes Evelina sees surveying her party "in a careless manner" (234)—women were supposed to lower their eyes. The prostitutes that Evelina encounters unwillingly at Marylebone are the only exception to this rule, yet they admire the "monstrous good stare" that Evelina directs at Lord Orville as he passes by, in hopes that he will rescue her (234). Therefore, although the male stare may be most in evidence, it appears that both sexes engaged in a play of glances and stares that composed the visual "space" of these social arenas.

The last of the three best-known social sites that Evelina goes to is Vauxhall, which, as I have said, attracted a broader audience than either Ranelagh or the Pantheon.[117] Although it opened in 1661 under the name of Spring Gardens, Vauxhall was modernized throughout the eighteenth century by its owner, Jonathan Tyers. Under his direction, it became "an unashamedly commercial exploitation of a garden tradition hitherto available only to a select few, adapted and democratized . . . to cater to the . . . expanding middle-class market."[118] Vauxhall was so successful in cultivating a broad clientele that, despite downswings in its popularity, it managed to stay open until 1859. In *Evelina,* Vauxhall's appeal to the middle and lower ranks is attested to by the fact that Evelina's cousins, the mercantile Branghtons, take her there. Mr. Branghton's rhetorical question to Evelina—"I suppose that you was never so happy in your life before?"—indicates his pompous faith in Vauxhall's status as the ultimate resort (194).

Unlike the Rotunda and the Pantheon, most of the attractions of Vauxhall were outside, encouraging more active forms of entertainment. Indeed, as Evelina recounts in her adventure there, Vauxhall's straight, high-hedged, often unlit walks and trompe l'oeil vistas were the site of rough pursuits:

> A large party of gentlemen, apparently very riotous . . . seemed to rush suddenly from behind some trees, and, meeting us face to face, put their arms at their sides, and formed a kind of circle . . . [in which] we were presently inclosed. The Miss Branghtons screamed aloud, and I was frightened exceedingly: our screams were answered with bursts of laughter, and, for some minutes, we were kept prisoners, till, at last, one of them, rudely, seizing hold of me, said I was a pretty little creature. (195–96)

Despite its tolerance for rowdyism, Vauxhall was not a resort for the middle and lower ranks only: in *Evelina,* this is reflected by Sir Clement Willoughby's intrusion and rescue of Evelina; historically, Vauxhall was patronized by the Prince of Wales, among other aristocrats. Rowlandson's watercolor "Vauxhall Gardens" (c. 1784) pictures the prince, his mistress Mrs. Robinson, the duchess of Devonshire, her sister Lady Duncannon, and others attending a vocal concert, illustrating Vauxhall's cross-rank appeal (see figure 5). Moreover, as with the Pantheon and Ranelagh, Rowlandson's watercolor makes it clear that Vauxhall's chief attraction was visual: rather than listening attentively, members of the audience are in the process of gawking at each other.

Vauxhall's visual features and its appeal to a broad spectrum of individuals are also illustrated by its facilities and its decorations.[119] In fact, Vauxhall was not only the most widely accessible of the three social arenas I have discussed, it was also the one in which explicitly visual attractions were most developed. To begin with, as I have mentioned, the gardens were constructed in a series of high-hedged alleys that effectively structured not only the direction of walks, but the movement of the visitor's eye. At the end of many of these alleys were placed trompe l'oeil paintings that gave them illusory endings, depicting such things as a

5. Vauxhall Gardens, *Thomas Rowlandson. Courtesy of Yale Center for British Art, Paul Mellon Collection.*

landscape with ruins and running water, the Temple of Neptune, the ruins of Palmyra, a Chinese garden, and niches with genii and flora in them.[120] One trompe l'oeil landscape was shown only at nine o'clock, when its cloaking curtain was raised and an illuminated country scene was shown, including hills, a vale with a mill, and a moving picture of a cascade, "created by releasing strips of tin, which produced a noise similar to flowing water and shimmered with the reflection of the light."[121] It is this scene that Evelina "thought extremely pretty, and the general effect striking and lively" (194). These illusions undoubtedly lent a theatrical air to the gardens, and it may be that stage scenery artists were employed to create them, along with various other "props" like the three triumphal arches that overhung the Italian Walk, or the Gothic obelisk at the top of the Dark Walk, both of which were made of wood frames covered with painted canvas.

In addition to this theatrical element, Vauxhall, like Ranelagh, had a

Rotunda in which self-display and spectatorship were emphasized for the visitor as appropriate roles or modes. The Vauxhall Rotunda was added in 1749–50 as a way of competing with Ranelagh and as a shelter for concertgoers on rainy nights. Although much smaller than its Ranelagh progenitor, the Vauxhall Rotunda was—like the interior of the Pantheon—more ornate, decorated with a flower-festooned, domed ceiling, walls painted in mosaic, sixteen oval mirrors, and an eleven-foot, seventy-two-candle chandelier at center. Not only was the chandelier embellished with a plaster model of the rape of Semele by Jupiter (referring, perhaps, to the kind of misadventure that Evelina nearly experiences), but, as J. Lockman noted in his *A Sketch of Spring-Gardens, Vauxhall* (1752), the visitor positioned under it "might see himself reflected at once [in all sixteen mirrors], to his pleasing Wonder."[122] Samuel Wale's painting of the Rotunda, entitled "The Inside of the Elegant Music Room" and engraved c. 1751, removes the chandelier in order to show the interior and the annex better (see figure 6). In the Vauxhall Rotunda, the visitor was thus confronted not only with a mythological analogue that suggested his or her potential role in the pleasures of Vauxhall, but also with a vision of him- or herself as desirable "other," multiplied sixteen times and located at the center of a brilliantly illuminated social space.

The final way in which the visual entered into the visitor's experience at Vauxhall was through paintings that decorated the Rotunda's "saloon," or annex, and the dinner boxes that lined the gardens. The four paintings in the Rotunda annex were commissioned from Francis Hayman in 1760, and depicted "scenes of national glory," such as the recent defeat of the French, and military heroes like Lord Clive.[123] Although these were undoubtedly impressive and may have been connected with the nascent trend toward panoramic, epic-sized visions of contemporary events that I have discussed, they were but a small part of, and were later additions to, Vauxhall's store of visual representations. The majority of the paintings at Vauxhall—over fifty of them—were placed inside the dinner boxes, where they were in more intimate contact with viewers. Commissioned by Tyers for his opening in 1732, the dinner-box paintings were designed principally by Hayman, although Hogarth permitted the copying of some of his designs. Judging primarily from their titles (since only a few survive), T. J. Edelstein has concluded that they presented the viewer with "a catalogue of leisure activities," ranging from games and sports to music-playing, singing, fishing, and more amorous pursuits.[124] Continuing the theatrical vein that we have seen in the "props" of the garden, some paintings depicted scenes from contemporary plays and

6. The Inside of the Elegant Music Room in Vauxhall Gardens,
*H. Roberts after Samuel Wale. Courtesy of Yale Center for British
Art, Paul Mellon Collection.*

Shakespeare. Although Edelstein judges that "such subjects reflect that behavior of the visitors to Vauxhall—the concerts, eating, drinking, and amorous intrigues," I would suggest that they also stimulated such activities by providing visual models for visitors to emulate[125]. The influence of these paintings should not be underestimated: most were engraved and sold in printshops, and many were given allegorical, emblematic significance that was reinforced in broadsides like "Frank Hayman A True Story," written by John Taylor, Hayman's student.[126] Furthermore, Isaac Cruikshank's borrowing of several Vauxhall images for his series of "drolls" (1794) shows that the paintings became part of the cultural repertoire of representations.[127] In this way, Vauxhall was the means by which "ways of seeing" the self—this time in leisure activities—were popularized and added to the options or models available for envisioning selfhood.[128]

Evelina's rejection of the model of selfhood that Vauxhall seems to impose upon her—that of a prostitute, or at least a Semele ready for a Jupiter's ravishing embrace—is partly the cause of her distaste for the place, but she objects more to the company with which she goes: Mr. Smith, Mr. Brown, Mme Duval and the Branghtons. Evelina's visit to Vauxhall marks the beginning of a series of visits to sights that attract a mixed clientele: from debuting at the theater, attending private balls, visiting Ranelagh, and staying on respectable Queen Anne Street with Maria and Mrs. Mirvan, Evelina moves with Mme Duval to rooms rented by a hosier in Holborn and goes to Vauxhall, the Hampstead Ball, Marylebone Gardens, and a host of smaller attractions with Mr. Smith and the Branghtons. While Evelina's reputation is occasionally endangered by her own naïveté in the former environs, her person is threatened at Vauxhall and Marylebone, reflecting their more popular clienteles: "An 'affray' of the kind familiar at Vauxhall and not infrequent at Marylebone was practically unknown at Ranelagh."[129]

Burney's combination of high and low characters and sites, with Evelina as their nexus, is strategic in at least two ways. First, it allows Evelina to present the reader with a tour of London's sights. I have already remarked on how the popularity of tour books like William Gilpin's both reflected and created a new emphasis on the power of the individual "eye"; while Gilpin's tours are rural, there were also available innumerable guidebooks to London, Bath, and other more urban areas. Part of *Evelina*'s popularity as a novel, one might speculate, was based on the fact that it was structured similarly to guides to London like Robert Wilkinson's *Londina Illustrata* (1819) or Rudolf Ackermann's *Microcosm of London* (1810), which combined illustrations with written descriptions.

Second, *Evelina*'s combination of "high" and "low" allows the development of its protagonist to be illustrated through her progress in ability to discriminate between worthless and worthy entertainments. In fact, one key difference between guides like Ackermann's and Wilkinson's and *Evelina* is that in the latter the "sights" are the subject of dialogue on their aesthetic and instructional merits. This dialogue is often implicit, as in the case of the comparison that readers must draw between Evelina's positive opinion of the opera on her visit with the Mirvans (38) and the disgust of the Branghtons when they take her subsequently (83–94). It is also explicit, as in the scene of debate between Lord Orville, Sir Clement Willoughby, and Capt. Mirvan that begins with the merits of the Pantheon and ends in a consideration of all public places, focusing on the theater, the opera, Cox's Museum, and Ranelagh as examples (106–10).

This debate literally foregrounds the "eye" as the aesthetic sense, with Lord Orville asking, "Will not your eye, Sir, speak something in its [the Pantheon's] favor?" and Sir Clement criticizing the "cool eye of unimpassioned philosophy" that would place the attractions of the Pantheon's architecture and decor above the beauties of the ladies in attendance (107).

Here it is clear that "taste," or aesthetics, is being used by both Orville and Willoughby as yet another way of asserting their individual subjectivities and of associating themselves with a particular set of values. Capt. Mirvan deflates their debate by arguing that taste is inherently personal, and thus relative: "you may talk of . . . your eye here, and your eye there . . . to be sure you have two,—but we all know they both squint one way" (107). By taking "eye" out of the abstract, Capt. Mirvan reduces taste to "squinting," or to the narrowing of perspective and construction of values that is involved in aesthetics; moreover, he exposes the elevated, aesthetic conversation between Orville and Willoughby as simply a vehicle for their self-presentation. Still, *Evelina* does not allow Capt. Mirvan to remain unscathed as a bastion of "true" vision; rather, the conversation proceeds to show how limited his own perspective is, as he intolerantly silences Maria and Evelina's opinions and then claims that "in all this huge town . . . there i'n't so much as one public place, besides the playhouse, where a man, that's to say a man who *is* a man, ought not to be ashamed to shew his face" (110). Thus, by qualifying and showing the limitations of all the characters' aesthetic opinions, *Evelina* presents aesthetics as dialogue, into which the self can insert itself and establish a sense of identity.

Collections of "Curiosities"—Different Cultures, Mechanisms, Nature, and the Past

Still, for Evelina herself, there is a proper set of aesthetic opinions that are, to a great extent, embodied in Lord Orville. On one occasion, in his discriminating analysis of the attractions of Cox's Museum, we see his values most clearly revealed. Lord Orville's taste is directly opposed to that of the Branghtons but in accord, in this one instance, with that of Capt. Mirvan, who thinks Cox's "i'n't worth thinking about" (110).

Cox's Museum is *Evelina*'s glance at a kind of entertainment that was becoming very popular; as the visit there points out, "museums" in the eighteenth century were a mixture of what they have since become— displays of various types of knowledge, organized for educational benefit—and of elements of the "show" that we have already discussed.[130]

For example, Cox's "Museum" displayed ingenious toys designed by its proprietor, James Cox, but not in a way intended to inform. Instead, the toys were displayed in a manner intended to create what Willoughby derisively calls a "brilliant *spectacle*" (76). In his evaluation of Cox's Museum, Lord Orville articulates what seems to be the general sentiment of all the characters, save for Mme Duval: "The mechanism . . . is wonderfully ingenious: I am sorry it is turned to no better account; but its purport is so frivolous, so very remote from all aim at instruction or utility, that the sight of so fine a shew, only leaves a regret on the mind, that so much work, and so much ingenuity, should not be better bestowed" (110). This evaluation rests on the assumption that every entertainment must have two intents—it must be *dulce et utile,* both amusing and useful or instructional. Although aesthetics were gradually separated from ethics during the eighteenth century, the *dulce et utile* formula here entwines the two, thus enforcing a conservative "norm" for the novel. Still, though this evaluation rests on conservative, traditional standards, it is significant that the novel stages the evaluation as the result of public dialogue, again suggesting the omnipresence of the public sphere.

During the course of the eighteenth century, the concept of the museum evolved gradually from the "curious shops" that Evelina mentions (37) and that required a "connoisseur" or "curioso" to perceive the value and interest of each object, to a more democratic institution that emphasized the museum's responsibility for educating the general public.[131] Cox's and Don Saltero's, which Mr. Smith praises as a place where "many genteel people go" (187), are exemplary of the old-style, popular museum. Don Saltero's began as a combination barbershop/coffeehouse that gained customers through its proprietor's (James Salter's) use of displays. Among the items displayed were "a nun's penitential whip, four evangelists' heads carved on a cherry stone, . . . William the Conqueror's flaming sword, Queen Elizabeth's strawberry dish, . . . a petrified oyster, . . . [and] a fifteen-inch-long frog."[132] Although the collection was united in a catalog that sold for three pence, it was clearly an assortment of randomly gathered objects whose claim to historical or scientific interest was tenuous, at best. Other such miscellaneous collections were offered for view at the Chelsea Bun House and at Adams' Royal Swan. These museums definitely offered entertainment and may have provoked their visitors' curiosity about the past, different cultures (as with the nun's whip), and natural surroundings. Moreover, by separating certain objects out for visual display, they encouraged the public to think of the past, other cultures, and nature as separately organized categories or visual "spaces."

The Historical Context

These popular museums were, to a great extent, parodies of Sir Hans Sloane's collection, which, as the private collection of the president of the Royal Society, was practically inaccessible to the common public. Although in 1753 Sloane's collection was purchased by Parliament as part of the then-projected British Museum, it was still to become no more accessible because the museum's board of trustees was "a deeply conservative body drawn from the ranks of ecclesiastics and 'persons of rank and fortune' " who effectively restricted entrance to an elite number of visitors.[133] When the British Museum was opened in 1759, visitors were required to make written application for tickets, which, if granted, would be for a date specified by the museum. Not only was the flow of visitors thus narrowed by a background check and organized to suit the museum's staff, but visitors were not allowed to browse through the collections—instead, they were briskly ushered through. Moreover, the museum still assumed that the visitor should be a connoisseur who would need no help in understanding exhibits; in this way, too, it was effectively restrictive. William Hutton, a Birmingham bookseller whose account of his visit to the museum in 1784 is often cited, complained of the lack of clarifying information:

> If I see wonders which I do not understand, they are no wonders to me. Should a piece of withered paper lie on the floor, I should, without regard, shuffle it from under my feet. But if I am told it is a letter written by Edward the Sixth, that information sets a value upon the piece, it becomes a choice morceau of antiquity, and I seize it with rapture. The history must go together; if one is wanting, the other is of little value. I considered myself in the midst of a rich entertainment, consisting of ten thousand rarities, but, like Tantalus, I could not taste one. It grieved me to think how much I lost for want of a little information.[134]

From this account, it is clear that the museum had no pedagogical imperative; it was designed for visitors who could make sense of its exhibits by their previous education. For very different reasons, then, the popular museums and the British Museum were alike in their disregard for the public's intellect, neglecting the *utile* part of the *dulce et utile* formula.

The British Museum's recalcitrance in the face of the popularization of museums was countered by Sir Ashton Lever's "Holophusikon," often referred to more simply as the Leverian Museum. Whereas the British Museum's trustees refused to see their collection as a spectacle, Lever actively marketed his collection to the public: after first opening his house—Alkrington Hall near Manchester—to visitors, free of charge, he moved his collection to London's Leicester Square in 1774, where he charged from two to five shillings for admission. The price of this admission proved sufficient to exclude the lower ranks, but not the middling ones. Although, as in the case of the British Museum, detailed information was not provided for the exhibits, at least they were organized by room so that one room held monkeys, one birds, one suits of armor, another musical instruments, and so on. Lever's museum survived in various forms until it was auctioned off in 1806, but the length of its tenure is not as important as the precedent it created for public museums.

The history of Lever's collection points to two other ways in which collections that had been limited to the view of an elite audience were suddenly made popular attractions for the middle ranks—auctions and tours of great houses. Christies held the first public auction in 1766; suddenly, they were another London attraction, mentioned by Evelina in the same breath as the "curious shops," so that even the sixty-day auction of Lever's collection in 1806 was not unusual. Outside of London, touring great houses was a popular activity, so popular, in fact, that Lever was forced to move his collection to London in order to retain his privacy. Other country houses featured art collections, gardens, or architecture that made them attractive to visitors: "in 1774 . . . 2,324 members of the public visited Wilton, while at Hawkstone in Shropshire there were so many visitors . . . that in c. 1790 an hotel was built to accommodate them."[135] The business of touring such houses also spawned an industry in the printing of tour guides—ninety such guides were published between 1740 and 1840, while the guide to Stowe alone went through thirty-one editions.[136] Viewing the houses of the wealthy enabled the middle ranks to see objects that were considered worthy of collecting; visual images that formerly had been private; upper-class notions of style in houses, gardens, and furnishings; and lifestyles that were very different from their own. Therefore tours, too, contributed to the widening array of ways of defining the self of which the average, middle-rank Briton was aware.[137]

Although the aristocratic culture revealed in the touring of great houses was foreign to many viewers, it was not so foreign as those cultures that were increasingly represented in Britain through the visits of peoples from outside the European continent and through aesthetic vogues for foreign styles. Visitors—including American Indians, Eskimos, Africans, Asian Indians, and so on—were effectively turned into public exhibits, although the government often intervened to prevent their being marketed directly as "sights."[138] The 1710 arrival of four Iroquois sachems caused a great stir, as did the 1762 visit of three Cherokee chiefs, the 1772 visit of two Eskimos, and the most famous visitor of all, Omai the Tahitian, brought back from the South Seas by Captain Cook in 1775.[139] The attraction of these non-Europeans was something felt across ranks, as illustrated by the fact that one of the Iroquois and Omai separately sat to Reynolds—who specialized in painting the wealthy—for their portraits.

Although these exotic visitors certainly did not inspire a desire for direct emulation on the part of most British viewers, some were heavily influenced by these brushes with alien cultures. For example, the British were the earliest Europeans to exhibit widespread interest in Oriental art:

> It was in the 1770s that English collectors began to take the Indies and the Far East seriously. By the end of the wars, when a breath of wind had made Renaissance art expensive and fashionable, the English market was still paying more for the latest Oriental oddities. . . . English collectors were nearly a century ahead of the Continent in their interest in Persian and Indian miniature painting.[140]

In fact, there was a vogue for "Chinoiserie" as early as the 1740s, when some of the Oriental-style buildings at Vauxhall were constructed. Literary examples of "Oriental" taste are found in such diverse tales as Samuel Johnson's *Rasselas* and William Beckford's *Vathek*. At the least, the visits of non-Europeans, the popularity of accounts of Cook's voyages, and other contacts with alien cultures spurred a "greater understanding of the diversity of human society."[141] Although I would agree with Linda Colley's assertion that the "British after 1707 . . . came to define themselves as a single people not because of any political or cultural consensus at home, but rather in reaction to the Other beyond their shores,"[142] I believe that the solidifying of national identity was only the macroscopic effect of contact with other cultures. For the individual subject, this contact could show that eighteenth-century British culture and ways of seeing were relative; in this way the subject was made aware of more options and could potentially interpolate an imagined identity between the familiar, or everyday, and the exotic "other."

Although *Evelina* records no meetings between its protagonist and foreign visitors, part of the novel's appeal lies in its use of a naive center of consciousness and letter writing (Evelina herself) who approximates the alien perspective on British sights that foreigners have. Through this naive, alien perspective, *Evelina* records encounters with the past in popular museums and "curious shops"; with the social in visits to the Pantheon, Vauxhall, and so on; and with the explicitly theatrical at plays and the opera. Each of these encounters is encased in a discourse of aesthetic and moral discrimination, in which the individual subject might situate him- or herself according to personal judgment. In this way, *Evelina* demonstrates the verbal and visual complex of influences on subjectivity. In part because, as an orphan, she has no fixed place in culture, Evelina must construct her identity through interaction with these verbal and visual influences, learning to defend against having an unwanted identity thrust upon her, as well as to "discriminate" properly social, ethical, and aesthetic value.

In the narrative logic of the novel, the guarantee of her proper self-situation—and thus of narrative closure—lies in her eventual marriage to Lord Orville, whose comments and behavior show him to be the center of discriminatory power properly exercised. However, the novel still appears unsure of securing Evelina's identity for readers, possibly because she serves as the nexus where "high" and "low" conjoin inseparably throughout its narrative. While it offers a discriminating view of "low" entertainments and illustrates the jeopardy—both physical and social—in which they place Evelina, the novel nonetheless encompasses them, as if to say that they are an unavoidable element of contemporary social and aesthetic experience. Yet, the novel exhibits a resistance to these low, popular elements, sometimes exposing them to satiric laughter, as in Captain Mirvan's "jokes" on Mme Duval, sometimes dissecting them rationally, as in Lord Orville's discussion of Cox's Museum, and sometimes expressing a sense of fatigue and subtle disillusionment at their multiplication, as in Evelina's comment that "we have not been to half the public places that are now open, though I dare say you will think we have been to all. But they are almost as innumerable as the persons who fill them" (49). In order to disengage Evelina from this populous, dialogized realm, marriage to Lord Orville is not enough—he, too, is mixed in with it. Therefore, Evelina must be raised above dialogic, discriminatory means of determining identity by discovering her parentage, a "natural" source of identity. When she is finally acknowledged to be the daughter of Sir John Belmont, her birth alone confirms her "high" status and removes her from the circulation of the verbal and visual. *Evelina*'s ultimate reliance on the "birth equals worth" equation, despite its seeming proof of the protagonist's merit through her discriminating behavior, reveals an anxiety about the fixing of social identity that I will discuss further in the following chapter.

2
Circulation and Specularity in Social Space

I begin my analysis of psychosocial spaces with social space, the space of the present, because it is most accessible and encompassing for individual subjects. Through readings of Tobias Smollett's *Humphry Clinker* (1771), Jane Austen's *Persuasion* (1818), and various aspects of eighteenth- and early nineteenth-century social history, I want to show how the social space of this "period" is characterized by a sharply increased emphasis, in social practice, on circulation and specularity. "Circulation" is a concept and an eighteenth-century phenomenon that I have discussed in the preceding chapter; "specularity," on the other hand, is new: it indicates the spatio-visual element of this circulative flow for the individual, including theatricality. Although the words "specular" and "speculum" are often associated with the theoretical work of both Jacques Lacan and Luce Irigaray, I use these terms somewhat differently here, based on the eighteenth-century definition of "speculum" as a diagram of planetary bodies that shows their relative positions.[1] Subjects, as I conceive of them, continually plot their own relative location, as expressed in a spatio-visual understanding of the world. This figure of the speculum, then, suggests situating or mapping out the shifting positions inherent in circulation.

My discussion here is governed by a set of critical assumptions about the relation between culture, representations, and subjectivity. First, I assume that the linearity of traditional narratives, both novelistic and historical, excludes the broader appreciation of culture as spatial network; while a linear narrative represses divergence from its focus on political discourse, a cultural history encompasses a multiplicity of discourses. Second, I assume that, in their capacity as audience and agents, eighteenth-century individuals constructed spatio-visual impressions of both the social structure they inhabited and their own positions within it. These impressions can be divided into a series of psychosocial spaces that, totalized, constitute what John Bender calls the "architecture of mind."[2] However, if we examine the social field in practice and on an individual level during the late eighteenth and early nineteenth centuries, it is clear that the effect of representations that attempted to mirror or diagram power relations in a way that would fix individual identity according to a single norm—traditional "rank" in the aristocrat-to-peasant hierarchy, for example—was disrupted by the inherently democratizing proliferation and circulation of images. Moreover, these spatio-visual impressions were not passively received by individuals, but rather were actively collected and composed from fragmentary, circulating images that permitted the construction of a variety of selves under a variety of norms.

Although the visual and the spatial as I conceive of them are inseparable, the visual may be further characterized as an interpretation of the spatial arrangement of entities. Because of this, Jacques Lacan's work concerning the interpretation of space provides a useful model for this analysis: he defines the visual, encountered first by the infant in the "mirror stage," as the locus of the Imaginary, which is a process of self-definition. In the mirror stage, a child's first recognition of its own image in a mirror is the determining step in forging a unified concept of the self and subjectivity. As Lacan points out, the Imaginary is not a developmental phase that the individual undergoes only during infancy; rather, it is an ongoing process that inhabits the individual. Therefore, although the self is determined in a totalizing fashion through visual perception, this totalization is continually broken down and reenvisioned. I want to show how the Imaginary continues to be a force, via the spatio-visual, throughout the social experiences of eighteenth-century selves. In the phenomena examined here—the novel, social practice, and visual representations of the social—the spatio-visual element is ambivalent, implicated both in the conservation of the status quo and in the disruption of it, if only on a momentary microlevel.

Humphry Clinker and the Politics of Circulation

I begin with the picaresque because it is a form of the novel that, in its insistence on adventure, carries its protagonist and readers vigorously forward, in a linear motion, to its close. The linearity and resulting repression of spatiality in the picaresque is curiously duplicated in the traditional historiographical view of eighteenth-century society, according to which eighteenth-century life offers a placid contrast to that of the nineteenth century. Both the picaresque novel and traditional historical narratives exclude the spatiality of the social.

Yet even the picaresque, which I take as paradigmatic of the desire for simple, linear causality both in narrative and in life (in so far as readers identify with the protagonist and, as a result, mimeticize the world of the novel), ultimately diverges from linearity and expands into a more spatial plot. For example, Tobias Smollett's *Humphry Clinker* is, to a large extent, a complication of his earlier efforts at standard picaresque fare such as *Roderick Random*.[3] Although the title page of *Humphry Clinker*, which announces that it is written by "the Author of *Roderick Random*," may be taken as an effort to capitalize on the earlier novel's popularity, it is also an invitation to compare the two. *Roderick Random* exemplifies the democratic scope of the picaresque, which conventionally embraces all ranks in the variety of characters encountered in the travels of its rascally protagonist. However, this protagonist is ultimately separated from the general rout of characters by his benevolence and social superiority. In contrast, *Humphry Clinker* fuses this range of characters to the protagonist, Matthew Bramble, deemphasizing his separateness from the rest of society and expanding the range of voices that are heard on a more or less equal footing.

Thus *Humphry Clinker* moves its focus from the lone picaro or rogue, who makes the linearity of the standard picaresque possible, to a group of individuals who represent the spectrum of British citizens: Bramble, an irascible, melancholic, fifty-five-year-old Welsh squire; Jery, a younger, more pleasant version of Bramble; Lydia, a young lady of the finest sensibility, trained in the latest modes; Tabitha, Bramble's avaricious, vain, and ignorant sister; Winifred, her maid; and Humphry Clinker, the postilion, Methodist preacher, and jack-of-all-trades. The voices of these characters are blended in the letters that we, as readers, receive in this epistolary novel, disrupting and expanding the traditional, single-voiced narrative of the picaro. As Ronald Paulson has noted, by positioning Bramble as "only one of five letter writers," Smollett effectively critiques the perspective of the lone traveler, producing "a commentary on satirists of Bramble's type."[4]

Inevitably, the characters mix as a group during their travels, as imaged in the overturning of the coach, when all the members of the Bramble party tumble together.[5] The fact that this accidental mixture occurs early in the novel, and at the point when the title character first appears, marks it as an emblematic incident. Here Smollett literalizes a metaphor: travel, represented by the figure of the coach, causes the mixture of various individuals. Jery notes the inevitable process of mixture that occurs during travel when he comments on his relationship with his uncle, Bramble: "his disposition and mine, which, like oil and vinegar, repelled one another at first, have now begun to mix by dint of being beat up together" (45).

In fact, by means of the device of following a heterogeneous party of travelers on a journey through Great Britain, the novel suggests that differences in disposition may be just as profound a barrier between individuals as those of social rank, if not more so. Yet, as Jery indicates, even dispositional barriers can be overcome. In *Humphry Clinker,* "disposition" clearly indicates not only matters of personality, but physical states of being; constant references are made to the humors—melancholy, choleric, sanguine, or phlegmatic—in connection to Bramble's illness, while Tabitha is lovesick, and Clinker himself has both been sick and now suffers the "disease" of poverty. Paulson has pointed out that Bramble's illness may indicate Smollett's desire to qualify Bramble's critical perspective—to satirize the satirist—but disease and disposition in *Humphry Clinker* also serve another function.[6] Rather than being associated with large-scale social structures, as are barriers between social ranks, disposition is radically individual. Therefore, *Humphry Clinker* displays an inherently democratic ethos in using illness as a metaphor to mark the importance of disposition in social relations.

The democratic implications of singling out disposition as the chief source of distinction among individuals are strongly signalled by the novel's close, in which matrimonial mingling brings together a series of odd, cross-rank matches, including Lydia and George Wilson, who, although the son of Bramble's friend Dennison, has chosen to lower himself to the profession of actor; Tabitha and Lismahago, a Scottish lieutenant and adventurer; and Winifred and Clinker, who is revealed to be Bramble's son. These matches are made not on the basis of social status—which is shown to be a surface detail—but rather according to disposition. By ending the novel on a typical comedic note through this series of marriages,[7] Smollett's judgment of the democratizing effects of circulation seems to be quite positive: in the process of mixing with one another in various social settings, the characters find a dispositional way of defining themselves that is shown to be "truer" than conventional social definitions of their individual worth.

Still, while the final effects of circulation are shown to be positive, the circulative process itself is not embraced wholeheartedly in *Humphry Clinker*. The novel's ambivalence toward circulation is expressed in one of the central ironies of the novel, the fact that Bramble, the author and paymaster of this agglomerated party, also decries such mixing of ranks as unhealthy. In this way, his character reflects the conflict between more dynamic, democratic, circulative visualizations of social space and static, hierarchical models. His critique of the democratizing trend in society occurs in his letters from the city of Bath, which he takes as exemplary of the evils of this trend. Upon arriving at Bath, Bramble indignantly remarks how

> Every upstart of fortune, harnessed in the trappings of the mode, presents himself at Bath, as in the very focus of observation. . . . Knowing no other criterion of greatness, but the ostentation of wealth, they discharge their affluence without taste or conduct, through every channel of the most absurd extravagance; and all of them hurry to Bath, because here, without any further qualification, they can mingle with the princes and nobles of the land. Even the wives and daughters of low tradesmen . . . are infected with the same rage of displaying their importance. (66)

In this passage Bramble marks out the two principal characteristics of democratization as it appears in Bath: circulation and specularity. Extending his preoccupation with his own health, Bramble uses bodily circulation—indicated by his emphasis on mingling, discharges, and channels—as a metaphor to figure the breaking of social boundaries as both a disease and a madness.

In addition, Bramble identifies Bath as an intensely specular field in which presentation and display are the primary activities; the city is "the very center of observation" (66). This is reinforced by Jery, who writes that "another entertainment, peculiar to Bath, arises from the general mixture of all degrees assembled in our public rooms, without distinction of rank or fortune" (78). In contrast to Bramble, who sees this mixture as a vulgar display, Jery sees it as a spectacular, unique entertainment.

Less detached in her appreciation is Lydia, who remarks happily that in Bath, "the eye is continually entertained by the splendour of dress and equipage" (68). Through their voices, the reader is provided with multiple perspectives on Bath's specular aspects rather than with a single-note evaluation. Nevertheless, all of them agree that Bath is a distinct realm in which observation—the specular—is a preferred mode. Because of its imperatives for visitors to both observe others and display themselves, Bath continually provokes the Lacanian Imaginary, engaging individuals in the process of redefining themselves.

Humphry Clinker's singling out of Bath as the site where circulation and specularity are most evident probably derives from Smollett's own experience of the town. Smollett's residence in Bath from 1766–68 must have provided him with many concrete details about social practice; given the vast number of visitors to Bath, he would have been aware of how qualified his readership would be to check his authenticity.[8] Given the foregrounding of social issues in the heterogeneity of the Bramble party and in the poverty of Clinker, as well as in the key position of Bath as the site of the first substantial exchange of letters, Smollett must have considered Bath to be particularly suited to the purpose of thematizing social experience. Indeed, *Humphry Clinker* gives a great amount of detail concerning the city and common social activities. Among other things, the reader is told that Bramble's party settles in Milsham Street after a false start in the South Parade, and that Jery subscribes to the dress ball series held at the Assembly Rooms (70). Via Bramble, a discourse on the architectural features of Bath is delivered, including evaluations of Queen's Square and the Circus (62–65), while Lydia provides a description of the baths themselves and the entertainments available: "we have music in the Pump-room every morning, cotillions every forenoon in the rooms, balls twice a week, and concerts every other night, besides private assemblies and parties without number" (68). Besides the novel's own testimony as to its documentary character, since the moment of its publication in 1771 it has been treated as social commentary: from June 15–18 of 1771, the *Whitehall Evening Post* made *Humphry Clinker*'s descriptions of Bath the basis of an article entitled "The Present State of Bath." This use of *Humphry Clinker* as social document has continued, from R. E. M. Peach's 1891 study of its architectural accuracy in *Bath, Old and New* to R. S. Neale's 1981 social history of Bath. Thus, both the structure of the novel and the history of its reception urge that it be read, in part, as a report on social practice.

To confirm the implications of *Humphry Clinker*'s description of the social realm of Bath, we need only turn to the well-documented history of the city. An examination of the social institutions of Bath shows an ambivalence in attitude toward circulation that is similar to the irony in Bramble's being simultaneously the author of a mixed-rank party and a critic of the mixture of social ranks. The symbolism of the office of Master of Ceremonies, for example, shows such a split in attitude. The Master of Ceremonies presided over the social functions held in the Bath Assembly rooms, welcomed newcomers to the city, attended to visitors' particular needs, and enforced an official code of regulations designed to preserve decorum and promote social interaction. For this reason, the Master of Ceremonies was often referred to as the "King," because his social authority within the city of Bath was regarded as absolute. The chronicles of the city offer many examples of noble and even royal personages who suffered the rebuke of the "King" for their violations of the rules of the company. Corresponding to his power, the Master of Ceremonies possessed regalia in the form of a medallion. For example, Le Bas, the Master of Ceremonies for the Lower Assembly Rooms[9] in the early nineteenth century, wore a gold medallion picturing Venus holding an apple; it was inscribed with the motto "Venus decens" (Venus the Beautiful) on one side, and "Arbiter Elegantiarum, Communi consensu" (Arbiter of Women's Elegance, by consent of the community) on the other. The mythological referent here is the judgment of Paris, in which Paris selected Venus as the most beautiful of the goddesses; the medallion clearly positions the Master of Ceremonies as the Paris of Bath. According to *The Improved Bath Guide* (c. 1809), the elaborateness of this medallion was not unusual; from the extent to which such regalia imitated that of the state, one may conclude that the kings of Bath had at least symbolic importance. The prestige of the kings is also indicated by the fact that several had their portraits painted by leading artists: Thomas Hoare painted the second and most famous king, Richard "Beau" Nash (1674–1761), whose biography was also written by Oliver Goldsmith, and Gainsborough painted the fourth king, Captain Wade. Furthermore, their importance is illustrated in the details that *The Improved Bath Guide* gives in describing the history of the office and in tracing the succession of kings.

On the one hand, the existence of this office and the attention and power given to the kings exhibit the desire for some sort of authority or control over circulation; on the other hand, the setting up of a social king subverts the established sociopolitical order, declaring the social to be a separate realm in which the rules of class distinction do not apply. Goldsmith's *The Life of Richard Nash* (1762) includes several examples in which Nash acted as "King," directly against the privilege of rank. One of the most famous incidents took place at an Assembly Room ball, when he stripped an apron from the Duchess of Queensbury. He did this, first, because he disapproved of the apron's "rustic associations" and, second, because it was a very expensive lace apron—one that could only be viewed as an assertion of exceptional wealth and social standing.[10] Nash's dominance in this instance suggests that Bath was a realm in which, at the very least, the rules of social distinction were reconstituted differently, to participate in what Terry Castle would call the "carnivalesque."[11] In this way, the office of the Master of Ceremonies contributed to the impression that Bath was a place of, if not "festive misrule," at least suspension of everyday rules, leading Lydia to exclaim that "Bath is to me a *new world*—All is gayety, good-humour, and diversion" (68).[12]

The sites of such diversion, Bath's Assembly Rooms, had rules that were designed to facilitate the circulation that Bramble detests. Like most regulations, the rules of the Assembly Rooms conserved power. Still, they also provided for easy mixing of disparate ranks. As the first King to attain widespread acknowledgement of his power, Nash established a set of eleven rules that were intended to do away with distinctions of rank: for example, "he reprimanded women who invoked social precedence in the dance."[13] He also used his influence to prevent private parties and balls from creating an exclusionary atmosphere at Bath. Jery describes the resulting democratic mixture of individuals at a dance: "The ball was opened by a Scotch lord, with a mulatto heiress from St Christopher's; and the gay colonel Tinsel danced all the evening with the daughter of an eminent tinman from the borough of Southwark" (78). By the time of the publication of *The Improved Bath Guide* in the first decade of the nineteenth century, the list of rules had escalated to twenty-two items, among them one that stated that "the three front seats, at the upper end of the room, [are] reserved for ladies of precedence of the rank of Peeresses of Great Britain or Ireland."[14] This particular expansion of the Assembly Rooms rules may reflect a certain defensive interest in conserving rank; in any case, expansion in general indicates a growing disciplinary structure being applied to channel and control circulation.[15]

Another institution that both reflected and created circulation in Bath was the town's architecture. It is no coincidence that Bramble introduces readers to Bath via an architectural critique of Queen's Square and the Circus, for they, too, reflected and shaped new social patterns. When Bramble indicts King's Circus as an ornament, part of the social artifice of Bath that he despises, by saying that "the Circus is a pretty bauble, contrived for shew" (63), the implication is that the buildings most associated with Bath's character as a site of social circulation have no substance and offer an illusory, contrived prestige. Bramble's description of the Circus as a "bauble" connects it not only to the feminine show of jewelry, which he implicitly derides, but also to the medallions and illusory or contrived authority of the kings of Bath. As a whole, Bramble seems repulsed by the new architectural projects, lamenting that "what sort of a monster Bath will have become in a few years, with these growing excrescences, may be easily imagined" (65). Through the architecture of the city, he attacks what he sees as the unnatural erasure of rank and the monstrous growth of a new social order based on circulation.

One architectural form, mentioned only briefly by Bramble, is even more closely associated with late eighteenth-century circulation and specularity—the crescent. This new form of row housing, or terrace, appeared first in Bath and then spread to other locations where growth was rapid and land was available.[16] Bramble's mention of the crescent is scant because Royal Crescent, built between 1767 and 1774, was the first of its kind, and construction on the crescent had only just begun during Smollett's tenure in Bath (see figure 7). Royal Crescent was followed by Lansdown Crescent, constructed in 1789–93, and by numerous others around Bath.[17] What is significant about the crescent form is that it created a *social* space that was in the field of view of all the residences. Previous to this development, squares like Grosvenor Square in London and circuses like King's Circus in Bath had enclosed space, but the potential social function of this space had instead been devoted to traffic, formal gardens, or a centrally located building like St. Paul's in Covent Garden.[18] These squares and circuses were designed according to a Roman or continental model that made them more appropriate for the formality and ceremony of a palace.[19] In the particular instance of King's Circus, R. S. Neale has argued that the architect responsible for its design, John Wood, meant it to symbolize the "awfulness and omniscience of God" through "the deliberate exclusion of all nature."[20] In theory, then, the formality of squares and circuses could be linked to the disciplinary discourses of British culture. Later, in discussing historical space, I will connect disciplinary discourse to the "regime of tradition," an attitude toward history that was governed by the desire to maintain the status quo of social hierarchy. Lydia, who is not attuned to this disciplinary, religious level of signification that Wood may have intended in the Circus, comments that "the Square, the Circus, and the Parades, put you in mind of the sumptuous palaces represented in prints and pictures" (68),

7. *Royal Crescent, Bath.*

showing how, even to those untrained in architectural allusions, they at least seemed distanced from, or inaccessible to, the individual subject, part of a realm of representation rather than of physical reality.

In contrast, the crescent was left open, creating a commons area without a formal or symbolic dimension. Whereas the square and circus forms were based on the exclusion of nature—including humanity—for the austere, inhuman coldness of paving stone, the crescent welcomed its inhabitants to a partially enclosed "green space." The crescent furthered movement toward a decentralized pattern of circulation in featuring only an *implied* center, rather than the designated, enclosed center of the square or circus forms. In connection to other Bath social institutions, this substitution of an implied center for a formal one seems most comparable to the substitution of a social king for the sociopolitical reality of the British monarchy. Like the institution of the social King, the crescent was a form that created social and spatial order in Bath, yet by the fact of its partial openness it appears to have encouraged a sense of freedom from all-encompassing authority.

Arguing a position that is somewhat different from this social interpretation of crescent architecture, Mark Girouard suggests that the "implied center" of the crescent was nature. Judging from the remarks of the residents of Lansdown and Royal Crescents who expressed marvel at their view of the "green space" before them, he concludes that in the crescent, "art and nature were consummately brought together."[21] In support of Girouard's hypothesis, R. S. Neale shows how John Wood the Younger, the architect of Royal Crescent, forced the lessor of the land on which the Crescent stood to agree not to build anything on the land upon which it looked out.[22] However, it must be noted that these residents were primarily pleased with their *view,* which included more than grass, sheep, and trees: they had the opportunity, in many cases, to overlook the city of Bath, and to observe their fellow residents in the crescent. This is indicated by one of the Royal Crescent's lease restrictions, according to which the landowner "was prevented from growing any tree more than eight feet high."[23] The view thus preserved at Royal Crescent was also one of the admired characteristics of Camden Crescent (1788), whose vantage point was described in 1819 by Pierce Egan as "command[ing] for miles a most interesting, extensive, picturesque prospect."[24]

In this way, the crescent literalized Bramble's characterization of the social space of Bath as "the focus of observation" because the dwellings were pointed inward, toward each other: "the crescent insured easy and perpetual visibility; everyone standing in the Royal Crescent can be seen by invisible viewers behind hundreds of viewers."[25] Indeed, the specular architecture of the Bath crescents seems most analogous to that of the theater: the crescent's windows are equivalent to the theater's boxes, and the implied center—Bath—is comparable to the stage.[26] Sir John Summerson offers another, similar analogy, one that he believes to have influenced both John Wood and his son. Summerson contends that the Circus was built as a miniature of the Roman Colosseum, which is synonymous with spectatorship in the ancient world. He argues further that "The [Royal] Crescent is likewise a Colosseum; but it has retained its elliptical plan, been turned inside out and then cut in half."[27] *Humphry Clinker* substantiates the relevance of this analogy in Bramble's comment that the Circus "looks like Vespasian's amphitheatre turned outside in" (63). The implication here is that the Circus inhabitants, like the audience at the Imperial Roman shows, were arranged so as to view a kind of spectacular production.

As Eric Rothstein has shown, analogy is a structure of reading that pervades both novelistic theory and practice throughout the eighteenth century, forming one of the central epistemological systems of order. Analogy works in the eighteenth-century novel in a way that "permits inquiry and creates order when the plot does not."[28] In terms of narrative movement, analogy supplements and, to a degree, subverts the simple causality of the linear plot. We see the analogical process deployed in *Humphry Clinker*'s presentation of the chaotic, undifferentiated social space formed by Bath, where circulation works as an analogical means of tying together bodily fluids and disease, Bath's supposedly healthful waters, and the "whirl" of social activity, mixing social ranks; on the level of the novel as a whole, the same analogy works to describe the mixture of Scots, Welsh, and British in the Bramble party, the circuitous path taken by the party, and even the "health" of the nation. This last analogical referent—the health of the nation—points to my next direction of inquiry. I suggest that *Humphry Clinker*'s depiction of Bath can be taken as a metonymic representation of late eighteenth-century British culture as Smollett saw it, and therefore that circulation, specularity, and the democratization of social space were endemic to that culture.

In fact, these qualities are found not only in the social space of Bath, but in London as well. Their visual metaphor was the Rotunda at Ranelagh, which I have discussed in the previous chapter (see figure 8). Peter Borsay has anatomized the eighteenth-century enthusiasm for formal walks such as that featured in the Rotunda, concluding that they were designed for "the pursuit and acquisition of status."[29] Here I would like to consider more specifically how the Rotunda literalized circulation and specularity. While it stood, the Ranelagh Rotunda was the largest structure of its kind: it was 150 feet in interior diameter, and was designed so as to provide a circular parade ground for strolling ladies and gentlemen. Those who chose not to stroll, or who needed rest, could observe the parade grounds and take refreshment in one of the booths in the surrounding arcade. One contemporary observer, Samuel Rogers, found the circulation of the strollers especially impressive: "all was so orderly and still that you could hear the whishing sound of the ladies' trains as the immense assembly walked round and round the room."[30] However, the silence that Rogers notes was not usual: from the date of its original conception to its demolition in 1805 Ranelagh always had a spot for an orchestra and organ. Music was combined with the stunning

8. An Inside View of the Rotundo in Ranelagh Gardens, *Nathaniel Parr after Antonio Canaletto. Courtesy of Yale Center for British Art, Paul Mellon Collection.*

visual effect of lighting provided by "numerous chandeliers, each ornamented with a gilt crown and containing crystal bell-lamps of candles" to create an almost theatrical setting.[31] On the frequent masquerade nights, the costumes of Ranelagh's visitors must have complemented the Rotunda's theatrical aspects, producing a real spectacle.

Architecturally, as in the crescents, the design of the Rotunda, with its fifty-two upper and lower "boxes," was analogous to that of a theater.[32] The theatricality of the Rotunda's circular space was probably no accident, since its alleged developer and principal owner was Lacy, the patentee of Drury Lane theater. Thus the Rotunda models circulation and specularity as social trends, having been designed to facilitate both; for those who came to the Rotunda, the most important thing was literally to circulate, expanding the number of fields of view in which one was seen.

Given *Humphry Clinker*'s preoccupation with social space, it is not surprising that, like Burney's Evelina, the Bramble party visits Ranelagh upon arriving in London from Bath. Bramble's description of the Rotunda highlights the circulative movements of its visitors: "One half of the company are following at the other's tails, in an eternal circle; like so many blind asses in an olive-mill, where they can neither discourse, distinguish, nor be distinguished; while the other half are drinking hot water, under the denomination of tea . . . to keep them awake for the rest of the evening" (120). In this passage, Bramble condemns the inability to distinguish or make social distinctions in the Rotunda, and connects it to the company's movement "in an eternal circle." It is no coincidence that this description follows on the tails of Bramble's critique of the city of London, in which he argues that "there is no distinction or subordination left—The different departments of life are jumbled together—The hod-carrier, the low mechanic, . . . the shopkeeper, the pettifogger, the citizen, and courtier, *all tread upon the kibes of one another* " (119; emphasis Smollett's). In essence, he claims that the vast circulation of London—in social, financial, and cultural terms—undermines the proper "subordination" of social hierarchy; this erasure of distinction is represented in the smaller, more polite circle of the Rotunda.

However, Bramble's is not the last word on the Rotunda: in accordance with the novel's practice of mixing the heterogeneous voices of the Bramble party, Lydia's commentary immediately follows Bramble's, and contradicts his negative impression of its attractions. Where Bramble feels that the the company "can neither discourse, distinguish, nor be distinguished," Lydia emphasizes the visitors' ability to see in an arena "enlightened with a thousand golden lamps, that emulate the noon-day sun" (123). Lydia's enthusiasm recalls Evelina's description of the Rotunda as "some *inchanted castle"* (37). Moreover, while Bramble considers the strollers to be "blind asses" who are tied to a laborious, tedious task—milling olives—Lydia glorifies them as the "exulting sons and daughters of felicity," who "tread . . . [a] round of pleasure" (123). Yet Lydia's description of the strollers is much like Bramble's, in that both are images of homogeneity: Bramble's is a vision of universal debasement, while Lydia's is one of universal transcendence. Both visions are enabled by a social space, embodied in the Rotunda, that gives at least the impression of egalitarianism and the erasure of social distinction. In this realm, both Lydia and Bramble feel free to impose their own idiosyncratic wishes on the company in characterizing them. In this way, both show that the Rotunda is a realm of psychosocial freedom. Of course, because their descriptions are dominated by wish-fulfilling impulses, Bramble and Lydia can testify only to the circulation and specularity of the Rotunda, not to the degree that its effects are concretely democratizing.

Indeed, the extent to which the Rotunda's visitors were drawn democratically from throughout the ranks of London's population is debatable. On the one hand, there is some testimony to indicate the diversity of the crowd that frequented Ranelagh. For instance, according to Horace Walpole, Ranelagh's clientele was very diverse: "the company is universal; there is from His Grace of Grafton down to the children out of the Foundling Hospital."[33] Similarly, in his *London Pleasure Gardens of the Eighteenth Century,* Warwick Wroth concludes that "at all periods the company was a good deal mixed" at Ranelagh.[34] On the other hand, the group who enjoyed the Rotunda must have been restricted by the price of admission, which was half a crown normally, a shilling during the day, and a minimum of half a guinea on masquerade nights.[35] In light of this somewhat contradictory evidence, it seems reasonable to conclude that, while the Rotunda was not entirely inclusive and democratic, the range of those familiar with its attractions extended from relatively prosperous citizens to professional families to the servants of the nobility, in addition to the wealthy and privileged.

The qualities of the social space that the Rotunda presented to these visitors become clearer if we compare its architecture to that of Jeremy Bentham's plans for a "Panopticon," which he first proposed in 1791.[36] In *Discipline and Punish,* Foucault uses the Panopticon as a metaphor for the disciplinary structure of modern society. Although the Panopticon and the Rotunda had very different intended functions—one a prison, the other a pleasure dome—they had surprisingly much in common architecturally. Both were circular structures whose circumferences were lined with a stacked ring of boxes or cells; both featured a central column separated from the circumference by an open, circular space; and both were designed to maximize specularity.

While these similarities are interesting, the differences between the two structures illuminate the unique features of the Rotunda's space. First, whereas the Panopticon, as Foucault describes it, held in its central column a place for the "unseen seer"—a stand-in for God or the State—to watch over prisoners, the center of the Rotunda was blind, occupied merely by a large furnace. This blind center can serve as a metaphor for the decentralization of power that was occurring within social space, transforming it into a field or market in which power and status were continually shifting, or circulating. Interestingly, this center space had originally been the site of the orchestra; within a few years of Ranelagh's opening, the orchestra was removed from the center to the side of the Rotunda, literally decentering the only rival attraction to the company's circulation. Second, whereas the Panopticon's structure defined power as the ability to see without being seen and conserved specularity as observation in its central column, the structure of the Rotunda dramatized how power within social space had come to depend on mutual specularity, emphasizing that the ability to display one's self as an object of attention was just as important as the ability to view others. In this way, both circulation and specularity may be seen as decentered functions in which the site of power is no longer fixed and protected, but rather is dispersed into the functions themselves.[37]

Humphry Clinker and social practice in the late eighteenth century show that the dispersal of power had contradictory effects, at once both restrictive and democratizing. The key to this ambivalence lies in the concept of circulation, which Jon Klancher has adeptly historicized in *The Making of English Reading Audiences, 1790–1832*. Tracing circulation as a metaphor in the work of the political philosopher Arthur Young and other writers of the late eighteenth and early nineteenth centuries, Klancher concludes that "cultural circulation means . . . an intricately prepared system of channels through which people, things, or writings connect and move."[38] As such, circulation was an ideological goal to be worked toward, a form of social order that pre-Revolutionary and Revolutionary France, for example, lacked: in Young's view, France's turmoil was caused by the fact that the old system, which was based on a linear, top-to-bottom hierarchy, fragmented before it could be replaced by a circulatory system. In its ordering aspect, circulation reinforces the cultural status quo; in this way it can be attached to Foucault's sense of a repressive, disciplinary structure. However, as Klancher points out, circulation also provides for movement within its "intricately prepared system"—movement not only of goods, but also of people and ideas. Thus circulation is ambivalent in its social effects: it imposes a decentralized yet restrictive order while it democratizes by offering channels for individual initiatives that may, indeed, cause the movement and change in social order that Bramble sees in *Humphry Clinker*.

In fact, one indication of social instability, what Lawrence and Jeanne Stone describe as a name change made to establish "fictive direct lineage," occurs in *Humphry Clinker*: as a young man, Bramble himself took the name of Lloyd for a time in order to secure a distant relation's estate.[39] The fact of his name change is treated as nothing very unusual; however, it ironically becomes the occasion of his engendering an heir in Clinker, whose legal name is revealed to be Matthew Lloyd, Jr. Although many name changes probably had little influence on the social order, Humphry's sudden elevation from Clinker to Lloyd and from impoverished, diseased, dissenting (Methodist) vagrant to heir is emblematic of the drastic changes that they could effect.

As we have seen in the previous chapter, nearly all ranks were affected by the increase in circulation and specularity and the growing inclusivity of the social. For those outside of the elite who still had ready access to the social field that I have described, circulation and specularity were its defining characteristics. In a social field dominated by a market ethos in which there were no fixed positions of status and in which the relative power of each individual's standing was determined by specularity—the ability to see and be seen—it was necessary to "circulate" in order to maximize one's personal prestige and create social rank. The new social arenas created a battle-like atmosphere in which individuals vied for attention:

> they were intensely public places in which it was known large numbers of eligible combatants and spectators would turn out and be fully exposed to the minutest assessment. . . . The instruments of battle, the means used by individuals to acquire status on the walks, were twofold: aspects of behavior, such as carriage and conversation (both the product of educational investment), and various types of material acoutrements, like dress, wigs, hats, and jewelry.[40]

Moreover, social space itself was decentered, moving out of specialized environments like Ranelagh, Vauxhall, and so-called pleasure gardens to domestic or residential settings like the crescent, and out of London to provincial locations like Bath, Scarborough, Tunbridge Wells, Bristol, Epsom, and Harrogate.[41] Bath combined both of these movements with a history of circulation of various kinds, including the circulation of its supposedly therapeutic waters, the poor or impeded circulation of its visitors, the circulation of money at its gaming tables, and the circulation of marriageable men and women.

Persuasion and the Articulation of Social Space

Bath's status as a marriage market and a center of social space make it a particularly felicitous setting for Jane Austen's *Persuasion,* a novel that deals explicitly with social space in terms of the tenuous positions of both its protagonist, Anne Elliot, whose age renders her increasingly unmarriageable, and of her family, whose self-indulgence leads them to an overextension of their finances. On the one hand, Anne's vulnerable social position and the narrative's close proximity to her perspective give the reader a microscopic, personal look at social space in practice, foregrounding the difficulties of existence on its margins. While they are treated quite seriously in *Persuasion*, these difficulties are seen in *Humphry Clinker* either unsympathetically, as in the case of the lovesick spinster Tabitha, or only distantly, as in the case of Clinker, who only once enters into the "conversation" of letters and hence is limited to being reported on by others. On the other hand, the financial plight of Anne's family provides us with the type of social experience described macroscopically by the Stones as the threat of "drop-out" from the gentry. Thus, *Humphry Clinker* serves well as an extensive introduction to the circulative and specular mechanisms of social space, while *Persuasion* offers an intensive, detailed case study of their workings.

On one level, *Persuasion* operates like *Humphry Clinker* in that it uses a topographical analogy to describe social space. However, while Smollett's novel uses the circular route of the Bramble party to image all kinds of social circulation, Austen's depends on the topography of the city of Bath to produce a static diagram of the relative positioning of individuals within social space (see figure 9). Moreover, this diagram is associated with the representatives of traditional, hierarchical social order—Sir Walter and Elizabeth Elliot—but not with the heroine, Anne Elliot. It delineates the repressive force of social power that Foucault describes by showing how topography is used both to ghettoize individuals and to reduce their identity, working in each case against circulation. For instance, topographical references are consistently given in place of personal names, as if we are expected literally to map out relations between individuals, families and "parties": when "the Bath paper one morning announced the arrival of the Dowager Viscountess Dalrymple . . . all the comfort of No.—, Camden-place, was swept away for many days";[42] or later, "Anne was already engaged, to spend the same evening in Westgate-buildings" (169). Here Camden-place becomes a shorthand for the Elliot family and their acquaintances, while Westgate-buildings serves to indicate Anne's impoverished, widowed friend, Mrs. Smith (see figure 9 for a map of the major characters' residences).

Topography therefore not only supplants individuals in name, but also denotes their status in *Persuasion*. Thus the house in Camden-place (which is frequently called "Camden Crescent") is much to the satisfaction of Anne's father, Sir Walter, because it is "a lofty, dignified situation, such as becomes a man of consequence" (151).[43] Still more dignified— perhaps because of its square, palatial design—is Laura Place, the residence of Lady Dalrymple, whose company is coveted by Sir Walter. In

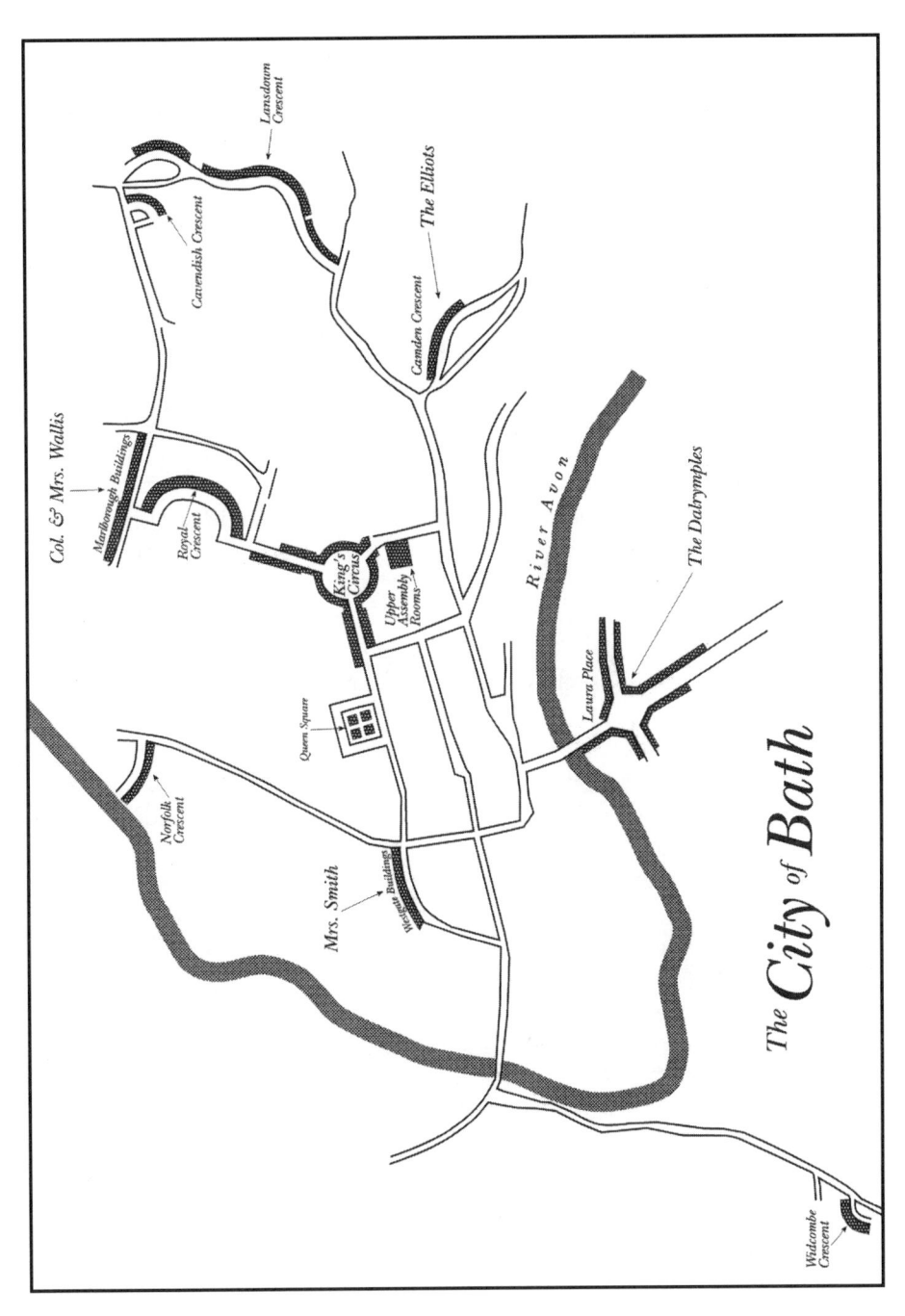

9. The City of Bath.

contrast, both Sir Walter and Anne's sister Elizabeth automatically disdain Anne's friend Mrs. Smith, though they have never met her, simply because of where she lives—the apparently undistinguished Westgate buildings. Nikolaus Pevsner notes that the part of Bath in which Westgate buildings were located "had been fashionable about 1730–40," but "had indeed come down" by the time of *Persuasion*.[44] Irked by Anne's going to visit Mrs. Smith, Sir Walter exclaims, "Westgate-buildings must have been rather surprised by the appearance of a carriage drawn up near its pavement! . . . A widow, Mrs. Smith, lodging in Westgate-buildings!—A poor widow, barely able to live, between thirty and forty—a mere Mrs. Smith, an everyday Mrs. Smith, of all people and all names in the world, to be the chosen friend of Miss Anne Elliot" (170). In this passage the names Smith and Westgate-buildings clearly contend in their relative ability to inspire Sir Walter's revulsion. Both in terms of her inferior family connections, as indicated by the commonness of her name, and in terms of her poverty, which is indicated by the location of her dwelling, Mrs. Smith is judged by Sir Walter to be unworthy of attention. In other words, she cannot be situated on the "map" that Sir Walter has drawn of Bath society: Camden place and Westgate buildings should never meet, and, in Sir Walter's eyes, any such meeting is a distortion of "proper" social topography.

In this respect, *Persuasion* documents a way of spatializing social relations that corresponds with efforts to fix social identity to a single-norm standard: each inhabitant of Bath's social space is reduced to the status of his or her residence. However, Anne frees herself from the social gridlock produced by the ghettoization that Sir Walter supports, refusing to restrict herself to fashionable patterns of circulation. Instead, she insists on taking advantage of the heterogeneous population of Bath by reclaiming Mrs. Smith, an old school friend. Outside the social space of Bath, such a meeting might never have occurred. Anne's practice within Bath's highly defined social space is an implicit critique of the static tableau or rigid social hierarchy that Bath seemingly enforces. In this way, *Persuasion*, like *Humphry Clinker*, presents both the repressive and the potentially liberating aspects of circulation.

Persuasion also goes beyond the antidemocratic analogy it reveals between Bath's topography and the topography of social relations in order to focus on the construction of social space on the microlevel of practice and the event. This focus is seen especially in the concert scene of chapter 20, which takes place at the Bath Assembly Rooms. In this scene, Austen emphasizes the strategic positioning of bodies within the social field. At least two movements are present in the scene: the self-representation of the Elliot party to the crowd attending the concert, and the attempted rapprochement between Anne and the suitor she rejected upon the advice or "persuasion" of her friend Lady Russell over a year before, Captain Wentworth. The detail with which the former is described creates a highly spatio-visual impression on the reader and carries the topographical analogy into the realm of practice, while the latter supplements and qualifies the reader's resulting visualization of the concert scene by providing details of the motivations for movement or inaction.

Both Anne and Wentworth have feelings for the other that they find difficult to articulate, in part because of their past, and in part because of the formal social aspects of the concert setting. The chapter opens with the Elliot party arriving at the Bath Assembly Rooms and entering the octagon room, where they take "their station by one of the fires" (see figure 10 for a plan of the Assembly Rooms). Upon Captain Wentworth's entrance, a detailed description of social moves follows that would be equally appropriate to an account of formal battle maneuvers during the Napoleonic Wars: Anne's slight "advance" to greet him "brought him out of the straight line"; meanwhile, Anne draws support from having her party in the "back ground." Despite the fact that Captain Wentworth is a "friendly party," social demands force Anne and Wentworth to translate their tentative desire for reconciliation into a series of codified, acceptable "moves" that preserve the existing social topography. Moreover, the military metaphor used throughout the scene connects the social firmly to Foucault's instrumentation of discipline, since the military is one of the fields in which he locates its development.

Although Austen's intent here may have been ironic deflation of the social, she also makes a point about its significance for her characters: it is a field in which a struggle takes place, albeit one in which overt violence is sublimated. Marilyn Butler's assessment of the Bath scenes in *Persuasion* registers this serious note in claiming that they consist of "a nervous sequence of half-articulate meetings between Anne and Wentworth—as they shelter from the rain, pass on opposite sides of the street, are separated by circumstances and by Mr. Elliot at the concert. Such occasions are tracked in Anne's consciousness, woven in with intensity among the cold externals of the Elliots' social life."[45]

While I cannot agree with Butler's subsequent linking of this intensity of consciousness to incipient Evangelism, her emphasis on the difficulty of the encounters between Anne and Wentworth is completely to the point. Because they each recognize that their relationship to one an-

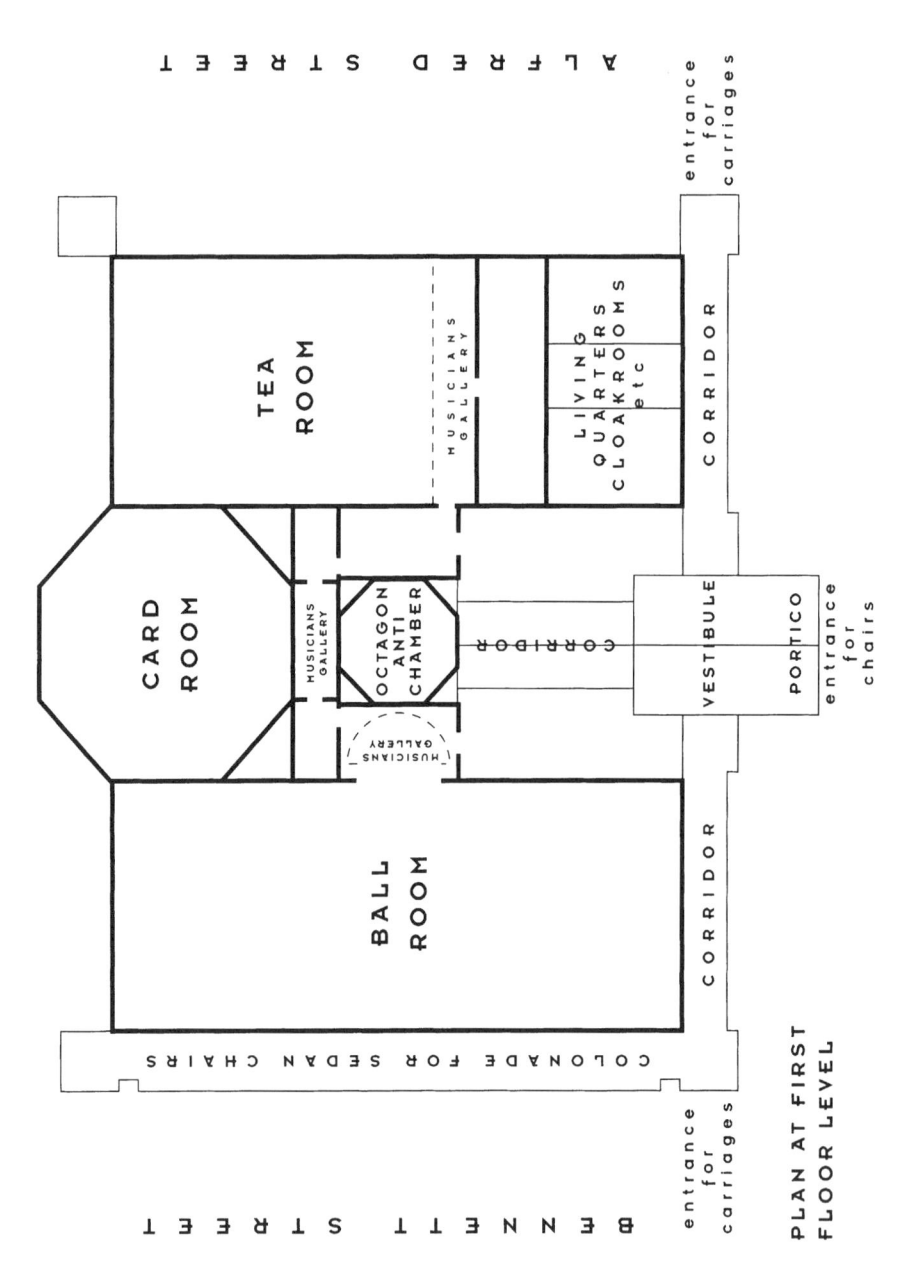

10. *Plan of the Assembly Rooms.*

other is, as of yet, undefined, their meetings are invested with a complex set of motivations that include sexual desire, insecurity about their attractiveness to the other, fear of rejection, anger over the truncation of their previous affairs, and the desire to be able to "read" the other completely in order to achieve proper definition of these vagaries. The strength of the motivations represented here signifies the importance of something beyond the tangible values of land and aristocratic birth through which the other Elliots sustain their self-images. The difficulties Anne and Wentworth face in defining their relationship are complicated further by the necessity of working through what Butler calls the "cold externals" of Bath's social space. Still, the fact that success is not a matter of separating these externals from an internal "truth" is indicated by Anne's refusal to apologize for the persuasions of her friend Lady Russell that originally caused her to break with Wentworth. According to D. A. Miller, " 'persuasion' is Jane Austen's subtle concept of social mediation, through which desire is nearly always made to pass."[46] In Anne's affirmation of persuasion, we see acknowledgement of the necessity of "social mediation," or the "cold externals" that channel individual social relations. For those like Anne and Wentworth who are working hesitantly, indirectly, and very separately toward a single purpose, the difficulty is to channel a very private, individual agenda into a formal, externally imposed set of conditions.[47]

In contrast, for the Elliot party as a whole, the concert scene is more clearly an arena for clear-cut, aggressive movement within the social field, signifying an assertion of specular, circulative social power. After entering the Octagon Room, the Elliot party waits for reinforcements—most notably, their noble relative Lady Dalrymple—to bolster their presence before moving into the concert room: "the whole party was collected, and all that remained, was to marshal themselves, and proceed into the concert room; and be of all the consequence in their power, draw as many eyes, excite as many whispers, and disturb as many people as they could" (194). In order to move, the party must "marshal," or organize itself spatially; the purpose of this organization is not only defensive—that is, to show their unity as a group and prevent unwanted intrusions—but also offensive in that it permits the Elliot party to exploit the specularity of social space, displaying itself as a desirable social commodity and as an integral part of the social field. In turn, this "disturbs" others, forcing them to consider their position relative to the Elliots. Thus each new entrant in the social field causes the deployment of new patterns of circulation and the realignment of social energies.

As the concert begins, it becomes clear that the music is mere accompaniment to a different kind of "orchestration," one based on arrangement of bodies: when the Elliots reach their seats, "the party was divided, and disposed of on two contiguous benches" (195). What becomes most significant during the concert is the control of the space next to Anne. While William Elliot, another suitor and Sir Walter's heir, initially maneuvers himself into this seat (195), Anne strives to make herself more accessible to Capt. Wentworth, who is not one of their party: "by some other removals, and a little scheming of her own, Anne was enabled to place herself much nearer the end of the bench than she had been before, much more within reach of a passer-by . . . she found herself at the very end of the bench before the concert closed" (198). Anne even secures a vacant space next to herself, and Wentworth draws near, "look[ing] down toward the bench, as if he saw a place on it well worth occupying" (199). This space clearly represents more than an empty seat: it is a site of access both to the Elliot party and to Anne in specific. As such, for Wentworth to take the seat would be to go beyond the tentative "advance" made by Anne at the chapter's opening, and to commit himself publicly to the project of forming a social and erotic alliance where, years before, his proposals of marriage had been rejected. Just as Wentworth seems ready to take the seat at Anne's side, William Elliot calls her attention away: "Anne could not refuse; but never had she sacrificed to politeness with a more suffering spirit" (199). Without another ally in Anne's party, and with what he sees as an obvious rival in William Elliot, Wentworth skittishly, or jealously, as Anne suggests, says a brief good-bye and withdraws. Wentworth's departure in spite of Anne's best efforts to encourage him signals the tenuous, momentary nature of social ties; he falters because there is no guarantee that he will be accepted, no fixed sociocultural standard that ensures his success.

In contrast to the broad, macroscopic social diagnosis performed by *Humphry Clinker, Persuasion,* and the concert scene in particular, show how the social is experienced on an individual, microscopic level as a phenomenon that is expressed partially in terms of the spatial articulation of bodies. More importantly, *Persuasion* shows that navigating social space is no longer a simple matter of locating proper acquaintances in a hierarchical system of rank. Rather, it is a process of measuring an entity—cultural capital—that is not so easily quantifiable. Furthermore, it is characterized by flux, uncertainty, and struggle: it is with quiet despair, considering her past history with Wentworth, her father's partiality for Mr. Elliot as a suitor, and the social impossibility of actively seeking

Wentworth out, that Anne contemplates "the peculiar disadvantages of their respective situations" (199). Her despair illustrates how incursion into social space in *Persuasion* is represented as a difficult necessity, while in *Humphry Clinker* it is merely an entertainment, although one that is ultimately both beneficial and useful in that it "cures" Bramble. In essence, the characters in *Persuasion* seem to depend upon their interactions in social space for their sense of self, while the characters in *Humphry Clinker* have subjectivities that are independent of the social and therefore can choose whether or not to participate in it. Thus the contrast between Anne's and Wentworth's persistence in the face of frustrating obstacles and, on the one hand, Jery's sense of detached amusement and, on the other, Bramble's wholesale rejection of the social experience typified by Bath.

This contrast points to a more basic difference between *Persuasion* and *Humphry Clinker*: forms of authority and centralization of power are negated in the former, whereas there is an implicit center—like that of the crescents—in the latter. Although the reverse might seem true on the level of narrative perspective, with *Persuasion* dominated by Anne's point of view and *Humphry Clinker*'s perspective divided among the letter writers, Bramble's voice is clearly "the most equal among equals." Moreover, while Bramble is very much in control of his party, Anne's power to act is circumscribed by her family and its nominal head, Sir Walter. Therefore, the narrative point of view is implicitly tied to traditional, patriarchal power in *Humphry Clinker,* and dissociated from it in *Persuasion.* In addition, standing apart from considerations of narrative technique, traditional male centers of power in *Persuasion* are shown to be weak. Although Sir Walter's authority governs his daughters, his bankruptcy in power is illustrated not only by the effective loss of his estate to renters and mortgages, but also by his character: "Few women could think more of their personal appearance than he did; nor could the valet of any new made lord be more delighted with the place he held in society" (36).[48] Here Sir Walter is emblematic of the "feminization" of the gentry; his vanity, which makes him "feminine," also undercuts his rank, as he is compared to a valet. The other males in *Persuasion* are only slightly better—William Elliot is an amoral chameleon (173), and Wentworth, although more sympathetic in his frustration, is clearly imperceptive if not stupid in failing to see Anne's persistent love for him.[49]

This is not to say that *Persuasion* simply replaces a male center of power with a female one. Rather, through Anne's active role in discussing aesthetic value and gender difference, traditional discourses of power are dialogized. She debates the differences between male and female psychology with Wentworth's friend, Captain Harville, arguing ultimately that these differences are inherently undefinable because no one is capable of escaping the prejudices of their own sex (235–38).[50] On another occasion, she argues with Captain Benwick about his taste for Romantic poetry; again, no unifying closure is achieved (100–1). Although Anne asserts her opinion strongly on each occasion, these debates cannot be regarded as establishing Anne as a center of power in the novel because they have little effect on the level of plot; they are similarly gratuitous on the level of characterization because they operate only to confirm her already-established intelligence. Instead, they serve to expand the novel's thematic focus from social circulation to include ideologies of gender and aesthetics. In this way, by illustrating the discursive circulation that Habermas has described, these passages contribute to the decentralization of power depicted in *Persuasion*.

In both of her discursive interventions, Anne can be seen as increasing fragmentation and diversity rather than constructing order and unity; however, it seems unlikely that either Anne or Austen is an advocate of cultural circulation. I would agree with Jay Clayton in his contention that Austen "does not view the acknowledgement of multiplicity as a potentially revolutionary gesture, but rather as an unavoidable recognition of the way men and women live in a complex—she might say overcomplex—social world."[51] This sense of circulative social space as "unavoidable" is perhaps indicated by the setting of the novel's time frame in the aftermath of Anne's decision to reject Wentworth and follow Lady Russell's advice. The air of resignation and even penance that Anne expresses early in *Persuasion,* upon encountering the self-absorption of her sister Mary's family, the Musgroves—"she acknowledged it to be very fitting, that every little social commonwealth should dictate its own matters of discourse" (69)—is connected to the penance that the Elliot family as a whole must undergo due to strained financial circumstances.

Both Anne and her family are dislocated from their proper positions, and this renders them vulnerable: Anne should be with Wentworth, but finds herself instead surrounded by unsympathetic family and friends; the Elliots should be at Kellynch Hall, but are forced to rent it out in order to support their extravagant lifestyle. We also see this family dislocation in the opening chapter, where Sir Walter is poring over the Baronetage, which is crowded with "the almost endless creations of the last century" at the expense of "the limited remnant of the earliest patents" (35). This sense of decline and of resignation is another way in which

Persuasion diverges from the representation of social space provided in *Humphry Clinker,* which treats circulation as a new grafting onto the old system, rather than its replacement.

Our sense of the passing of the old, hierarchical social order is furthered by the dead ends reached by the two Elliot scions, Sir Walter and his heir, William Elliot: the former is a vain man, the narrator tells us (36), whose expensive lifestyle has led him to mortgage his estate "as far as he had the power" (41), while the latter is a virtual outlaw to the family because "he had purchased independence by uniting himself to a rich woman of inferior birth . . . and shewn himself as unsolicitous of being longer noticed by the family" (39). While Sir Walter's irresponsibility shows the self-destructive tendencies of the old order, the younger Elliot's career further demonstrates the instability and weakness of this order by his success outside of it, and, indeed, by his contemptuous refusal to recognize its claim on him. Even when he does seek reentry into the family, his priorities are clear: having first secured financial stability, he now feels free to "purchase" his way back into the family through ingratiating behavior. William Elliot is the ultimate product of the circulative, specular social field, in that he has a different face for every circumstance—as Anne thinks, "various as were the tempers in her father's house, he pleased them all" (173)—and he has no identity of his own except a desire to accumulate wealth. Thus, the figure of the heir, which serves as a vehicle for redemption in *Humphry Clinker* (both in terms of continuing the lineage and in terms of Clinker's religious preaching), is employed by Austen instead to illustrate the complete transformation of social space from an emphasis on birth and a fixed system of values as the primary measure of social standing to an emphasis on capital and a corresponding flexibility and liquidity of character.

Although Anne's marriage is meant to provide an alternative lineage based on merit, it is presented as a very compromised, tenuous solution to the difficulty of assigning social value and thus closing off the narrative. To begin with, because authority is decentered in the novel, there is no guarantee of "proper" closure—that is, marriage between Wentworth and Anne: "the play of narrative complication is allowed to threaten the possibility of *incarnating* the right settlement."[52] Therefore, Anne and Wentworth's final understanding is attained not through the channels of circulative social space, but rather across them, in a desperate note from Wentworth that exposes his love for Anne as well as his ignorance of her feelings. In this way, their success can be regarded as an exception and not as a model. Furthermore, because Anne refuses to admit that she was wrong to give in to Lady Russell's persuasions against marrying Wentworth, there seems no "proper" reason for marrying him upon his second proposal: Anne excuses herself, claiming that "if I was wrong in yielding to persuasion once, remember that it was to persuasion exerted on the side of safety.... When I yielded, I thought it was to duty" (246). Indeed, the only change in Wentworth over the eight years between proposals is a material one—"he was rich" (86)—suggesting that Anne's motivation may be partially mercenary, like William Elliot's in courting her. Rather than presenting a series of healing marriages in closing, as does *Humphry Clinker, Persuasion* excludes several characters from happiness, including Elizabeth Elliot, Sir Walter, and William Elliot. Meanwhile, it portrays Anne and Wentworth's union as a reversal of, or a reaction against, the typical patterns of marriage in that Anne, a member of the gentry, brings neither wealth nor any family connections "which a man of sense could value" to her tradesman husband (252–53). Even in *Humphry Clinker*, where the rationale for marriages is based on compatible dispositions, this ground for happiness is not left unsupported by other criteria, as it is in *Persuasion*. Both in its reversal of norms and in its unbalanced dependence on compatibility of dispositions, Anne and Wentworth's marriage represents a radical undertaking that enlarges the breach between their position, which is already internally split over the value of persuasion and duty, and that of the Elliots.

Although I have done some violence to historical context by yoking together these novels, which are separated by nearly a half-century of social ferment, this is justified, I feel, by the more complete picture of social space that they present in tandem. Perhaps the more anxious tone of Austen's novel might be explained by the literally "revolutionary" events that took place on the European continent during the last decade of the eighteenth century, well after *Humphry Clinker*'s publication. This anxiety is also due to the fact that, in *Persuasion,* social space and persuasion are inevitable, as they are in *Evelina,* and can be repressive or threatening. In contrast, social space in *Humphry Clinker* is depicted as a national "wonder," an alternative to the the reality of the stay-at-home, which produces Bramble's illness. Although social space in *Humphry Clinker* is clearly the site of dislocations of traditional identity, these dislocations are ultimately not seen as threatening, but rather as playful and potentially liberating. In fact, Bramble's "circulation" results in the discovery of his "natural" heir, Clinker/Lloyd, implying that social space may offer a cure to what ails British culture, and may allow its perpetuation.

By their focus on social environments like Bath and Ranelagh, *Persuasion* and *Humphry Clinker* show the importance of circulation and specularity in determining individual identity at both the beginning and the end of the period with which I am concerned. Breaking down the illusory picture of "Neoclassic" social stability, *Humphry Clinker* depicts society as an "open" circle that permits changes in status for individuals like Clinker and his ex-servant wife, Winifred. In *Persuasion* that circle is fractured between hierarchical and circulative models of determining identity, resulting in the failure of even marriage, the device *Humphry Clinker* uses to restore social and narrative order, to halt the processes of the Imaginary. Through their constant reading of one another's behavior on the microlevel of practice, Anne and Wentworth continually shift and reconfigure their self-images. Thus, in comparing these two texts, one can see that the production of identity and social status in late eighteenth- and early nineteenth-century Britain was specular, circulative, and decentered, rather than being statically defined from the stable ground of any single norm or fixed social code.

3

The Ruin as Object of Desire

The Recess, Visual Art, and Historical Space

In addition to having their identities continually placed under circulative and specular scrutiny within social space, eighteenth-century subjects also had increasing access to the imagined psychosocial space of history, or the past. Although social space was most compellingly "present," historical space provided an alternate means of establishing identity. Throughout the century, the impulse to recover history was strong: besides the proliferation in exhibits of the past in museums (e.g., Queen Elizabeth's strawberry dish) and the popularity of historical painting, which I have discussed in the first chapter, this period saw the rise of antiquarianism, the birth of the British historical novel, and the renewal of history writing through the efforts of Gibbon, Hume, Catherine Macaulay, and Smollett, among others. Eighteenth-century Britain is also remarkable for its construction of "histories" of the arts, as Lawrence Lipking has noted.[1] Lipking's assertion that these histories were meant to establish traditions as grounds for contemporary artistic practice parallels my own contention that history in general was increasingly mined as a source for models of subjectivity, personal and ideological genealogies, and ways of seeing that were different from those of the present.

One of the primary assumptions of this investigation is that history is a cultural "space" that is useful to the individual's self-conception because it can establish the precedents by which one determines one's relation to culture. These precedents are largely what I would call "genealogical," in that they consist of a series of ideas, a set of beliefs, a tracing of family relations, or a knowledge of certain past events, all of which are recognized by the individual subject as important because they make up his or her heritage. This "genealogy" is in fact a private selection of history that disregards the antiquarian's attentive concern for an independent historical record while it may, nonetheless, absorb some of the historical materials that antiquarians reintroduce into cultural circulation.

Perhaps because of Freud's insistence on the recurrence of the past in the present, his work is very useful in exploring the historical dimension of the construction of identity. For instance, Freud's commonplace comparison of psychoanalysis to archaeology, from the very early *Studies on Hysteria* to the later *Civilization and Its Discontents,* depends on the connection between history and the search for identity. Of course, the notion of space is inherent to archaeology, which recovers and reconstructs the past largely through the establishment of spatial relations between artifacts and remains, mapping history as a set of culturally functional locations: the baths, the market, the temple, the small dwelling, the great house, and so on.

I would argue that the eighteenth- and early nineteenth-century audience's interest in history derives from a similar archaeological or "genealogical" impulse directed toward the private concern of representing identity. Just as psychoanalysis is haunted by the spectre of its transcendental signified—the primal scene—so a clearly defined historical space serves as the ultimate goal for the genealogical impulse, both depending on the excavation and recovery of the past. Here the operation performed on history is more one of *re*-construction than of construction; in other words, it is governed by the transference of desires to history in order to work history's latent content into a manifest that is acceptable to the individual. Thus the desire to "fix" history in an assimilable form can be seen as part of an effort to consolidate identity through the reconstruction and recovery of this "genealogical" heritage.

Frank Palmeri has pointed out how Freud's essay "Mourning and Melancholia" specifically relates to the desire for recovering history. In this essay, Freud explains mourning as the "process of working through in detail the memory of the lost object as a precondition to finally accepting the death of the preceding, generative culture as an unalterable fact."[2]

The Ruin as Object of Desire

Moreover, he defines the source of mourning and melancholia as identification with an external object whose proximity to the subject is subsequently disrupted (by death, absence, disillusionment, insult, etc.). Because of the subject's libidinal investments in the object, there is a dual process of withdrawal and mourning, rejection of the object and dwelling upon it. In terms of this investigation, the object is history itself. Eighteenth-century efforts to recover history are characterized by the ambivalence that Freud describes, a tension between the desire to reconstitute the past, thus conserving the subject's investment in genealogy, and the desire to withdraw from the past, celebrating its death and the subject's survival.[3]

This ambivalence is particularly manifested in the late eighteenth-century fascination with the figure of the ruin, in which archaeological, antiquarian, and historical interests were synthesized. Although popular interest in ruins is not a new phenomenon, as Rose Macaulay has shown in tracing it back to the Hellenistic period, the extreme passion for them in late eighteenth-century Britain—manifested in the construction of false ruins, or "follies"—points to a cultural need for representations of the past. The significance of the ruin as a representation of desire for history has been obscured by its very popularity as a feature of pleasure gardens, fantastic or picturesque scenes in paintings, and the "Gothic" in literature. Even Macaulay, who, writing about the eighteenth-century fascination with ruins, states that "the realization of mortality . . . seems to have been the dominant emotion to which ruins then led," suspects that this morbid mood "was only the emotion best understood" by writers on ruins, implying that the fascination with ruins had different motivations than those conventionally offered.[4] Conventional associations between the figure of the ruin and "the realization of mortality" suggest that the ruin simply represented death, and thus was connected to the imposition of psychosocial limits on subjects. Although this certainly does constitute part of the complex, ambivalent attraction of the ruin for eighteenth-century audiences, it also served as a point of entry to the past, connecting the public with historical "space."[5]

Although the eighteenth-century rage for ruins was most vigorous in Britain, some useful insights into the ruin's historical significance can be gained by placing it in the broader European context. Jean Galard observes that the historical significance of ruins is indicated by the fact that they are always institutional edifices—in England, primarily castles and churches—rather than private dwellings. To support this, Galard draws on the definition of ruins provided by the *Encyclopédie*: "*Ruine* ne se dit que des palais, des tombeaux somptueux ou des bâtiments publics. On ne dirait point *ruine* en parlant d'une maison particulière de paysans ou de bourgeois; on dirait alors bâtiments *ruinés*."[6] Roland Mortier testifies further that "la ruine appartient le plus souvent au style haut (palais, monuments), parfois au style moyen, jamais au style bas."[7]

The ruin's association with the grand, the public, the institutional, and the historical also works for the British setting. Wordsworth, for instance, is careful to entitle his poem of tragic peasant life "The Ruined Cottage" since a cottage could never be simply "a ruin." By its connection to grand, "historical" entities, the ruin offered subjects a contact with something that could not only propel their imaginations beyond the personal limits of their lives, but could also serve as a potential challenge to the status quo of eighteenth-century culture.

Writing of Europe in general and France in particular, Mortier concludes that "La présence de la ruine dans les tableaux du XVIIe et du XVIIIe siècle correspondait déjà à une volonté d'y intégrer le Temps en terms symboliques."[8] He also suggests that the ruin's popularity was due to a cultural malaise from which it offered a route of escape: "Libérant le spectateur des contingences spatio-temporelles, elle permet à l'imagination de plonger sans entraves dans le coulée du temps, de se rêver hors du présent, dans un passé sacralisé ou dans un avenir mystérieusement déchiffré."[9] In other words, for European culture in general, the ruin was a vehicle for fantasies, a means of escaping the troublesome reality of the present.

Ranging widely over the eighteenth-century European cultural scene, Elizabeth Harries's *The Unfinished Manner* discusses the significance of the fragment as the literary analogue of the ruin. Harries contends that gaps and discontinuities in eighteenth-century novels symbolize "the experiences society has repressed, made culturally invisible and untellable."[10] Furthermore, although her approach to the ruin is not explicitly feminist, Harries suggests that ruins and especially the literary fragment "were understood as a kind of feminine discourse, or an eighteenth-century écriture féminine."[11] Both Harries and Mortier thus argue that the ruin—whether real or represented in painting or writing—could serve as a potentially liberating vehicle for the individual.

The work of Mortier, Galard, and Harries on the figure of the ruin in European culture is complemented by several studies of the ruin's meaning for England specifically. Laurence Goldstein's *Ruins and Empire: The Evolution of a Theme in Augustan and Romantic Literature* treats the use of ruins in Spenser, Dyer, Defoe, Goldsmith, and Wordsworth, among others. Like Mortier and Harries, Goldstein approaches the ruin from a psychological perspective, emphasizing the ruin's ability to synthesize the consolatory virtues of retreat from the worldly pursuit of "empire." Thomas McFarland's *Romanticism and the Forms of Ruin: Wordsworth, Coleridge, and Modalities of Fragmentation* also uses a psychological approach to the ruin, but is both more limited in historical scope and perhaps more precise theoretically than *Ruins and Empire* in its specific focus on the ruin as a Romantic symbol. According to McFarland, "Incompleteness, fragmentation, and ruin—*ständige Unganzheit*—not only receive a special emphasis in Romanticism but also . . . define that phenomenon. . . . The sense of longing . . . saturates Romanticism."[12]

Whereas both McFarland and Goldstein treat the ruin primarily as an aesthetic object in order to situate it in "Augustan" or "Romantic" contexts, Anne Janowitz has attempted to historicize the figure of the ruin. Like McFarland, she notes the importance of the ruin's status as a fragment, but a fragment specifically of a past, ruined culture: "ruin imagery cannot help asserting the visible evidence of historical and imperial impermanence, for the ruin has been traditionally associated with human and cultural transience."[13] McFarland and Janowitz agree, likewise, that the ruin's fragmentariness is sublimated to its ability to point to a greater whole, but McFarland's observations are grounded in Romantic aesthetic theory, while Janowitz's are grounded in her sense of British imperialist imperatives. McFarland contends that "for Kant, as for Goethe, the symbol is a jaggedness that implies a wholeness" while it grants primacy to the fragment as the basis of poetic communication, the imperfect crystallization of the absolute in the specific present.[14] Janowitz, in contrast, analyzes a substantial number of late eighteenth- and early nineteenth-century lyric poems to show how the ruin "provides an historical provenance for the conception of the British nation as immemorially ancient, and through its naturalization subsumes cultural and class difference into a conflated representation of Britain as nature's inevitable product."[15] By arguing that the ruin is harnessed to a nationalist and imperialist agenda, Janowitz places the ruin more firmly in the context of British culture than either Goldstein or McFarland, while concurring with their general, theoretical, and aesthetic conclusions about the ruin.[16]

I hope here to continue the work of historicizing the ruin's attraction for eighteenth-century British audiences that Janowitz has thus begun; however, rather than emphasizing the ruin's purpose on the macroscopic level of nationalist ideology, I want to focus on the microscopic level of audience reception, where historical "space" is formed. Janowitz's emphasis on the "naturalization" of the ruin and the cultural occultation of its disturbing connotations—a process necessary to the nationalist agenda—tends to obscure the complexity of this level of individual practice, in which the ruin's significance is ambivalent, pointing both to the possibility of constructing history as a support for the status quo and to a past that is riven with forbidding discord and disruption.

Although Janowitz does acknowledge this last aspect of the ruin more than any other writer on ruins, it is not enough: the British ruin's association with violence, both intestine and iconoclastic (in a literal, idol-smashing sense), is what makes it distinct from the continental ruins described by Galard and Mortier, even if that violence is partially naturalized or occulted. In his essay "The Subversion of the Subject and the Dialectic of Desire in the Freudian Unconscious," Lacan refers to what is occulted as the "inter-dit." Of course, he is concerned specifically with the unconscious, but my point is that the ruin is a figure whose popularity stems, at least in part, from its significance within the unconscious, on both cultural and individual levels. The ruin belongs to the "inter-dit" in two ways: first, it represents what is "forbidden" (interdit) or "Other" for English audiences—a forsaken Catholic heritage; second, it represents what is said "between the lines" (inter-dit) or beyond its denotative meaning—a cultural desire for and anxiety about unity in history. In both cases, the ruin confronts the subject with potentially disturbing connotations, suggesting the potentially "ruinous" effects of seeking identity through historical excavation and reconstruction.

In order to achieve a more complete appraisal of the complexity and the social and cultural significance of the ruin for eighteenth-century British audiences, I will examine a variety of verbal and visual sources. Following an overview of the ruin's popularity that focuses primarily on constructed ruins and visual representations of ruins, I will examine the different uses and meanings of native British and ancient Greek and Roman ruins. By examining British ruins in the context of other ruins, the distinctive function of British ruins appears more clearly. These two kinds of ruins—British and "Classic"—can be associated with two opposing attitudes toward or uses of history that I call the "regime of tradition" and the "regime of change." After discussing the wide variety of ruins available to eighteenth-century British audiences, I will concentrate on the regime of change and native ruins, with particular emphasis on monastic ruins. Because they most clearly reflect an iconoclastic break with past British culture, monastic ruins serve as the focal point for eighteenth-century discussion of ruins, revealing the complex attitudes held on ruins in general. Finally, after a brief analysis of iconoclasm and the ruin, I will examine Sophia Lee's *The Recess*, a novel that exemplifies the fascination with native ruins and their importance in defining historical or genealogical space.

The Taste for Ruins

Eighteenth-century approaches to the past were influenced by two phenomena: late seventeenth-century antiquarianism and more contemporary discoveries of Greek and Roman ruins. On an intellectual level, the former spurred a renewed interest in the British past, while the latter stimulated consciousness of the relative "difference" of previous civilizations and stimulated attempts to bridge that difference by analogy and imitation. On a practical level, both phenomena were represented by the figure of the ruin.

During the course of the eighteenth century, antiquarian interests gradually became popular, moving from the status of a recherché topic for pedantic clergymen to a topic of fashion and great cultural influence. Coexisting with the Palladian fashions of the late seventeenth century, "Gothic antiquarianism, wistful though bibulous, had been typical."[17] Sir William Dugdale's *Monasticon Anglicanum* (1655–73) and Anthony Wood's *Antiquities of Oxford* (1674) exemplify the growing interest in native remains of the past.[18] For collectors and antiquarians, this culminated in the 1717 foundation of the Society of Antiquaries.[19] Still, a serious taste for the native or medieval past was rare in the early part of the century; because styles derived from the Italian Renaissance were fashionable, those involved in collecting medieval objects were often derided as eccentrics or pedants.

The taste for the native past eventually made its way into aristocratic circles through landscape gardening. At first, "hermitages" were created in parks; then they were given more historical accuracy and sometimes transformed into castles or monasteries.[20] One of the first such transformations occurred at the Earl of Bathurst's Cirencester Park, where, beginning in 1721 with the advice of Alexander Pope, Bathurst erected "Alfred's Hall," a mock castle. The building of such shams or "follies" accelerated during midcentury, spread from aristocratic to more public settings, and continued well into the nineteenth century.

Sanderson Miller, amateur architect and son of a wool merchant, was responsible for a number of the most well known follies of the 1740s. He constructed his own sham castle at Edgehill (1743–47) to commemorate the spot where Charles I raised his standard before going into battle against his rebellious subjects. This sham was so admired that Miller was commissioned to build ruined castles at Hagley Hall in Worcestershire (1747–48) for the first Lord Lyttelton and at Wimpole Hall in Cambridgeshire (1768) for Lord Chancellor Harwicke.[21] Miller's brief career as ruin-builder is exemplary of how popular ruins became—so popular that artificial ones were created throughout the country: Barbara Jones's *Follies and Grottoes* lists over 830 British follies and shams, many of them ruins, and most of them constructed during the eighteenth or early nineteenth centuries.[22]

The sham ruin's popularity is, of course, the result of the part it played in the theory and practice of landscape gardening, yet the building of artificial ruins also reflects a desire to appropriate history on a very personal level. There were real ruins enough dotting the English countryside, but wealthy men—even those who had just middling incomes—felt a desire not only to see ruins in the neighborhood, but to possess them. Sometimes this desire to possess the past resulted in the dismemberment of actual ruins and their reconstruction on an estate: William Shenstone had Halesowen Priory moved to his garden at The Leasowes (c. 1750), while Thomas Dummer had the north transept of Netley Abbey moved to Cranbury Park, in Hampshire (c. 1760).[23] Such cannibalization of the remains of the past indicates a lack of interest in historical accuracy and preservation, and literalizes Freud's notion that our uses of the past are always based on a personal reconstruction of it.

Thus, the effect of moved ruins and follies is, at least in one aspect, to personalize or "possess" history on an individual level. Barbara Jones notes that the personal quality of follies exists even for the modern viewer: "Follies are personal in a way that great architecture never is. Their amateur quality makes them our own: never expect too much from other people's favorite follies. You will find that some of those that most appeal to me are dull when you visit them."[24] Here Jones implies that, rather than having a "real," highly defined function—like "great architecture" that dictates its statement to the viewer—the folly has a subjective, less defined, psychological function for its audience. Thus, because the sham ruin need only be psychologically (and visually) effective, its artificiality is irrelevant. For this reason, although the resemblance between shams and theater props is often strong, as at Wimpole, where "no regard was paid to the rear of the building, which is backed by a stand of pines," this serves only to heighten our retrospective recognition of the ruin's "theatrical" role in representing the British past to imaginative viewers.[25]

The theatricality of the ruin is illustrated to the point of absurdity in one set of architectural plans in Timothy Lightoler's *Gentleman and Farmer's Architect* (1764) that presents the gentleman architect with a series of artificial ruins designed to cover "disagreable Objects" on an estate.[26] This exemplifies, in a very literal way, the ambivalent role of the ruin in the eighteenth century: it both represents history and, by its very stylishness, covers what is disagreeable or disruptive in history—or, as in this case, the pigsty, stable, barn, and so on.

Although access to ruins and shams was limited by their generally rural location to local inhabitants and "polite" visitors and tourists, the figure of the British ruin was virtually unavoidable for the general public, even in the city. For example, London pleasure gardens such as Vauxhall and Ranelagh featured artificial ruins as part of their attractions.[27] The 1752 *Sketch of Spring Gardens, Vauxhall* offers a description of the sham ruins: "Adjoyning to these Gothic Pavillions (in and near the grand Cross-Walk, where the Picture of Ruins is seen) is the Representation of two ancient Castles, with Turrets and Battlements."[28] In addition to seeing actual or sham ruins like these, the average Londoner (and visitors to the city) would also have been familiar with the many images of ruins that were available in print form through print shops. For example, even Miller's sham at Wimpole was engraved, and had the following verse attached to the resulting prints:

> When Henry stemmed Ierne's stormy flood
> And bowed to Britain's yoke her stormy brood,
> When by true courage and false zeal impelled
> Richard encamped on Salem's palmy field,
> On towers like these Earl, Baron, Vavasor
> Hung high their floating banners on the air.[29]

By supplying the imaginative, vague historical field that the sham was meant to conjure, the verses supplement the engraved image in an attempt to make the print substitute for the experience of actually seeing the sham. Although prints like this one were commonly sold at a price that would have made them accessible to a lower-middle-class buyer, even members of the lowest classes would have had access to pictured British ruins in print shop windows.

At the same time that antiquarianism was familiarizing a growing public with representations of the British past through native ruins, a series of discoveries of ancient Greek and Roman ruins brought the figure of the foreign, "Classic" ruin also to the public's attention. Heavily illustrated books like *The Ruins of Palmyra* (1753) by Robert Wood, *Antiquities of Athens* (1762–1800) by James Stuart and Nicholas Revett, and *The Ruins of the Palace of the Emperor Diocletian at Spalatro in Dalmatia* (1764) by Robert Adam announced new discoveries of "Classic" ruins that caused a stir of revision in the dominant, Palladian/Italian style of architecture and design.

Parallel to these discoveries, there was an enthusiasm in the artistic community for visual images of Continental, Classic ruins. The artists who were initially responsible for this enthusiasm were Marco Ricci (1676–1730), Giovanni Panini (c.1692–1765/68), Giovanni Battista Piranesi (1720–78), Hubert Robert (1733–1808), and Charles-Louis Clérisseau (1721–1820). The "capricci" that these artists produced were fanciful scenes packed full of ancient-looking edifices. These capricci were similar to sham native ruins in their expression of a lack of interest in historical accuracy and in their use of monuments of the past for personal rumination.[30] In contrast to the artists of the capricci, who were almost exclusively Continental, British artists like William Pars (1742–82), John "Warwick" Smith (1749–1831), and Francis Towne (1739 or 1740–1816) focused on depicting Classic ruins in a more mimetic, documentary style. Pars's "The Temple of Venus" or Towne's "Grotto of Posilippo, Naples" are exemplary of the architectural and topographical accuracy with which these artists approached their subjects (see figures 11 and 12). Unlike the "capricci" artists, who worked primarily in oils, the British painters of Classic ruins were generally watercolorists, whose works were often engraved and sold serially, as in the case of Smith's *Select Views of Italy* (1792–99), or in books such as Pars's *Ionian Antiquities* (vol. 1, 1769; vol. 2, 1797). Therefore, their works were at least technically available to a much larger viewing public.

However, the reception of and audience for Classic ruins was quite different than that for native British ruins. To a great extent, the appreciation of Classic ruins was limited to the "connoisseurs" of the upper ranks, who were trained as a matter of course in Greek and Roman literature, and who had the financial resources to take a "Grand Tour" of the European continent, viewing firsthand at least the relics of Roman culture, if not those of the Greek as well. These connoisseurs were most frequently responsible for commissioning drawings or paintings of Classic ruins, and their peers, who had likewise seen these ruins personally, were the most likely buyers for series and books like those by Smith and Pars. Smith, in fact, was not atypical in being sponsored in his European travels by an aristocratic patron, Lord Warwick, who purchased many of

11. Temple of Venus, Rome, William Pars. Courtesy of Yale Center for British Art, Paul Mellon Collection.

Smith's watercolors and kept them for his private viewing. Although Pars's work was more widely circulated, he, too, was sponsored by private persons—first the Society of Dilettanti, then Lord Palmerston.[31]

In general, the more exclusive audience for Classic ruins is illustrated by the Society of Dilettanti, which not only sponsored Pars but was involved in the publication of two of the "discovery" books mentioned above, *The Ruins of Palmyra* and *Antiquities of Athens*. This "Society" was founded in 1732 and has been described as "a closed circle, within which the conversation about works of art was almost as important as the works of art themselves."[32] Johann Zoffany's picture of one of the society's most prominent members, Charles Townley, surrounded by other Dilettanti and his collection of ancient objets d'art reflects the insular world of these gentlemen connoisseurs.[33] Their position as patrons of artistic efforts to represent Classic ruins indicates the control that they wielded over the circulation of such representations in financial and social terms; while

12. The Grotto of Posilippo, *Francis Towne*. ©*The British Museum*.

single engravings of some Classic ruins may have been available to a broader public, in contrast to the expensive "discovery" volumes, buyers would have been discouraged from purchasing them because of their association with the cultural interests of the upper ranks. The devotees of the classic ruin depended on the inaccessibility of Greek and Roman cultures—in terms of language, the distant settings of their ruined remains, and, in contrast to British culture, their "alien" status—to conserve these ruins as symbols intelligible only to an audience of aristocratic viewers.

Because of the distant setting of Classic ruins, British audiences were dependent on visual representations for most of their familiarity with Greek and Roman architectural remains. There were, however, some Classic ruins erected in gardens; as with the native ruins previously discussed, these were both reconstructed and sham. In fact, I have been discussing Classic "ruins" quite loosely, for in gardens the remains of the Greek and Roman past were usually encountered—by a very narrow public—not as fragments, like the remains of the British past, but rather as completed, intact wholes.[34] For the most part, Classic ruins in English gardens consisted of vases and statues—some of these authentic—and newly created imitations of ancient architecture that were given names such as the "Temple of the Four Winds" at Castle Howard, or the "Temple of Ancient Virtue" at Stowe. These edifices were "ruins" only in the sense that they drew on an ancient, dead culture for their design and allusive power. Although some gardens, like Stowe, were open to a certain public, as evidenced by the publication of "guides" for visitors, the emblematic or allusive deployment of Classic ruins within them would be intelligible only to an audience of connoisseurs who had the training to decipher it.[35]

To this point, I have delayed a full treatment of ruins as they appeared in visual representations because they were inseparable from the picturesque, a specifically British optic or "way of seeing" the past that deserves independent examination. Because British ruins are native, like picturesque theory, they— rather than Classic ruins—are picturesque objects par excellence. It would seem most likely that ruins would be found in history paintings, yet that is not the case for eighteenth-century England. While history painting became the dominant visual style in France during this period, as evidenced by the work of Jacques-Louis David and his school, it was largely ignored in England, even by Reynolds, its foremost proponent. As described in the first chapter on historical context, the British paintings done in this mode—by Benjamin West, James Northcote, George Romney, and others—were often not "history" in the strictest sense because they focused on representing more current events, such as the death of General Wolfe in the battle of Montreal. In contrast, the French "Grand Prix de Rome," awarded each year by the French *Académie,* effectively enthroned history painting as the "highest" genre by prescribing the depiction of a scene from Biblical, Greek, or Roman history as the grounds for competition among painters.[36] The analogies constructed between the new French republic and the Roman republic, in particular, show how historical painting was converted into a vehicle for nationalist sentiment.[37]

From the relative lack of historical painting in England, I postulate that the English taste for history was sublimated and represented by the picturesque. Even when it focuses on seemingly most unhistorical material, the picturesque still reflects an interest in time: "The typical picturesque object or scene—the aged man, the old house, the road with cartwheel tracks, the irregular village—carries within it the principle of change. All of them imply the passage of time and the slow working of its change upon them."[38] Indeed, the desire to make visual representation encompass time and change is what distinguishes the picturesque from the beautiful and the sublime, both of which tend toward the ideal and the static. Moreover, as mentioned in the first chapter, artists of the picturesque frequently portrayed other artists in the process of capturing a scene, thus dramatizing the moment of their own artistic production in time. Interest in time and the changes wrought by it characterize not only the thematic concerns of the picturesque, but also technical or formal aspects. There was a vogue for the sketch, the watercolor, and the blot drawing—forms that highlight process and thus the time involved in composition. In a curious parallel to Samuel Richardson's "writing to the moment," it may be said that artists became increasingly interested in forms normally considered incomplete, forms that appeared to have been "drawn up to the moment," according to the accidents of time. It is perhaps this emphasis on the depiction of time as an aesthetic goal that leads Martin Price to speak of the "Picturesque *Moment*."

The Regimes of Tradition and of Change

In order to fully understand the picturesque as the "carrier" of both history and the figure of the ruin, it is necessary to recognize not only how it represents time, but also why this sublimation of time into the picturesque occurs. In encounters with ruins there can be detected two different attitudes toward historical space—the "regime of tradition," which depends on a cyclical vision of history, and the "regime of change," which views history as a linear procession of events.[39] These regimes coexist and sometimes overlap in the arts of this period, the former associated with an older, aristocratic ethos, in which the individual's identity was fixed from birth, the latter associated with the new, mercantile and imperialist ethos, in which the individual's identity was fluid, and was constructed through personal activity.[40] Casting the opposition between the regimes of tradition and change in terms of the visual arts helps to explain the sublimation of time into the picturesque. The binaries involved in the opposition may be summarized as follows:

regime of tradition	*regime of change*
cyclical vision of history	history as procession
continuity with past	discontinuity
mourning for past/narcissism	use of past
classical ruins	native ruins
identification with and investment in past	skepticism of and resistance to past
discipline/control	fantasy/self-conception
socially fixed subjectivities	fluid subjectivities
social status quo	social change
land as power	commerce as power
beauty/sublime	picturesque

Above all, the last two terms in this series indicate how the visual arts fit into the regimes. The British artistic community was, as the opposition suggests, split between between members of the Royal Academy (led by Sir Joshua Reynolds), who claimed the depiction of the beautiful and the sublime as their aesthetic goal, and non-Academics such as William Hogarth, William Blake, and William Gilpin, who sought to broaden the Academy's conceptions of the beautiful.

Naomi Schor defines the contention between these two groups as a struggle over the role of the detail, or the particular, in representation: "In the first instance, Reynolds argues that because of their material contingency details are incompatible with the Ideal; in the second he argues that because of their tendency to proliferation, details subvert the Sublime."[41] The logic of the academic strictures against detail stems from the desire to find the universal and thus, to establish continuity with the past. Discussing Reynolds's portraits, Christopher Flint contends that in Reynolds's harmonic display of past and present, history either becomes attenuated, insofar as the artist prolongs the continuity between classical Greece and eighteenth-century Britain; or it disappears altogether, as the two periods generalize each other out of existence.[42] This clearly corresponds to the attitudes synthesized in the regime of tradition, as do the examples that Reynolds cites of Ideal and Sublime art, which he finds in the works of Italian masters such as Raphael and Michelangelo. By eliminating detail, Reynolds and other academics were attempting to represent the timeless—the detail, with its groundedness in the "real," was seen as an assault on the ideal.[43]

A further distinction between the regimes of tradition and change arises from the regime of tradition's tendency to look backward to a "Golden Age." This reverence for the distant past led to the belief that the world was gradually deteriorating; therefore, all change was seen as deterioration and departure from the ideal. In contrast, the regime of change developed the opposite tendency to proclaim any change as improvement or progress. Consequently, instead of looking back to a "Golden Age," those who participated in the regime of change envisioned a utopic future for humanity. As an aesthetic mode, the picturesque can fit into either regime, but its aptness in depicting the processes of change tends to place it within the regime of change.

Having outlined the ways of seeing represented by these two "regimes," I want to explore their ramifications, beginning with the regime of tradition. In essence, the regime of tradition uses the ruin to represent history as an eternal pattern of rise and fall determined by God and guaranteed by His instrument, Nature. In this regime, Nature encompasses and restrains humanity, keeping it forever within the "envelope" of proper activity established by God. It is for this reason that Lord Kames, in *Elements of Criticism* (1762), rejects Classic ruins in favor of Gothic ruins, which "[exhibit] the triumph of time over strength; a melancholy, but not unpleasant thought; [whereas] a Grecian ruin suggests rather the triumph of barbarity over taste; a gloomy and discouraging thought."[44] Here we may identify "time" as another of God's agents, one that is allied with Nature in causing decay to occur and in reminding the reader or viewer of mortality, which cannot be overcome by human exertion or "strength." The implications of this regime for the individual subject are clear: the subject needs no construction because it is bounded by a series of outside factors, including Nature, mortality, social station, and cyclical history, all leading to one great limiting force: God. The second half of Kames's evaluation of ruins reflects his desire to project this regime into the past and to establish continuity specifically with the Classical past.

The anxiety Kames expresses about Greek ruins is reflected in the purchasing habits of English collectors of Classical antiquities, who insisted on having their objets d'art whole and seemingly unaffected by the ravages of time. For many eighteenth-century English tourists, the ability to secure a perfect object of antiquity symbolized their trip's success: "[t]he appreciation of an untouched torso or some precious fragment of the sculptor's art was a long way off yet, so the 'restorer' had everything his own way. Milord wanted a complete statue or vase to take home with him, and Milord should have it!"[45] Besides the desire for historical continuity that this evinces, it also implies a desire to do away with discontinuities, which are represented by the marring that occurs with time, as well as with the whole process of archaeological retrieval, which is also indicated by incompleteness. In other words, the regime of tradition dictates that ruins of the valued past—the Classical past—must be made to seem immediately present, with any marks of their difference and distance from the cultural present obliterated. This complete identification amounts to a form of cultural mourning, like that which Freud describes on the individual level, in which the predecessor culture is both honored and triumphed over through the conversion of its art to souvenirs and trophies. Achieving the perfect "presence" of the past testifies to the power of the present to transcend the boundaries of time, asserting the dominance of the cultural present.

The Warwick Vase is one Classical artifact that not only illustrates the way in which the enthusiasm for ruins (and ruined, past cultures) attests to the desire for a recoverable history, but also gives us clues as to the character of this desire. The Warwick Vase is a huge Greek vase, measuring over eighteen feet in circumference, that was brought from Rome by the Earl of Warwick in the late 1770s (see figure 13). He made it the centerpiece of the conservatory of Warwick Castle, where it soon became so well known that its shape appeared as a model for wine coolers, saltcellars, and so on.[46] On the one hand, the immense popularity of the Warwick Vase indicates the strength of cultural desire for a sense of continuity with the past, a desire directed toward the appreciation of Greek and Roman art in part through the influence of Winckelmann's *History of Ancient Art*, first published in Britain in 1764. On the other hand, a close examination of the composition of the Warwick Vase may cause uneasiness about the gaps that were "filled in" in order to establish this sense of continuity: the vase is a collection of fragments that, as they were assumed to go together, were fixed upon a clay foundation in a manner dictated by their redesigner, Piranesi. Furthermore, as N. M. Penzer has shown, Piranesi freely added fanciful details to the vase wherever he felt that the reconstruction was somehow lacking. The Warwick Vase serves as an example of how the desire for historical continuity was frequently satiated by a pastiche of the past rather than an accurate retrieval of it.

In other words, within the regime of tradition perpetuated by aristocrats and connoisseurs, the desire for history was not motivated by an interest in understanding it as a cultural "Other," but rather by what justification it could give to the British cultural present. This desire uses identification to erase all differences between the past and present, save one: the survival of British culture, as opposed to the destruction of Classical culture. Cultural narcissism clearly comes into play here, in that British culture is shown to be alive and growing, in contrast to its defunct predecessor.

The most self-celebratory examples of the regime of tradition's use of the past are counterpoised, however, by an excessive sense of mourning in which the death of past cultures is projected onto the present. For example, Gibbon's pessimistic outlook on the nature of the comparison between past and present is revealed in his comment that "the Decline of the Two Empires, the Roman and the British, advances with equal steps."[47] Gibbon's attitude may well be the secularized, ironic version of the Christian tradition of pessimism, in which all worldly activities are judged to be worthless, and there is "nothing new under the sun." Ultimately, this worldview implies that, since humanity is locked into repeti-

13. *The Warwick Vase, Warwick Castle, Warwick, England.*

tive patterns of behavior, it is futile to attempt reform. In this way, although the pessimism sprung from the regime of tradition's mourning seems initially to be self-destructive, it results in the reinforcement of the status quo as the only possible—and therefore the best of all possible—world(s).

On the macroscopic level, the drive to use the past as authorization for the status quo manifested itself in the discourse of didacticism, which valorized the study of history as a way of controlling what it understood as humanity's obsessive/compulsive pattern of repeating the same behaviors. As a part of the dominant or "polite" culture of the late eighteenth century, the discourse of didacticism served as the official justification for historical enterprises. It is roughly analogous to what Robert Rosenblum has called the "Neoclassic Stoic," but also encompasses what others have called "Sensibility." Rosenblum cites the reconstitution of "the truth of an edifying historical moment" as the prevailing aim of the "Neoclassic Stoic," and he gives an excellent example of it in tracing the image of the grieving, virtuous widow.[48] By "excavating" and depicting scenes from antiquity that featured "proper" behavior upon the death of a husband or a son, these paintings sought to use history to instruct eighteenth-century women viewers on the necessity and propriety of grieving.[49] Another example of how didacticism seems an inevitable companion to explorations of the past comes from the critical reception of Sophia Lee's *The Recess*. I quote a critic, writing in a 1786 edition of *The Gentleman's Magazine*, who is troubled by the way that *The Recess* mixes historical fact with fiction: "we cannot entirely approve the custom of interweaving fictitious incident with historic truth. . . . These volumes, however, are calculated to supply not only amusement but *instruction*; and we recommend them with pleasure."[50] Thus, although the critic fears that history is being handled somewhat imprudently in the novel, he ultimately approves of *The Recess* because its imprudence does not obscure the lessons it offers to readers.

These lessons are viewed as eternal verities that are confirmed by "historic truth." In this way, history becomes the mine for materials to support the status quo of culture and the "proper" roles it prescribes for individual subjects. Even William Gilpin, the foremost promoter of the picturesque beauty of native ruins, occasionally lapses from purely aesthetic appreciations into the discourse of didacticism. For instance, speaking of Glastonbury's monastic ruins in particular, he claims that "When we consider five hundred persons bred up in indolence . . . [in] great nurseries of superstition, bigotry and ignorance; the stews of sloth, stupidity, and perhaps intemperance . . . we are led to acquiesce in the fate of these great foundations, and view their ruins not only with a picturesque eye, but with moral and religious satisfaction."[51] In this passage Gilpin moves from his ahistorical, formalist assessments of the aesthetic value of ruins toward a moral evaluation of their history, justifying the violence of their destruction and even taking "satisfaction" in it. He sees the ruin as representing indolence and a host of vices that he draws in opposition to the disciplinary values that he embraces, such as industry, sobriety, and rationality.[52] By describing the past in such negative terms, Gilpin "naturalizes" the violence represented in the ruin's remains, making it seem right and proper. Gilpin's comments on Glastonbury's ruins illustrate that the disciplinary, didactic discourse sponsored by the regime of tradition cannot be associated exclusively with the figure of the Classic ruin, but can be found in "appreciations" of native ruins as well.

Moreover, the Classic ruin itself was not wholly dominated by the tendencies of the regime of tradition. Its ability to provoke recognition of historical change and difference is most clearly revealed late in the century and on the European continent, however, not in England. On the continent, the neoclassical movement

> tacitly or openly challenged Christianity and replaced its sluggish observances with a fiery inspiration which . . . [had] the solid structure of fact: the fact of Rome and the exciting fact newly unearthed at Herculaneum and Pompeii, the marbles and terracottas, temples and houses, which all had the primary value of existing, of being true, and the secondary one of being beautiful. That wonderful world had set up its own standards, without the aid of Christ or the Virgin.[53]

This subversive attitude toward the Classic ruin is exemplified in the "Broken Column" folly house, located in the Désert de Retz, near Paris. While participating in the symbolism of freemasonry, the Broken Column's gigantic size is surreal, "signaling the visitor to prepare for an encounter with the bizarre."[54] In this way, the Classic ruin came to be associated with a revolutionary ethic whose "pagan" or even decadent tendencies would have shocked Gilpin. However, this association ultimately reinforces the Classic ruin's status as a symbol of the union of moral virtue and aesthetics that Shaftesbury and others had delineated early in the century. Therefore, despite its ability to relativize the status quo by presenting a vision of alternative cultures, the Classic ruin is in the end reattached to the discourse of discipline and control by its association with moral or ethical standards, whether Christian or non-Christian.

In sum, although the "way of seeing" offered by the regime of tradition actively sought out the past through the figure of the ruin, it did so while denying the potential for historical alterity or discontinuity. We see this both in the Classic ruins that were reconstructed and aestheticized as ideal objects, thus dehistoricizing them, and in the pleasure taken by Gilpin and others in seeing, as Kames puts it, the triumph of time over "strength" and the "barbarity" of a different culture. Through the regime of tradition's cyclical view of history and its projection of contemporary values onto the past, it managed to negotiate history without danger to the social status quo, repressing any sense of upheaval, rupture, or violent change.

However, if on the macroscopic level historical representation was thus co-opted as part of the disciplinary structure of society, on the microscopic level—the level of individual practice—the drive to reclaim the past was motivated more variously than admitted in the official discourse of didacticism and the regime of tradition. Particularly in the case of native ruins, such as those discussed by Gilpin, the ruin becomes a means by which the individual subject may appropriate history for private reconstructions of him- or herself. This use of the past corresponds with the vision of history as a linear procession of events that is espoused by the regime of change. In contrast to the regime of tradition, there is no developed sense of mourning in the regime of change because emphasis is placed on using the past as a source of creation and novelty rather than as a prop for the maintenance of the status quo. Moreover, in contrast to the boundedness of the subject in the regime of tradition, the regime of change stresses the subject's potential for growth and development.[55]

In this way, the figure of the ruin becomes the site for potential disruptions of the status quo and the unified vision of history upon which it relies. This can be seen in Gilpin's writings on the picturesque, which, although they attempt to recuperate the ruin within the regime of tradition, effectively place it outside the pale by considering it first and foremost as an aesthetic object that is subject to the modern viewer's powers of appreciation and evaluation. Two striking examples of the potentially disruptive effect of the figure of the ruin within the regime of change are offered in Joseph Gandy's "The Bank of England in Ruins; a Fantasy" (1832) and Hubert Robert's "The Grande Galerie of the Louvre in Ruins; a Fantasy" (see figures 14 and 15).[56] These two images subject

14. The Bank of England in Ruins, Joseph Gandy. By courtesy of the trustees of Sir John Soane's Museum.

national institutions—the Bank of England and the Louvre—to private vision. In the way that they express an unambiguous desire for future destruction, these images lay bare the character of the ruin as wish fulfillment. Thus, they show how the ruin could potentially become the site of liberating dislocations of cultural norms, creating a space of freedom in which the individual subject could reconfigure him- or herself.[57]

Nonetheless, while the regime of change encourages an attitude toward the ruin and history that could be freeing for the individual, it also reclaims history as a potential threat or disruption for the self. This occurs because it acknowledges the existence of rupture, discontinuity, and violent change in the past, the very elements repressed by the regime of tradition. Picturesque art demonstrates the resulting split in attitude toward the ruin, manifesting attraction to it as a symbol of the past, yet attempting to occult its reference to the violence, disruption, and difference of the past. Although this split superficially duplicates the ambivalence caused by mourning, it is different because the regime of change assumes no investment of libidinal energies in the past; any such investment is very tentative, in contrast to the full investment assumed under the regime of tradition.

15. The Grande Galerie of the Louvre in Ruins—a Fantasy, Hubert Robert. Musée du Louvre.

    The many representations of castles in picturesque art exemplify this split in attitude toward the past: on the one hand, they depict somewhat forbidding ruins; on the other hand, they naturalize these ruins by including tourists, hikers, or even lovers. Viewer identification with these human figures helps domesticate the ruins into a familiar pastoralism, allowing the spectator to internalize them as a symbol of the "friendliness" of the past. As we have seen, Freud explains how identification is related to mourning; however, identification has also been described as an aesthetic goal. In his study of late eighteenth-century French painting, Michael Fried finds the desire to "enter into" paintings to be a dominant theme. He further claims that a state of absorption on the part of depicted figures was a catalyst for the viewer's identification with them: "It was chiefly by virtue of the persuasive representation of the complete absorption of a figure or group of figures in various actions, activities, and states of mind . . . that the painter was able to establish the fiction of the aloneness of those figures, and by implication of the painting as a whole, relative to the beholder."[58]

By the term "absorption," he refers to a painted figure's loss of self through rapt attention to an object outside the self. According to Fried, the presence of such figures encourages the viewer, through the process of identification, to adopt an absorptive posture toward the painting. The active response thus demanded from the viewer by the painting has its eighteenth-century literary equivalent in the "non finito," which is "the art of making the reader or viewer supply what is unstated."[59] Of course, before this could occur, the reader had to be engaged with the text in an absorptive manner. Through this engagement, the reader was to construct an "ideal presence" that supposedly converted representation into an unmediated experience of the objects described. In both the non finito and the absorptive painting, the audience was expected to supply extraneous details to the scene or narrative through their intense identification with it and with the human figures within it. Thus, in terms of contemporary verbal and visual structures, identification was a common principle that we see extended within picturesque depictions of native ruins.

Constable's "Hadleigh Castle"[60] (1828) is a good example of how identification operates within the context of the ruin's split significance (see figure 16). "Hadleigh Castle" features the remains of the castle's two towers, the most complete of the two split by a black, craggy breach in its walls, and overlooking a precipitous drop to the sea. On its own, this ruin and its environs might seem threatening, if not sinister: the breach and the precipice literalize the potential for disruption or "breaches" in historical space. But Constable has seen fit to add a bit of human presence to his picture: a shepherd and his dog walk on the level of the ruins, while another man tends some cattle immediately below the castle. These figures—straight out of poetic idealizations of the country life—reassure the viewer and dissolve the threat embodied in the castle's war- and time-ravaged appearance.[61]

One of the most interesting aspects of "Hadleigh Castle" is the balance between threat and reassurance that it manages to maintain. In contrast, Michael Rooker's (1743–1801) watercolor of "The Chapel at the Greyfriars Monastery, Winchester" illustrates how pastoral accoutrements may overwhelm the ruin's difference from the cultural present (see figure 17). The human figures in this picture serve several important functions: to begin with, they are an indication of scale, permitting the spectator to judge the size of the ruins in human terms; second, because

16. Hadleigh Castle (1829), John Constable. Courtesy of Yale Center for British Art, Paul Mellon Collection.

the figures are at rest, eating and drinking, they place the ruin in the context of the repetitions of everyday life, thus "normalizing" it; third, the activity that the figures appear to have just abandoned—hay raking—situates the ruin within the reassuring framework of harvest, and the cyclical repetition of birth, death, and renewal embodied in the seasons. Because the probable viewers of this picture—city dwellers—would have felt greatly removed in social station from the peasants it depicts, it is highly unlikely that they were intended to identify with them. Rather, the gap in social station permits viewers to feel completely at ease and in control over the situation presented, as if they were landlords surveying their property. Greyfriars Monastery is fittingly thrust into the background, since this picture refuses to acknowledge either the potential for destruction or the cultural difference of the past that are figured in the ruin, preferring rather to emphasize the domestication of the ruin and thus the past. Because of this, and because of the way the watercolor depicts a static social order based on the traditional hierarchical differen-

17. The Chapel of the Greyfriars Monastery, Michael Angelo Rooker. Courtesy of Yale Center for British Art, Paul Mellon Collection.

tiation between landowners/viewers and landless/viewed, Rooker's vision of Greyfriars participates, at least overtly, more in the regime of tradition than in the regime of change.

Like Rooker's picture, Thomas Walmsley's (1763–1805 or 1806) watercolor "West End of Netley Abbey" deemphasizes the ruin's threatening aspects (see figure 18). However, it differs from Rooker's work as well as Constable's in that it gives the viewer human figures with which identification is possible. Unlike the figures in "Greyfriars" and "Hadleigh Castle," these figures are not engaged in any sort of labor; instead, like the viewers of the picture, they are engaged in viewing, directing their gaze out to sea. Because these two—a man and a woman—are standing close

18. West End of Netley Abbey, Thomas Walmsley. *By courtesy of the V & A Picture Library.*

to one another, apparently leaning toward one another, it is logical to assume that they are lovers, connecting the ruin—and its viewers—with a type of desire or wish fulfillment far less destructive than that expressed by Gandy and Robert.

This association between ruins and love is not uncommon: in his analysis of Diderot's meditations on ruins, Jean Galard argues that "Les ruines sont le lieu idéal de l'amour; la pudeur y est moins forte, le désir plus entreprenant. Entrer dans . . . un tableau de ruines, ce seraient rejoindre la scène sublime (primitive?), pénétrer dans le lieu mythique."[62] For English audiences, the ruin was perhaps not connected so overtly to the notion of greater freedom or a state of nature, but its romantic connotations are nonetheless clear. These connotations may have been transferred from the enthusiasm for Italian landscapes populated with ruins, vulnerable women, and supermasculine banditti, to native English ruins.[63] The "foreignness" or historical alterity of the culture represented in the ruin helped to free viewers from their everyday self-conceptions and encouraged them to "try on" different selves within a semitheatrical atmosphere.

Walmsley's picture suggests, through the proximity between the lovers and Netley Abbey, that the past, as figured by the ruin, may serve as the basis for creative acts of self-definition like erotic attachment to another individual. The overall structure of the picture also permits it to be read as a vision of continuity: as the lovers are "backed" or supported by the past, represented by the ruin, they look forward, or to the future, represented by the spectacle of the ships coming and going from shore to horizon. These ships compose a scene in which commercial and technological dynamism is illustrated; its positive evaluation of the national future may be regarded as a promise of prosperity for the lovers.[64] Walmsley's watercolor, like Constable's, uses the ruin to give the viewer access to the past, but it also ties that past to both private and national aspirations for the future in a manner corresponding to the mercantile and imperialist preoccupations of the regime of change.[65] Still, the personal, individual quality of this process indicates the significance of the ruin on a private, subjective level, as well as on a public or national level.

The analysis of these three representative ruin images shows the breadth of response to the native ruin's historical implications. Moreover, as examples of picturesque art, these ruin images show how the picturesque was the visual carrier of history, and how it was inhabited by both regimes. Within the picturesque, then, the figure of the ruin is ambivalent, conveying simultaneously the threat of disruption and discontinuity in the past and potential liberation from the status quo. As we have seen, identification moderates these tendencies: in the regime of tradition, the difference between past and present cultures is treated as a scandal to be overcome and repressed through a masking, complete identification, while in the regime of change, identification is used as a point of access to cultural and historical difference.

Repressed Violence and the Monastic Ruin

The sequence of picturesque ruins that I have discussed—moving from ruined castles like "Hadleigh Castle" to monastic ruins like "Netley Abbey" and "Greyfriars Monastery"—foreshadows the narrowing of this investigation to the role that monastic ruins and iconoclasm played in determining the character of British encounters with historical space. I choose to focus on iconoclasted ruins because iconoclasm marks a more profound ideological break with the past than the threats of civil discord or foreign invasion embodied in ruined castles. Moreover, because iconoclasm was such a distinctively English phenomenon, it is central to determining the specifically English characteristics of both the figure of the ruin and historical space.

Ronald Paulson has argued that English heritage is unique among European cultures because it features the institutionalization of iconoclasm as an official power of the State: "England was the only country of any size where iconoclasm—as an important part of the Protestant Reformation—was carried out as a government policy with a fair amount of consistency and so produced a mind-set that was national rather than factional or local and continuing rather than sporadic."[66] The forbidding aspect of British monastic ruins is a result, above all, of the fact that they are reminders of the iconoclastic destruction of English monasteries, a violation perpetrated by Henry VIII and repeated during the Commonwealth period. The destruction of the monasteries is most frequently called the "Dissolution," a term that acts, like the pastoral accoutrements of ruin images, to mollify or cover the violent connotations of the ruin. The English tradition of iconoclasm actually begins *before* Henry VIII, in the fourteenth century with the iconophobic followers of the religious reformer Wycliffe.[67] According to Paulson, what the English iconoclasts feared most of all was *their own* tendency to "idolatry," the replacement of God by an image. The iconoclasted ruin thus represents not only a threatening rupture of genealogy and history, but also the schismatic separation of England from the Continental tradition of visual representation exemplified by the Catholic Church.

In eighteenth-century British culture, the figure of the iconoclasted, monastic ruin thus represents the repressed Catholic past as a half-destroyed yet still threatening "Other." Under the banner of "Catholicism," the ruin represents the repression of a complex of values, conjuring the spectres of iconophilia, sensuality, mysticism, secrecy, rebellion, and irrationality, in addition to religious difference. It also does not fail to represent the violent, iconoclastic spirit necessary to keep this complex controlled. In this way, the ruin reveals a split or duality in the past that is threatening to the regime of tradition and at least challenging to the regime of change; on the level of the individual subject, this split suggests that attempting to consolidate identity through historical space is a tenuous project at best.

Moreover, through its association with Catholicism, the monastic ruin possesses connotations of secrecy and repression that reinforce the notion of the private and hidden nature of individual identity. This is true both because of Catholic practices and doctrinal beliefs, and because of the fact that Catholicism was at one time an officially outlawed religion in England. For instance, the sacrament of confession makes the church, in the person of its priests, a repository of secrets. The very structure of Catholic churches, with their chambers for devotions to particular saints "hidden," as it were, in side alcoves, promotes the association of Catholicism with secrecy and with the expression of desires, prayers, and confessions that cannot be uttered under the scrutiny of the larger public.[68] In this way, secrecy and privacy are spatially represented in the cellular, chapeled, and chambered plans of Catholic churches and monastic buildings (see figure 19). Furthermore, because of its emphasis on inner faith—something that is empirically unmeasurable and contained wholly within the individual "soul"—the Catholic church virtually discounts the visible self in favor of a hidden self that is undiscoverable except to God.

These elements of practice and belief, among others, are by themselves enough to explain the existing cultural association between Catholicism and the privatized, secret self. However, the historical persecution of Catholicism in Britain also helps to impose the same association. Because of persecution, Catholics were forced to conduct their religious rites in secrecy and to hide their priests in what were called "priest holes," hidden rooms whose entrances were deviously concealed. Sophia Lee probably witnessed the anti-Catholic Gordon Riots of 1780, which resulted in £100,000 of property damage in London and the deaths of over 290 citizens; liberalization of laws restricting Catholics in Britain did not come until the nineteenth century.[69] It is easy to see how, given its outlaw status and the concealments its adherents were forced to practice, Catholicism in England came to stand for a dangerous divergence from the cultural values, as well as for a reality that was present, yet hidden from detection by "normal" scrutiny. This divergence was further reinforced as a political reality in the split between Stuart/Catholic pretenders to the throne and its Tudor/Hanoverian/Protestant possessors, a split that is evident in the Elizabethan era dramatized in *The Recess*. Indeed, for English audiences of the late eighteenth century, it is no overstatement to claim that Catholicism represented the repressed, irrational, "Other" side of the self.

Because of this, one of greatest reasons given for condemning Catholicism was its supposed encouragement of superstition, which, it was claimed, served the purposes of church leaders in allowing them to manipulate and repress ignorant believers. Idolatry was but one type of superstition of which Catholicism was accused. In its mildest form, this condemnation is seen in George Keate's poem, *The Ruins of Netley Abbey* (1764), where he urges those who look on the ruins to abandon the

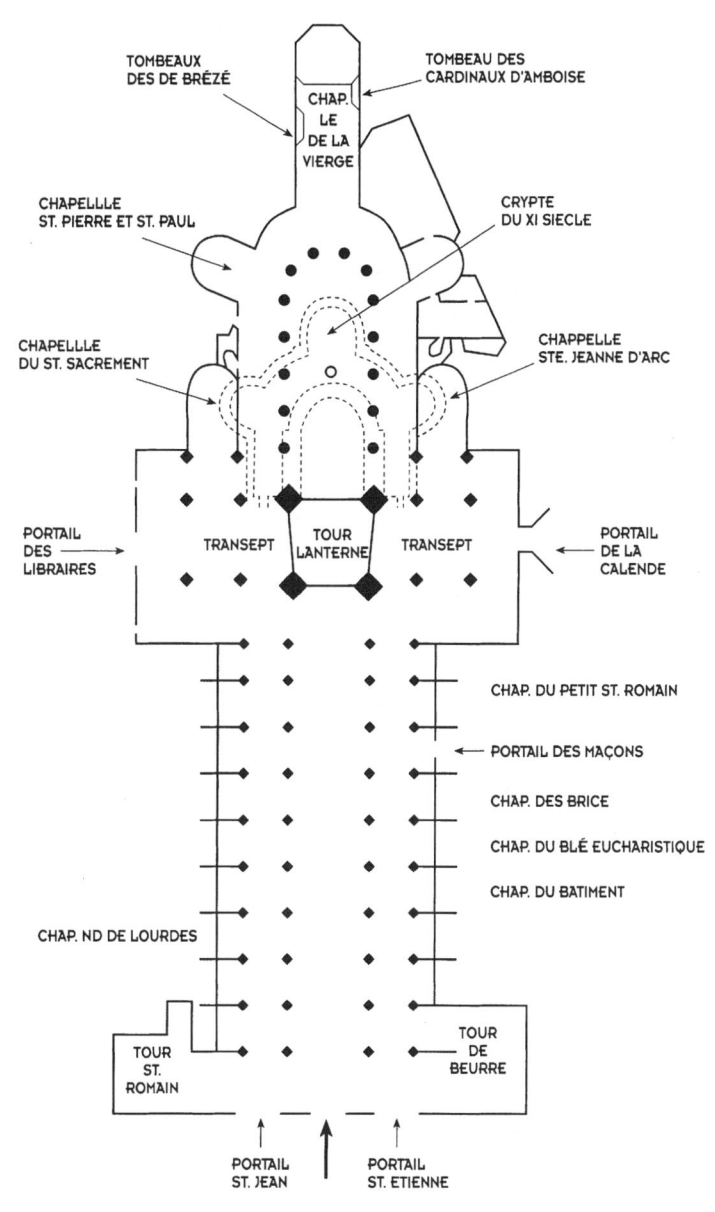

19. Plan of the Cathedral of Rouen.

search for worldly beauty, which he associates with the iconoclasted, "idolatrous" ruins, and to pursue Reason and Sense instead.[70] The Reverend Dr. Joseph Jefferson is less equivocal when he writes triumphantly in *The Ruins of a Temple* (1793) that "No more the cowl or rosary is known;/The Monkish garb and worship are no more;/Those walls are moulder'd where the list'ning stone/Heard Superstition frame its solemn roar"[71] Both writers dichotomize Protestant and Catholic differences by associating the former with "Reason," "Sense," and belief in empirical reality, and the latter with "Superstition" (the irrational), "beauty" (the aesthetic or sensual), and belief in a supernatural reality. Given the Freudian dictum that superstition (and, indeed, all religion) is the result of projected unconscious fears, the strength and frequency of denunciations of Catholic superstition by ruin-ponderers may indicate that these fears were only obscured by iconoclastic violence, not banished. In other words, as Paulson suggests, the iconoclasts and their eighteenth-century apologists still felt within themselves an attraction to idolatry and the irrational that they believed might rise once more if not controlled through violent opposition.

The eighteenth-century fascination with ruins—especially native, monastic ruins—suggests that this attraction was still very strong among the viewing public. In turn, this shows both the persistence of an unreconciled ideological split that could be simultaneously threatening and exciting to the individual subject, and a longing for the unclaimed, forbidden "Catholic" past.[72]

History and Ruins in the Novel

In literature, the implications of the ruin for subjectivity are most clearly expressed not in poetry, which has been the focus of previous "ruin scholarship," but in the novel, where narrative length permits the development of interaction between characters and the ruins that surround them. In the tradition of novel criticism, the appearance of ruins leads a novel to be categorized as "Gothic," and the ruins to be considered as part of the conventional apparatus of that literary mode. However, in view of the foregoing discussion of the ruin's wider cultural significance, novelistic ruins may be attached to something beyond literary convention: an ongoing fascination with the ruin's reflection of the past and its impact on visualizing the individual subject's identity. Sophia Lee's neglected novel *The Recess* (1783–85) was immensely popular when originally published, due in part to its use of monastic ruins as setting.[73] In contrast to the delineation of a complex social space that we have seen in *Humphry Clinker* and *Persuasion, The Recess* focuses on the individual subject outside of society: social space is limited to the repressive Court of Queen Elizabeth, where all forms of identity production are directed toward reinforcing the importance of the Queen alone. I will argue here—in a vignette discussion of *The Recess*'s more than nine-hundred-page, three- volume bulk—that the ruins it features can be attached to contemporary fascination with historical space and that, furthermore, this novel constructs an analogy between the ruins it presents and the protagonist's sense of identity, thus literalizing the psychological dimension of the ruin's popularity that is suggested in visual representations.

From the date of its publication, critics—and readers, one might assume—have focused on how *The Recess* deals with the past. Although one modern critic warns that "the modern reader of historical novels . . . may well be surprised and disappointed" with *The Recess*'s sense of historical accuracy (i), Lee's contemporary, a *Gentleman's Magazine* reviewer, concluded that "[t]he writer seems well acquainted with the times she describes. The truth of character is rigidly preserved, for the peculiarities of Elizabeth and James are not delineated with more exactness in Hume or Robertson."[74] Thus, according to the standards of at least one eighteenth-century reader, part of the novel's value was its plausible representation of the past.[75] Most critics suggest that *The Recess* is a blend of historical and Gothic interests, following its Gothic predecessors *The Castle of Otranto* (1764) and *The Old English Baron* (1777) yet adding an attention to history that neither possessed.[76]

The Recess also exhibits the conjunction of the picturesque and the historical: Harriet Lee (Sophia's sister) commented that *The Recess* depends upon "picturesque descriptions" for at least part of its interest to readers.[77] For the most part, these descriptions are directed toward the remains of Catholic, monastic edifices. The recess referred to in the title is a hidden chamber within an iconoclasted convent, within which the two daughters of Mary, Queen of Scots, are raised in secrecy. As described by their guardian and "more than mother" Mrs. Marlow, "it was once a Convent, inhabited by nuns of the order of St. Winifred, but deserted before the abolition of Convents, from falling into decay . . . [it was] devoutly visited by those travellers whom chance or curiosity brought this way."[78] During the dissolution, when "Henry . . . robbed the monks of their vast domains," the monastery with which the convent was associated was confiscated, torn down, and rebuilt as a modern estate called St. Vincent's Abbey (1:43).[79] The first owner of St. Vincent's was nominally

Protestant but sympathetic to Catholicism; because of this, he fashioned the convent's ruined, subterranean chambers into a "priest hole" that was connected to the abbey by a secret passage more than a half-mile long. Hidden in the recess, the priests "by degrees formed two other passages from the Recess, one of which ends in the Hermit's cave, where the eldest of them lived, and the other in the midst of the ruins" (1:44). These ruins and the habitable recess shaped within them draw together the notions of secrecy, retreat from the world, and religious repression that are visible in picturesque representations of ruins.

The principal narrator of *The Recess,* Mary's daughter Matilda, completes our impression of the picturesque setting of the novel with her descriptions of the passage from the abbey to the recess and the entrance located in the ruins of the convent. In the abbey, the entrance to the passage is hidden by a false-backed clothes press that opens to "several subterraneous passages built on arches, and preserved from damps by cavities which passed thro' every statue that ornamented the garden;" this passage ends at the door to the recess, which is concealed by one of the portraits of Matilda's parents, Mary and the Duke of Norfolk (1:22–23). The most immediate entrance to the recess is in the ruins of the convent, and is disguised as a tomb: "It was at the foot of a high-raised tomb, at each corner of which stood a gigantic statue of a man in armour, as if to guard it, two of whom were now headless. Some famous knight . . . lay on the tomb. The meagre skeleton had struck an arrow through his shield into his heart; his eyes were turned to the cross which St. Winifred held to him" (1:85). In these descriptions, the hidden reality of the recess lies just below their picturesque surface, which becomes somewhat more threatening and "Gothicized" in its evocation of damp, unlit passageways, tombs, and gigantic warriors.

Moreover, these descriptions are always framed by an explicit consideration of the visual. For instance, although the tomb entrance to the recess provokes "trepidation" in Matilda and her sister, she remarks how "[n]othing could be better contrived . . . for, however rude the sculpture, the ornamental parts took the eye from the body of the tomb" where the door is concealed (1:85). Here she is not only more concerned with the movement of the eye than with the tomb's gruesome sculpture, but also becomes a critic of its apparently poor representational quality ("however rude the sculpture"). Immediately after the description of the tomb entrance, Matilda gives the reader a very visual, painterly impression of its surroundings:

> For a vast space beyond the tomb, the prospect was wild and awful to excess; sometimes vast heaps of stones were fallen from the building, among which trees and bushes had sprung up, and half involved the dropping pillars. Tall fragments of it sometimes remained, which seemed to sway about with every blast, and from whose mouldering top hung clusters and spires of ivy . . . the intricacies of the wood beyond added to the magnificence of art the variety of nature. (1:85–86)

The roughness, wildness, and disordered state of the ruins here is something in which Matilda and Ellinor, the two sisters, clearly take pleasure. Therefore, the threat seemingly represented in the "awful" dimensions of the iconoclasted convent and in the morbid sculpture of the tomb is only one aspect of the encounter with the figure of the ruin.

The more pleasant, and even romantic, aspects of the ruin-dominated landscape are symbolized by the fact that Matilda meets her first love, Robert Dudley, Lord Leicester, in this setting. Although his presence is initially threatening by default, because the sisters are discovered unawares, the near-immediate romance between Matilda and Leicester soon causes the scene to resemble Walmsley's depiction of ruins and lovers in "West End of Netley Abbey." In another example of the important role visual and picturesque taste plays in *The Recess*, Leicester shows his worth as a suitor by describing how, after an absence of years from his now-deceased wife, the first thing he did upon his return was to exhaust himself "in surveying the gardens, and directing many necessary alterations" (1:137). Matilda also seeks to recommend him to the reader by describing his estate, Kenilworth, which "[h]e had greatly improved" (1:170). Kenilworth's gardens consist of a

> magnificent lake . . . in whose clear bosom the trees were reflected, and round which the sheep and deer grazed on rich pasture: swans and waterfowls innumerable play'd on its surface, and an aight in the center was made highly picturesque by several half-seen cottages, and emblems of agriculture. . . . Several gilded boats, and little vessels, danced on the bosom of the lake, and added, by the various streamers which played upon the surface, to the gaiety and richness of the prospect. (1:173)

Like the "emblems of agriculture" that adorn his gardens, Leicester's taste for the picturesque and ability to produce a pleasing "prospect" serve as emblems of his virtue and merit. In this way, the picturesque is harnessed to the novel's strategy of characterization.

The overarching importance of the descriptions of the recess is indicated by the frontispiece to *The Recess* (see figure 20), which neatly tabulates its content: it shows the two sisters fleeing from the intruding male

20. *Frontispiece to Sophia Lee's* The Recess *(1783–85)*.

presence of Leicester, their first discoverer. While his facial expression indicates no malice, they clearly perceive him as a threat and cringe toward their refuge, the recess. The ruins are present in the background, shrouded in foliage and guarded by the two stone knights-at-arms who sit at either corner of a remaining wall; two Gothic arches, bereft of the roof they once supported, are silhouetted against the sky. By picturing the ruined convent both in the frontispiece and in verbal descriptions within the text, *The Recess* reinforces the image of history as at once a space of safety and of menace.

The Recess focuses on history not only symbolically, through the figure of monastic ruins, but also explicitly, as indicated by its subtitle, *A Tale of Other Times,* which promises a vision of the "otherness" or difference of the past from the present. Furthermore, Lee explicitly critiques the selectivity of conventional historical writing in the "Advertisement" to *The Recess:* "History, like painting, only perpetuates the striking features of the mind; whereas the best and worst actions of princes often proceed from partialities and prejudices, which live in their hearts and are buried with them" (1: unpaginated). The restoration of "otherness" to history—as opposed to "striking features"—and "partialities and prejudices" (personal practice)—as opposed to law—is exemplified in the novel's focus on an other, alternative lineage of rulers. The twin daughters of Mary, Queen of Scots, Matilda and Ellinor, must be protected from the wrath of Mary's enemy, Queen Elizabeth, by their foster mother, Mrs. Marlow, and a stern Catholic priest, Father Anthony. When Matilda and Ellinor eventually enter the world outside of the recess, they are forced to conceal their identities because of the threat of persecution. In the course of the novel, their efforts to shield their identities are progressively undermined, and both they and the recess itself come under attack. Matilda is driven to madness by this persecution, but recovers and lives to tell her tale despite her "shattered constitution" (3:219), while her sister, Ellinor, eventually dies from the effects of the same type of treatment (3:221). Telling her tale in retrospect, Matilda exclaims at one point, "How have I wept the moment I quitted the Recess—a moment I then lived but in hope of!" (1:11). The outside world clearly represents a threat to identity; in contrast, the recess is a protected, private sanctuary for the protagonists.

Throughout *The Recess,* Lee invests the monastic ruin with the protagonists' sense of identity. In this way, the ruin literalizes the psychosocial concept of genealogical or historical space in which their heritage is conserved. This occurs most prominently in the fact that the recess contains Mrs. Marlow, their only human tie to their imprisoned mother; a casket that contains "proof" of their birth in the form of letters (1:78, 81); and full-length portraits of their parents. Mrs. Marlow is the only person who can inform them of facts about themselves such as who they were named after: she tells them that Matilda was named after her aunt, Lady Scroope, while Ellinor was named after their father's mother (1:66). Their source of such unrecorded yet important information, their "only tye on earth," is lost to them when Mrs. Marlow dies of fever (1:20, 81).

Among the other ties to genealogy that the recess contains, the most interesting are the portraits, which were commissioned by Matilda and Ellinor's aunt (1:75). The casket of letters plays a comparatively minor role, registering the progressive loss of genealogy when they are removed from the recess and lost at Kenilworth when new owners replace Leicester. In contrast, the portraits are much more a part of the identity-stabilizing apparatus of the recess. As we have seen, one of the portraits conceals the entrance to the recess from St. Vincent's Abbey; as a literal door, the portrait's status as a "door" to the past and to genealogical ties is revealed. Even before the sisters know the identity of the pictures' sitters, they are instinctively affected by them. Gazing on what they later learn to be the portrait of their father, the Duke of Norfolk, Matilda feels "[a] sentiment of veneration," while Mary's portrait "seemed to call forth a thousand melting sensations; the tears rushed involuntarily to our eyes" (1:9). This reaction to the paintings first occurs when Mrs. Marlow, who has hidden the sisters' identity from them, is absent. In the "space" of her absence, genealogy reasserts itself and the portraits are activated as parental figures: "we lived in the presence of these pictures as if they understood us, and blush'd when we were guilty of the slightest folly" (1:9). In order for the portraits to play this parental role, it is important that they are "whole length" and thus offer to Matilda and Ellinor, as nearly as possible, replicas of their parents, Mary and Norfolk. The sisters' involuntary, instinctive reaction to these portraits illustrates the strength and "naturalness" of the tendency to anchor identity in the genealogical space of family ties.

The confirmation of genealogy as a source of "natural" identity is also expressed in Matilda and Ellinor's resemblance to the portraits. Matilda first recognizes her sister's resemblance to the pictured Duke (1:9); then, when Mrs. Marlow wishes to describe their mother to the sisters, she says instead, "I would describe the Queen of Scotland to you, my dear children, had not nature drawn a truer picture of her than I can give.—Look in the glass, Matilda, and you will see her perfect image" (1:55). Matilda's recognition of her duplication of Mary's beauty leads her to fear that her resemblance may inadvertently betray the secret of her parentage. Because of her telltale features, Matilda disguises herself upon first encountering Elizabeth and her entourage, "letting my hair curl more over my face and neck, enwreath[ing] it fancifully with flowers; then mixing with the villagers in habits resembling theirs" (1:199). The portraits testify to Matilda and Ellinor's identities by showing their near-facsimile resemblance to their parents.

Through the portraits and other ties to the genealogical past that are held in the recess, an analogy is constructed between the recess and the identity of the sisters. Through this analogy, the recess's ruined features are transferred to Matilda and Ellinor's genealogical or historical heritage. The first human "ruin" that the narrative introduces is Matilda herself, who opens the novel by proclaiming her readiness for death: "After a long and painful journey thro' life, with a heart exhausted by various afflictions, and eyes which can no longer supply tears to lament them, I turn my every thought toward that grave on the verge of which I hover" (1:1). Given the personal losses that Matilda sustains throughout the narrative, losing her husband, mother, sister, best friend (Rose Cecil), and foster mother, this longing for death is understandable. In addition to the family losses that Matilda experiences, her own trials are so extreme that, in the end, Matilda is a relic like the ruins that hide the recess.[80]

The analogy between the recess and the sisters' identities is extended in the fact that the progressive "ruining" of Matilda and Ellinor is accomplished through the revelation of those two interrelated secrets, the hidden, protective space of the recess, and the concealed identity of the sisters. At the start of Matilda's tale, her own identity and even that of her foster mother, Mrs. Marlow, is concealed from her; both secrets are kept from the reader, too, until Mrs. Marlow's illness and death. As the novel progresses, the secrets of Matilda and Ellinor's identities and the location of the recess are increasingly revealed, and their vulnerability and woes mount. The public, daylight world is dominated by Elizabeth's evil allies, who bring death and destruction to the protective, beneficent netherworld of the recess. Although Mrs. Marlow is allowed to die peacefully, Father Anthony is murdered by Williams, an intruder bent on revenging himself on Leicester and Matilda (2:3); Williams also converts the recess into a prison and torture chamber: "I [Matilda] every where perceived a variety of instruments, nameless to me, . . . the means of torture and death" (2:2). The recess is finally destroyed by usurping owners who gain possession of the St. Vincent's Abbey estate through their cooperation with Elizabeth in advancing her web of vindictive, persecuting designs. Furthermore, the protective qualities of the recess, itself a ruined convent, are effectively effaced and reversed when Matilda is held captive in a convent and threatened by the evil fanaticism of the nuns, who "saw the absolute necessity of winning me over, or entombing me alive" (2:83). In essence, the destruction of Matilda and Ellinor, their heritage, and the past is figured in the destruction of the recess by the dominant powers of the present.

As figured in the relationship between Elizabeth's court and the recess, the relationship between the past and present in Lee's novel is a reversal of Gothic literary conventions. In the Gothic tradition that, according to J. M. S. Tompkins and Devendra Varma, Lee supposedly follows, the past continually returns to—often literally—"haunt" the present.[81] This feature and others typical of the Gothic tradition are found in Claire Kahane's description of the general pattern of Gothic fiction:

> Within an imprisoning structure, a protagonist, typically a young woman whose mother has died, is compelled to seek out the center of a mystery, while vague and usually sexual threats to her person from some powerful male figure hover on the periphery of her consciousness. Following clues which pull her onward and inward . . . she penetrates the obscure recesses of a vast labyrinthean space and discovers a secret room sealed off by its association with death. In this dark, secret center of the Gothic structure—typically a bedroom—the boundaries of life and death themselves seem confused.[82]

This description seems particularly appropriate for *The Recess* because of its emphasis on a motherless, female protagonist and "obscure recesses" that hide a secret. Although Kahane implies the potential involvement of the supernatural when she claims that the center of the Gothic unsettles the boundaries between life and death, I think that this includes more prosaic forms of the return of the past than just ghostly ones. In the context of this discussion, what is most striking about Kahane's pattern is how *The Recess* inverts it. Rather than moving from the light of day into the "Gothic world," penetrating "the obscure recesses of a vast labyrinthean space," the sisters are born into the obscure recess and consequently penetrate daylight reality, what might be called the labyrinthean space of Elizabethan England, with its court intrigues, jealousies, intense passions, and devious plots. Indeed, one might say that, rather than being haunted themselves, Matilda and Ellinor are the "ghosts" of the past that haunt Elizabeth, indicating by their "reincarnation" of Mary and Norfolk's looks the persistence of a lineage that she thought she had destroyed forever. Moreover, whereas the conventional Gothic novel associates the forces of the "real" and the present with virtue in their conquest and exposure of the evil shadow world that is composed of the imaginary, the irrational, and the past, *The Recess* reverses this association by making the recess the site of not only virtue but also happiness and shelter from a threatening "real" world.[83]

The inversion in *The Recess* of the Gothic pattern described by Kahane effectually turns the world of the present, the world in which Elizabeth is dominant, into the true location of horror in the novel. In the context of this inversion, the fact that Lee avoids the supernatural also works to convince the reader of the reality of horror, in the daylight world of everyday life.[84] What is ultimately most "horrifying" about the present in *The Recess* is that it has the power to repress and obliterate the complexity of the past. This power operates on both the national, ideological level, as reflected in the representative obliteration of Mary's Catholic lineage, and the personal level, as reflected in Elizabeth's hatred of Matilda and Ellinor and her destruction of the genealogical means by which they seek to establish their identities.

As in the case of picturesque visual depictions of ruins, identification is key to the reader's perception of the "horrors" involved in the relation of the past to the present. Through the bond of identification that develops between reader and protagonist in *The Recess,* the reader is invited to sympathize with an alternative history, one born among the ruins of an abandoned religious and cultural heritage and persisting in the real world despite persecution by the dominant strain. The struggle to survive that occurs between Elizabeth on the one side and Mary and her daughters on the other dramatizes the inherent multiplicity of history, and consequently exposes canonical history as a highly political choice made between diverging "lineages."[85] Although *The Recess* thus stages the construction of history on a macroscopic, national level, dealing with conflicts between royal lines, it also has ramifications for the microscopic, personal level: the process of identification between the reader and Matilda can only encourage the reader to internalize the importance of the past to his or her personal self-conception. The reader is complicit with the protagonists, identifying with their efforts to maintain their secret identity in a hostile, prying world. In this way, the "horrors" that Matilda must face in order to protect her identity serve as analogues to the risks that one must entertain in attempting to use genealogy as a foundation of psychological stability.

Like the figure of the ruin in visual representations, the ruin in *The Recess* is shared by the regimes of tradition and change. On the one hand, the regime of tradition's cyclical vision of history is perpetuated in the novel's elaborate system of doubles and the discourse of fatalism. The doubling occurs primarily between generations, and thus implies the inevitable recurrence of behavioral patterns. The secret marriage between Matilda and Leicester, for example, parallels the earlier secret marriage between Mary and Norfolk. As we have seen, Matilda's looks duplicate those of Mary, who has a namesake in Matilda and Leicester's child, Mary. Unjust imprisonment is also a pattern that recurs and produces doubles: "Bloody" Mary imprisons Elizabeth, who, upon reaching the throne, imprisons Mary Stuart. Finally, the principal male characters—Leicester,

Norfolk, and Ellinor's lover, Essex—are all overconfident, prone to unwise anger, and easily duped and destroyed by Elizabeth.

This pattern of recurrence and doubling is accompanied by a discourse of fatalism in which Matilda depicts herself as a helpless victim of Fate. For example, at her tale's beginning, Matilda tries to impose a coherence on her history by claiming that she was "marked . . . out [as] a solitary victim to the crimes of my progenitors" (1:2). The nature of these crimes is never explained, but Mrs. Marlow states that, at least in Elizabeth's eyes, "Mary's greatest crimes . . . were the graces she received from nature," implying that "nature" or God determined Mary's persecution (1:51). Indeed, when the sisters visit her prison and see her from afar, Mary is described not only as a human ruin, but as a symbol of necessary resignation:

> [O]h how chang'd, and yet how lovely!—damp rooms had weakened her limbs—her charming arms were thrown round the necks of two maids, without whose assistance she could not move—a pale resignation sat on her still beautiful features . . . .
> —Her beads and cross were her only ornaments, but her unaffected piety, and patient sufferance, mingled the Saint with the Queen, and gave her charms beyond humanity. (1:191)

While the Mary who reigned as Queen of Scots was prone to error, as Mrs. Marlow remarks, the ruined Mary, like the ruined monasteries about which Gilpin rhapsodizes, is elevated in an apotheosis of resigned suffering and, ultimately, martyrdom. Through this apotheosis, in the details of her cross and rosary, the death of the preceding, Catholic culture is celebrated by its successor and naturalized as the work of Providence. Nearing death, Matilda imitates her mother's resignation, arguing "that consummate misery has a moral use, in teaching the repiner at little evils to be juster to his God" and to see how "[g]lorious though inscrutable are all his ways" (3:355). Thus, the image of continuity that is valued in the regime of tradition is maintained both by the discourse of fatalism—blended with didacticism in Matilda's comments—and by the series of doublings evident in *The Recess*.

On the other hand, the regime of change is also evident in *The Recess*'s representation of the past as an "Other" time. Rather than standing apart from the events of the present as an invulnerable, inviolate symbol of history, the recess becomes the site for modern struggle over the fate of Mary and her two daughters. In demonstrating Elizabeth's ruthless control over Mary, Ellinor, and Matilda, over the recess, and thus over historical space, *The Recess* shows that the key to power and to constructing a stable identity is dominance over the past. If we persist in reading the recess as a stand-in for history, the implications are clear: history is not a static tableau, as the regime of tradition would have it be, but is instead imbricated in and transformed by the events of the present. As Jayne Lewis argues, Lee uses her narrative to illustrate the struggle over historical interpretation: "Lee's representation of Mary forces the authors of history to share authority with its subjects and readers. At the same time, this sharing is not idealized as a solution to the problem of how modern cultural authority is arranged."[86] In showing that history itself is fluid, and that it is a construct defined by the dominance of the present culture over the past, *The Recess* participates in the ideology of the regime of change.

Still, it might be argued that, in emphasizing the complexity of history, Lee's novel shows how individual subjects are blocked from historical space: against the background of political, artistic, and religious iconoclasm provided by the convent ruins, *The Recess* tells a tale of personal disruption originating in the separation of Mary from her children and ending in futile attempts to repair the damage. For Matilda, this seems to be true; however, for the reader of *The Recess,* the space of history it offers is somewhat different. Despite its projection of certain eighteenth-century sensibilities onto the Elizabethan past, *The Recess* nevertheless represents a time and culture that was very different from that of its readers. Therefore, it provides readers with alternate models of subjectivity, and even provides an image of Elizabeth's playful recreation of herself as the "Lady of the Lake" in a masque, although Matilda colors this episode with disgust at Elizabeth's self-indulgence and selfish arrogation of all theatrical presence (1:204–5). Thus, the fatalism and didacticism found in *The Recess,* and its acknowledgement of discontinuity in the space of the past, do not necessarily prohibit the reader's appropriation of parts of its representation of history for the purposes of self-(re)creation.

Examining narrative and visual configurations of the ruin in tandem helps to delineate the pressure placed on history as an "anchor" for the construction of the self. On the one hand, by looking at visual representations of ruins we can recognize the narrative ruins described in *The Recess* and other texts as more than "Gothic" or "Picturesque": in other words, we can see them as an elaboration of the ruin's role in harnessing history for private, individual purposes. On the other hand, by looking at literary ruins we can discern the psychological element that is occulted in the visual. Most importantly, treating both the visual and the literary manifestations of ruins together exposes the fact that ruins were part of the larger public consciousness, and were not an aberrant interest among artists of a single genre.

This examination of the figure of the ruin has led to several conclusions, not the least of which is that the ruin was a nexus for ambivalent emotions concerning the past. This ambivalence can be further broken down into two distinct ways of regarding the past: the regime of tradition, which relies on the past as a prop for the maintenance of the status quo, and the regime of change, which acknowledges the more threatening aspects of historical consciousness while making use of its "spatial" diversity. Part of the threat involved in historical or genealogical excavation stems from the British tradition of iconoclasm, which has resulted in the association of the ruin with violence and with the forbidden. For this reason, the British ruin is frequently the vehicle for the expression of wish fulfillment and unauthorized aggression (in terms of exploration of the forbidden past). Furthermore, the artistic strategies of absorption and the non finito reflect the fact that identification was the principal means through which audiences were meant to assimilate the ruin's implications. All of these conclusions serve to reinforce the ruin's principal status as an attempted contact with history.

The complex emotions surrounding the ruin indicate the strategic importance and desirability of history. As one of the "spaces" that defines social reality, history can—no matter how tenuously—serve as an anchor for both national and personal identity. Jean Baudrillard marks the continuance of this role for history in contemporary Western society when he claims that "we need a visible past, a visible continuum, a visible myth of origin to reassure us as to our ends"; he further asserts that "our entire linear and accumulative culture would collapse if we could not stockpile the past in plain view."[87] The figure of the ruin in the late eighteenth and early nineteenth centuries underscores Baudrillard's belief in the stabilizing use of historical artifacts. Moreover, his emphasis on vision and the necessity of displaying the past "in plain view" coincides with the motivations of Lord Kames and others who seem to have been compelled to preserve and exhibit signs of the past as "proof" of their society's status as heir to classical antiquity.

However, Baudrillard's characterization of Western society as "linear and accumulative" points to an aspect of historical or genealogical excavation that he does not discuss—its potential to disrupt conventional linearity. The plot of *The Recess,* for instance, tells the story of the suppression of one political and familial "line" in favor of another; the monastic ruin—both in general and within *The Recess*—tells the same story of suppression, substitution, or replacement, this time in religious and artistic terms. This exemplifies the ruin's disruptive connotations: it deconstructs the monolithic linearity of history by pointing out the existence of other "lines," forming a spatial network.

In sum, the ruin mobilizes complex emotions because of the fundamentally ambivalent nature of the encounter with history—history is both threat and opportunity. Ultimately, although history may be initially turned to as an escape from the pressures of social space, a developed historical awareness—a sense of historical and cultural difference—renders the individual's conception of reality more complicated because it reveals identity and cultural formation to be contingent rather than immanent, multiple rather than monolithic, and fluid rather than fixed.

4

Erotic Space

Amelia
and the Miniature

This chapter focuses on erotic space—a space of desire that is constituted in figured relations between human bodies. Like historical space, erotic space is a sub-version of social space through which individual subjects can supplement, or nearly substitute for, an identity formed in the space of the present. Because the erotic is related to deferral, and thus to the future, it is a space that is characterized by absence and desire. *The Recess,* for instance, blends historical space with the erotic in that it is governed by the absence of Matilda and Ellinor's mother, Mary, and by the frustrated attempts of the sisters to forge stable, romantic bonds with a series of noble, ill-fated heroes. Thus, the erotic arises out of the absence of a beloved; this absence is camouflaged by representations that promise to make the beloved one continuously accessible. As the most "bodily" of the spaces I will describe, the erotic is composed of efforts to define the body as the substance or expression of beauty and to make the absent, desired body present.

Perhaps because of the more private nature of erotic space, it is delineated in a language of minutiae that requires close reading of details. In this way the erotic contrasts greatly with the social, in which public display indicates the necessity of externalizing the internal in order to achieve self-representation. Erotic space manifests itself in the liminal grounds between public display and hiddenness, where "common" forms of communication are too visible, yet some subtle demonstration of attachment is desirable. In Jane Austen's novels, for instance, "the quietness, the virtual negativeness of . . . proposal scenes arises from . . . a belief that language is in itself inadequate to the expression of strong emotion"; for this reason, "the smallest gestures . . . are very highly charged with emotional significance."[1] However, the silent "language" of the body is difficult to perceive: because of Wentworth's inability to read the details of Anne's gestures and behavior, their final romantic reconciliation is carried through by default, via the indirect means of a letter that, for all its intensity, indicates a failure to communicate face to face, on a personal, immediate level. The potential ambiguity of the minute, silent language with which the erotic is expressed often leads erotic space to be fraught with anxieties and blockages.

Frequently, the "text" that is necessarily read to detect erotic ties is the lover's dress, which, by its concealing and embellishing of the body, indicates the importance of the body in erotic space. Although love letters, rings, and other tokens of affection are clearly markers within erotic space, they can offer only indirect, metonymic assurance of an erotic tie. In contrast, visual images of the beloved offer the metaphoric assurance of complete (bodily) possession; therefore, I will focus here on portrait miniatures as the most popularly accessible way of representing the absent, beloved "other." Although the enormous popularity and relative inexpensiveness of portrait miniatures alone make them a significant cultural phenomenon, I will argue that, throughout the eighteenth century, portrait miniatures served as means of defining their owner's identity by advertising the owner's possession of an "other" body. In fact, the inherent qualities of the miniature as both visual and narrative mode—its stylization of beauty and its tendency to become self-referential—ultimately erase the need for the "other" and narcissistically return the focus of erotic energy to the self.[2]

Following a discussion of the erotic function of portrait miniatures, I will examine Henry Fielding's *Amelia* (1751), in which the title character is effectively "miniaturized." The miniature appears in *Amelia* not only as a narrative movement but also as a plot device, when a portrait miniature is introduced as a measure of the two main characters' love for each other. Since *Amelia* is, to a large extent, the story of these characters' struggle to maintain love within married life, this novel exemplifies the conjunction of the miniature and the erotic. I suggest that the appearance of portrait miniatures in novels such as *Amelia* hints at the action performed on the erotic by the narrative—the "miniaturization" of the beloved "other." However, before addressing portrait miniatures or *Amelia* directly, I will follow the example of my subject by offering a miniaturized paradigm—through a brief reading of Mary Shelley's *Frankenstein* (1816)—of the ways in which the novel and the miniature represent erotic space.

The Miniature as Visual Image

In *Frankenstein,* the miniature worn by Victor Frankenstein's brother, William, is both a symbol of desire and, indirectly, a motive for murder. The creature, after he has killed William because he "belong[s] . . . to my enemy," sees the portrait miniature:

> I saw something glittering on his breast. I took it: it was a portrait of a most lovely woman. In spite of my malignity, it softened and attracted me. For a few moments I gazed with delight on her dark eyes, fringed by deep lashes, and her lovely lips; but presently my rage returned; I remembered that I was forever deprived of the delights that such beautiful creatures could bestow.[3]

The creature reacts to the woman's portrait as an erotic object, taking "delight" in the details of her represented body. Furthermore, he explicitly associates the image with the sexual delight that he is denied by his own ugliness. If the portrait is a symbol of the creature's general exclusion from erotic pleasure, however, it is something far more particular for William and Victor: unbeknownst to the creature, the portrait is an image of their mother, Caroline Beaufort, who died when Victor was a young man. For William and Victor, then, the portrait represents the ideal of motherly love, a love that they no longer possess; for both of them and for the creature, the portrait figures an unfulfillable desire.[4]

Through the William's murder, the miniature is transformed from a signifier of erotic space characterized by desire, absence, and deferral of possession to an indicator of guilt, violence, and foreclosure of desire. After he has killed William and taken the miniature, the creature flees to find a hiding place. Inadvertently, he discovers Justine, the Frankenstein family servant, asleep in a barn. She then becomes the object of the creature's erotic fantasies, which have been stimulated by the portrait miniature: he immediately compares Justine's beauty to that of the woman in the portrait, then role-plays a lover, whispering to Justine, "Awake, fairest, thy lover is near" (137). Despite this erotic movement and Justine's vulnerability to sexual attack, the creature neither rapes her nor even wakes her. Instead, he commits an equally grievous wrong by slipping the miniature into Justine's pocket: in this clearly sexual movement, he passes on the symbol of his lustful urges and, more importantly for the plot, the token of guilt in William's murder. Thus the miniature in *Frankenstein* represents erotic space and the "staging" of desire.

This use of the miniature clearly reveals its erotic value, but one might argue that any portrait could have the same function. Indeed, Norman Bryson further blurs the distinction between miniature and other visual art by claiming that all art is a form of miniaturization:

> for ourselves, for humanity, art begins where an artificial barrier between the eye and the world is erected: the world we know is reduced, robbed of various parameters of its being, and in the interval between world and reproduction, art resides. An image by [the sixteenth-century miniaturist] Hilliard may well stand for the universal type of the work of art, for very deep in human thought, as the anthropologists tell us, lies the idea of art as miniaturisation.[5]

As Bryson suggests, the portrait miniature can be taken as an emblem of all forms of visual representation, but it is, of course, most closely attached to the genre of the portrait. Portraits in general not only represent the sitter's physical appearance, but also define their possessor's identity by establishing a relation to the sitter(s).[6]

This is perhaps most evident in a particular form of portrait, the nude. In his analysis of this genre, John Berger alleges that the nude portrait served to advertise its male owner's virility. Writing of the "secret" nude portrait of Nell Gwyn commissioned by Charles II, Berger concludes that "the painting, when the King showed it to others, demonstrated . . . submission and his guests envied him."[7] For the man with a desirable mistress—an aesthetic commodity among wealthy, aristocratic men—possessing her portrait was perhaps more valuable than possessing her body itself in the task of representing himself as the master of his own erotic gratification.[8] For the sake of the portrait's display value for its owner, then, the nude does a kind of violence to the sitter by exposing his or, more typically, her body as a mark of submission. By the nude's reduction of the sitter to a single attribute, sexual attractiveness, it also miniaturizes, demonstrating Bryson's claim.

The miniature is thus imbricated in the concept of visual representation. One might protest, however, that the difference between the nude and the portrait miniature in their manner of presentation—one offering a whole-body facsimile of its exposed sitter, the other a tiny version of well-clothed head and shoulders—would seem to illustrate the comparatively limited representational capacity of the portrait miniature. In fact, although this difference in presentation is important, it does not indicate the limitedness of the portrait miniature: because of its size, the miniature accepts a different, less stringent level of mimesis as constituting a "realistic" likeness of the sitter. In his essay "On the Nature of that Imitation which takes place in what are called The Imitative Arts" (c. 1777), Adam Smith attempts to explain this phenomenon, claiming that "where the disparity [between imitating and imitated objects] is very great, . . . we are often contented with the most imperfect resemblance."[9] As an example, Smith uses the conventions of statuary: "A painted statue, though it certainly may resemble a human figure much more exactly than any statue which is not painted, is generally acknowledged to be a disagreeable, and even an offensive object; and so far are we from being pleased with this superior likeness, that we are never satisfied with it."[10] Both Smith's example and his conclusions point to the fact that the "distance" of the miniature from the sitter's physical reality ironically make it capable of seeming more "like" the sitter, just as the unpainted statue is somehow more satisfactory than the more mimetic painted statue. Similarly, Richard Wendorf speaks of "the great compression to be found within the boundaries of the miniature" that actually offers "more intense scrutiny of the human face" than portraits closer to life-size.[11] This ability to provide likeness despite artificial distance from the sitter is paired with the foregrounding of the miniature's status as object, just as the statue's lack of paint foregrounds its materiality as carved and polished stone. Therefore, the portrait miniature combines superior representational qualities (while sacrificing all claim to life-size mimesis) with an accentuated materiality; together, these qualities permit its "talismanic" use, which I will describe further in the following.

Another distinctive quality of portrait miniatures that results from their small size is their increased accessibility to purchasers and exposure to the viewing public. All portraits, like that of Nell Gwyn, had the power to establish the identity of their owners by associating them with the subject of the portrait; however, portrait miniatures were even more effective in this respect than other forms of portraiture. This is true first of all because they were affordable for a broader range of the populace, and, second, because their smaller size made them more portable and wearable, thus enabling the image of the beloved to be physically associated with the body of the lover.

The standard-size portrait was a costly item: in the years 1782–91,

Sir Joshua Reynolds charged an average of fifty guineas for the smallest kind of oil portrait, the head, which measured 24" × 25"; for larger portraits, the larger the canvas, the greater the cost, ranging up to 200 guineas for a whole-body portrait. In contrast, over nearly the same period of time, 1788–95, the king's painter of miniatures, George Engleheart, charged between eight and twelve guineas for a portrait miniature.[12] Admittedly, this comparison is somewhat exaggerated: Reynolds's prices after the mid-1760s "left all rivals far behind," while Engleheart's are far more representative of high to average prices in his field.[13] Nonetheless, it still shows that miniatures could be as much as five times cheaper to commission than standard-size portraits.

In fact, this relative affordability is one of the features of the eighteenth-century portrait miniature that distinguishes it from miniatures of the sixteenth and seventeenth centuries. In these former times, the high cost of miniaturists' work limited their clientele to the political elite: among courtiers of Elizabeth's reign, it was considered a badge of loyalty to wear a portrait of the queen. The miniatures of at least one artist, Nicholas Hilliard, "were often linked to spy missions."[14]

In part because of their new affordability, during the eighteenth century portrait miniatures became common possessions among the middle class. Throughout the eighteenth century, but particularly in its last quarter, there was "an insatiable public demand for" miniatures.[15] As a result of this demand, fashionable miniaturists like Richard Cosway often painted twelve sitters a day,[16] leading "some portrait painters in the Royal Academy whose income was most threatened by the ever increasing popularity of the miniature" to suggest that "miniaturists were . . . a mercenary corps more interested in personal gain than in the loftier aims of high art."[17] Thus the miniaturist turned out his or her product with assembly-line efficiency and flooded the market with cheap but often high-quality images of loved ones. Still cheaper and faster to produce were silhouettes, or, as they were referred to contemporaneously, "shades" or "shadows."[18] These "shades" miniaturized the image of the beloved even more than the portrait miniature, reducing it to a profile in black and white, yet their popularity was remarkable. The importance of the democratization of the personal image caused by both portrait miniatures and "shades" cannot be overestimated: for the first time in English history, the common middle-class citizen had access to a means of representing an absent "other."

Not only were miniatures easily purchased by the common citizen, they were frequently set out in public view as jewelry, since they were small enough to be worn. Among the settings in which portrait miniatures and silhouettes were found were on the wrist, as a bracelet; around the neck, as a choker or locket; on clothing, as a brooch or pin; or hanging below gentlemen's waists, as watch fobs.[19] They also were frequent adornments of snuff boxes. In fact, one of the greatest miniature combinations produced during the eighteenth century is the Ancaster box, which Cosway adorned with enamel portraits of the Duke of Ancaster's family, and which "was made . . . to be carried in [the Duke's] vest pocket, and was used to contain toothpicks and patches."[20] This use of the miniature contrasts greatly with that of Elizabethan times, when miniatures were more frequently kept in cabinets or worn discreetly within a locket, hidden underneath clothes. The connotations of secrecy and exclusivity that the sixteenth-century miniature carried were diluted, to say the least, by the portrait miniature's status as a commonplace eighteenth-century fashion accessory. Moreover, the political import of the sixteenth-century miniature, which could attach the possessor to Stuart or Loyalist parties or reveal international alliances, was removed as the miniature became privatized in the eighteenth century. By wearing a portrait miniature as jewelry, an individual maximized the image's display or "advertising" potential and associated the miniature image with their own body, thus locating themself in the network of personal desires that make up erotic space. In this way, portrait miniatures were part of the theatrical apparatus of the eighteenth-century presentation of self.

Yet, while portrait miniatures worked to establish the identity of their possessors, they miniaturized that of their subjects. Their small format permitted the reduction of an erotic tie to a simple sign of possession. This reductive effect is common in many forms of miniaturization; it fosters an artificial sense of security and complete familiarity. For example, although one may tend to forget that maps are miniaturizations, they are, in fact, exemplary of how the miniature in general claims to convert something that is inherently too large and complex for the comprehension or control of the individual eye into something that is easily mastered. Similarly, the portrait miniature designed for display, like those fashioned into jewelry, helps to map out the individual's position in erotic space, depicting his or her bond with an absent loved one.

The appearance of miniatures in standard-size portraits offers a special case in which the miniaturization of the loved one stands out. For example, in two portraits by Pompeo Batoni, "Sir Sampson Gideon and an unidentified companion" and "Sir Edward Dering" (c. 1759), miniatures are displayed by the sitters, who are surrounded by other art objects, among them classic ruins and various statuary, including a replica of the Apollo Belvedere (see figures 21 and 22). The conscious gesture by which the miniatures are displayed, as well as the context of other aesthetic objects, highlights the miniature's use as a diminished, pocket-sized stand-in for the absent loved one. This use can also be inferred from the fact that these portraits were done in Rome, while the sitters were on "Grand Tours" of the continent, were separated from family, friends, and lovers, and were presumably missing them. Yet, the context of the portraits' making also suggests another use for the miniature: at least in the case of "Sir Edward Dering," it appears that Batoni was commissioned by Dering's aunt-in-law, Lady Guilford, to paint her nephew; this indicates that the portrayal of the miniature being displayed was designed to confirm the sitter's (Dering's) continued devotion to his beloved while they were separated by so great a distance. In both uses, the miniature serves to mark absence and the deferral of the erotic to the future. The reverse function of the miniature—in which the beloved's identity is confirmed—is something that is limited, however, to the apprehension of "insiders" like Lady Guilford, and is almost always unrepresented unless staged, as in Batoni's paintings. Thus, the ultimate effect of the miniature was directed toward the reduction of the beloved to the status of aesthetic object in order to confirm the identity and erotic "competence" of the miniature's possessor.

To an extent, the miniature also represents the domestication of the desired "other." Thus Susan Stewart claims that "if the miniature is a kind of mirror, it is a mirror of requited love," arguing that the miniature image presents its possessors with a sense of security arising out of assurance of their affection being returned by the beloved.[21] In larger terms, I would argue that the "requitement" or security offered by the miniature is not attached to any specific beloved, but rather to the ideal of beauty that it depicts. A sense of control or mastery over this ideal, and, implicitly, over the beloved, is expressed in three aspects of eighteenth-century portrait miniatures: their stylization of beauty, the potential anonymity of the sitter, and the care lavished on their settings.

Of all the portrait miniatures painted in the eighteenth century, Richard Cosway's are perhaps most illustrative of the way in which the desire to codify beauty translated into a high degree of stylization.[22] Because of his tendency to stylize, when compared to the miniatures of his contemporaries, Cosway's work is likely to seem "a trifle insipid" to at least some modern viewers, although he "was the most successful both socially and financially" of all the miniaturists of his time.[23] Cosway biographer

21. Pompeo Girolamo Batoni (1708–87) Italian. Sir Sampson Gideon and an unidentified companion (1767). Oil on Canvas. 275.6 x 189.0 cm. Everard Studley Miller Bequest, 1963. National Gallery of Victoria, Melbourne, Australia.

22. Sir Edward Dering, *Pompeo Girolamo Batoni. 294.1970. Italian, 1708–87. Oil on canvas. 136.5 × 99.5 cm (53¾ × 39½ in.) Private collection. Courtesy, Museum of Fine Arts, Boston.*

Erotic Space

George Williamson claims that "The dainty miniatures produced by Cosway were in many ways the antithesis of the work of the older school that had preceded him. The painters of the sixteenth and seventeenth centuries were . . . 'pure realists.' "[24] In other words, while preceding miniaturists had attempted to emulate the mimesis found in standard-size portraits, Cosway arrived at an ethereal style that was reminiscent of Fragonard, and that fully explored the miniature's difference from standard-sized portraiture.[25]

According to Williamson, Cosway's style was the result of his principal innovation: before Cosway, "no one appears to have properly appreciated the charm of its [ivory's] brilliant surface, the exquisite transparent effect that could be obtained upon it, or the manner in which the ivory itself could be left to suggest some of the lights in the portrait or some of the airy effects desired by the painter."[26] Paired with his characteristic use of pale blue-white backgrounds, Cosway's light, wispy touch resulted in his sitters seeming almost heavenly in their airy luminescence.

Of course, this technique already tended to reduce the particularities of his sitters, but Cosway's prescription for painting the face was even more leveling of differences: "there should be room in the face for an eye between the two eyes; hair should always be represented in masses, and then lightly touched out; there should be a ray of light along the nose and a white dot at its tip, and a stream of light should flow on the cheek, while the ears and nose should be equal, level, and equally forward."[27]

Although this formula sounds as if it would produce uniform results no matter what the features of the sitter, if we examine two of Cosway's many portrait miniatures of Georgiana Cavendish, Duchess of Devonshire, it is clear that his technique was not so static as he suggests (see figures 23 and 24). Still, his distinctive light touch, his use of blue backgrounds, and his desire to regularize the features of his sitters all show Cosway's tendency to reduce individual differences in order to portray an unstated, implicit ideal of beauty.[28]

The underlying project of miniatures like Cosway's is to remove the particularity of the individual sitter and subject it both to the idealized vision of the artist and to the need of the possessor to consolidate his or her identity within erotic space.[29] This project results in the diminution of the sitter's identity and erotic power: "What is, in fact, lost in this idealized miniaturization of the body is sexuality and hence the danger of power. The body becomes an image, and all manifestations of will are transferred to the position of the observer, the voyeur. The body exists not in the domain of lived reality but in the domain of commodity rela-

23. Georgiana, Duchess of Devonshire, *Richard Cosway.*
*Devonshire Collection, Chatsworth. Reproduced by permission of
the Duke of Devonshire and The Chatsworth Settlement Trustees.*

tions."[30] To say that sexuality is lost in the miniature may be somewhat imprecise—after all, the display value of the miniature is founded upon its erotic appeal, which is built into the ideal of beauty—but it is nonetheless quite reasonable to trace the rise of the voyeuristic power of the miniature's owner to a compensating decline in the power of the sitter. Thus, although the portrait miniature originates as a representation of a particular individual, it is drained of direct reference to that individual and becomes instead a sign of the owner's taste in beauty and control over the erotic. In this way, the sitter is rendered virtually anonymous to all but the owner, for whom, as we shall see, the miniature becomes a sort of "talisman."

24. Georgiana, Duchess of Devonshire, *Richard Cosway*.
*Devonshire Collection, Chatsworth. Reproduced by permission of
the Duke of Devonshire and The Chatsworth Settlement Trustees.*

This process of anonymization is reflected in the fact that the identities of so many eighteenth-century miniatures are today unknown: unlike full-size oil portraits, portrait miniatures rarely bear the signature of the artist and even more rarely give any indication of the sitter's name; their referentiality was determined exclusively by their possessor. In the final analysis, the stylization common in the portrait miniature implies that the identity of the sitter was only one of the elements represented, and that, ultimately, the value of the sitter's image may have lain more in its ability to confirm the owner or wearer's attractiveness and to attach him or her to the ideal of beauty it depicted.

Besides stylization, there is another phenomenon that indicates how desirable an aspect of portrait miniatures anonymity was: the eye miniature (see figure 25). Even in "normal" portrait miniatures, the eye was frequently made a specific focal point: Cosway, for one, exaggerated the pupils of his female sitters. This points both to the existence of an ideal of beauty implicit in the miniature, and to the sexual appeal that is conventionally associated with the eye.[31] According to one commentator, the genre of the eye miniature was invented by George Engleheart, who painted the eye of the Prince of Wales' mistress, Mrs. Fitzherbert.[32] This set a trend which lasted well into Victoria's reign. Because the eye miniature guarantees the anonymity that stylization tends toward, it may be seen as the ultimate fulfillment of the miniature's reductive force. Moreover, by its overt attempt to conceal the identity of the sitter from all but the lover, the eye miniature foregrounds the hidden, private nature of the lover's erotic ties, thus drawing the attention to the lover.

As I have already mentioned in connection with Adam Smith's discussion of statuary, the miniature's smallness permits it to be treated not only as an image, like the large-scale portrait, which verges on presenting a life-size facsimile of the sitter, but also as an object. The portrait miniature's materiality was, in fact, celebrated by the elaborate and valuable incrustations of gold and gemstones that sometimes surrounded it.[33] For instance, at one point in *Frankenstein,* Justine refers to the miniature of

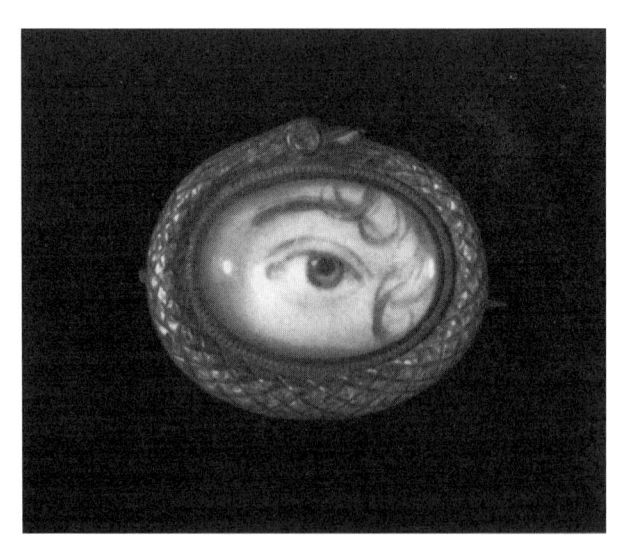

25. Miniature of a Lady's Eye Set in a Brooch, *Anonymous.*
Reproduction by permission of Fitzwilliam Museum, Cambridge.

Victor's mother as "the jewel" (80), a usage that was neither uncommon nor inappropriate: besides the wealth that was often worked into its casing, the portrait miniature was normally painted on ivory, a surface that could only have been selected because of its value since it is inhospitable for painting.[34] Indeed, in the first reports of William's murder, it is speculated that the motive was theft of the "very valuable miniature": Victor's father writes to him that "this picture is gone and was doubtless the temptation which urged the murderer to the deed" (70). A nonfictional example of the ornament frequently bestowed upon the miniature is found in the case of an eye miniature found in the Fitzwilliam Museum: its gold setting is fashioned in the shape of a garnet-eyed snake.[35] The investment of labor and precious stones and metals in the miniature suggests that it is an analogue to the investment of erotic energies in ties between lovers.

Moreover, the materiality of the miniature also acts to confirm the portrait's status as figural equivalent of the beloved. This is accomplished through the addition of physical relics of the beloved, most frequently locks of hair, which are ornately plaited and arranged in the glass-encased backs of the portraits. In some cases, the entire back of the miniature was enveloped with the beloved's woven hair; in other cases, a single lock was decoratively arranged. The Latter-Schlesinger collection of miniatures in the New Orleans Museum of Art provides several examples of the decorative use of hair (see figures 26–28): in one case, it is placed so as to form a wheat sheaf cinched with seed pearls.[36] Besides locks of hair, another frequent inclusion was the monogram of the beloved: the back of one of Cosway's miniatures in the Latter-Schlesinger collection features a "monogram 'PP' in diamonds in the center of [a] medallion of hair, surrounded by [a] border of dark blue enamel."[37] In accompanying the portrait, these minute tokens of the beloved move the function of the portrait miniature beyond simple representation to a talismanic status. In other words, whereas the portrait alone is linked to the beloved by resemblance or metaphor, the portrait matched with bits of the body—hair—and a reduced, coded name—the monogram—claims a metonymic, partial identity or equivalence with the beloved. Thus, the miniature becomes a "talisman" in the etymological, root sense of the word: "telesma," from Greek, meaning completion, or consecrated object. In the combination of metaphoric and metonymic traces of the beloved, the miniature promises the lover a full or complete representation—one that approximates presence—of the object of his or her desire.

Ultimately, the material uniqueness of the portrait miniature and its

26. *Portrait miniature back:* Woman in a White Dress *(ca. 1790),* Thomas Hull. *New Orleans Museum of Art: Gift of Mrs. Richard B. Kaufmann.*

claim to do more than simply represent the beloved make it an important signifier of erotic space. These qualities are similar to what Walter Benjamin called the "aura" of a work of art. I would agree with Benjamin that, at least in the case of personal images, this aura is destroyed by mechanical reproduction: once the image is subjected to reproduction, "the quality of its presence always depreciates."[38] For instance, modern wallet-sized photos of loved ones do not serve the same cultural function that portrait miniatures once did because they are not unique, and have thus forfeited the one-to-one relation with their subjects that portrait miniatures claimed. Furthermore, these photos have none of the qualities of erotic investment that the miniature displays through its status as jewelry or its association with physical relics of the beloved. Finally, the display value of the miniature is very different from that of the wallet photo, in that the former was frequently on automatic display while the latter is normally hidden from view. Poised as it is upon the brink of the age of photography, the portrait miniature remains distant from the claim of the

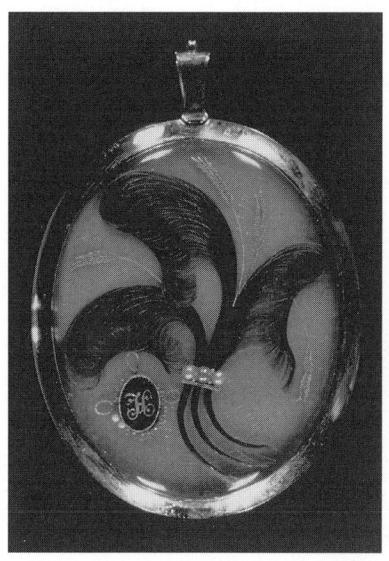

27. *Portrait miniature back:* Mrs. H. *(ca. 1790), George Place. New Orleans Museum of Art: Gift of Mrs. Richard B. Kaufmann.*

photograph to offer an objective, mechanically reproducible vision of reality.

The Miniature as Narrative Movement

In Henry Fielding's *Amelia* (1751), not only is a portrait miniature used in the plot, but the role of its title character is also effectively "miniaturized": even though the novel's title is *Amelia,* it begins and ends with her husband, Captain Booth. On the one hand, *Amelia* suggests the reductiveness of ideals of beauty by contrasting the heroine's disfigured nose with the "beauty" of her manners and fidelity to an unfaithful husband.[39] On the other hand, in focusing almost entirely on Booth's moral meanderings, the novel restricts readers' appreciation of Amelia, who becomes a simple, monolithic foil to Booth. Ultimately, *Amelia*'s narrative works to package its title character as an erotic object that we, as readers, are asked to decide if Booth is worthy of possessing. *Amelia* achieves this effect through several different techniques of narrative miniaturization, including its allusions to Greek and Latin texts, its arrangement of male characters in an "expressive circle" surrounding Amelia, its use of explicitly theatrical scenes and references, and its overall "presentational" strategy.

28. Portrait miniature back: P. P. (1790), Richard Cosway. New Orleans Museum of Art: Gift of Mrs. Richard B. Kaufmann.

    The title page announces the narrative's focus on Booth, despite the title's emphasis on Amelia. The first epigraph, from Horace's *Odes,* indicates that marriage will be a central focus: "Thrice happy and more are they whom an unbroken bond unites."[40] The second, from Simonides' *Iambics,* specifies the perspective from which marriage will be examined: "A man can possess nothing better than a virtuous woman, nor any thing worse than a bad one" (3). In effect, this second epigraph assumes a male perspective, defining women as possessions whose moral value is to be determined through male scrutiny. Moreover, this intertextual use of Greek and Latin passages marks Fielding's narrative as the product of his traditional, upper-class, academic training and attaches it to a canon of "classical" texts that constituted part of eighteenth-century disciplinary discourse by defining women through the male gaze. Flaunting such training already places an immediate distance between Fielding and the average female reader, to whom it was denied; this distance is increased by the novel's mockery of one woman, Mrs. Bennet/Atkinson, who attempts to rival men in teaching herself from the Greek and Latin "classics." Although the eighteenth-century British attitude toward classical antiquity was not naively idolizing, Fielding certainly seems to refer to his Greek and Latin precedents here without irony, as authorities upon which he founds his narrative perspective.[41]

In fact, irony in *Amelia* arises because, although the narrative does accord with Fielding's classical sources by circumscribing Amelia perfectly within traditionally "proper" models of feminine behavior, it draws the reader's scrutiny not to her, but to the moral behavior of her husband. In other words, while the title page might lead one to expect a narrative in which the husband's moral stance is unquestionably correct and that of the wife consistently dubious, the reverse is true in this case. Our doubts about Booth's moral character, and thus about whether or not he deserves to be Amelia's husband, are inaugurated by the opening book of *Amelia,* in which Booth finds himself separated from Amelia and reunited, in prison, with a former lover, Miss Mathews. This inadvertent tryst is prolonged, in the narrative sense, by Booth's tale of how he met and won Amelia as his wife. Thus, the reader is presented with two forms of tantalizing, erotic deferral: as long as Booth remains in prison, he is separated from Amelia, yet she is made figurally present through his telling of her; furthermore, his telling serves as foreplay for "criminal conversation" with Miss Mathews (154).

The episode culminates not when Booth and Miss Mathews make love (off-scene, of course), but rather when Booth, Amelia, and Miss Mathews meet accidentally upon Booth's discharge from prison. This meeting between Booth's acknowledged and unacknowledged, licit and illicit lovers is the first of a series of theatrical tableaux that punctuate the narrative, allowing its reduction to a series of visual scenes. In the 1780 *Novelist's Magazine* version of *Amelia,* this scene is represented by an illustration that reflects the latent visual element of the narrative (see figure 29). The content of the scene is explicitly erotic: while Booth's desires are triangulated between the real (Miss Mathews) and the ideal (Amelia), Miss Mathews's desire for Booth is both staged and stimulated, with Miss Mathews playing the role of passive viewer and Amelia playing the role of rightful possessor of Booth's affections. Furthermore, although on the surface this meeting causes Booth the utmost anxiety, it stages at least a subconscious desire on his part to possess two women at the same time. In the final analysis, this scene shows that the network of desire that defines erotic space is not only one of the primary concerns of *Amelia,* but is also effectively miniaturized or encapsulated through the use of static

29. *"Prison Scene from* Amelia," *Harrison ed. of* The Novelist's Magazine *(1780)*.

theatrical tableaux; this tableau is only the first of a series that I will return to.[42]

In addition to Fielding's use of Greek and Latin "authorities" and the narrative strategy of theatrical tableaux, his consciousness of the miniature as a mode of the erotic is reflected in his plot use of a portrait miniature of Amelia. The miniature is first introduced when Captain Booth describes the contents of a "casket" that "was her [Amelia's] own work" (105) and that she gave to him to carry with him to the siege of Gibraltar.[43] Having thus identified this casket with Amelia, Booth characterizes its contents as "trinkets" (105) and "little matters" (108), items whose smallness and preciosity he transfers, by association, to Amelia. He goes on to describe the contents in a more detailed fashion: "It contained medicines of all kinds, which her mother, who was the Lady Bountiful of that country, had supplied her with. The most valuable of all to me was a lock of her dear hair, which I have from that time to this worn in my bosom" (108).

It is most appropriate that the casket contain medicines, for the novel suggests that Amelia's steadfast love must "cure" Booth of his irresponsible behavior and his predilection for deist philosophizing.[44] Such philosophizing is clearly connected to his lack of firm attachment to Amelia: he claims that "the doctrine of the passions had been always his favourite study," and uses this doctrine or theory to rationalize his ability to forget about Amelia when he is enjoying himself away from her (103). Booth's description of Amelia's lock of hair as "the most valuable [medicine] of all" indicates its metonymic ability to conjure up her image and thus restore him to a "healthy" order in his passions. In this way, the casket already "miniaturizes" the novel's plot, presenting the problematic essence of Amelia's and Booth's relationship.

However, the full impact of the casket is registered by what is not there, but should be: the portrait miniature of Amelia. Marking his dismay at having had to leave Amelia without it, Booth exclaims, "What would I have then given for a little picture of my dear angel . . . ?" (108). He goes on to say that "next to Amelia herself, there was nothing which I valued so much as this little picture" (108–9), indicating the extent to which he has drawn an equivalence between his possession of Amelia and his ownership of her image. In contrast to the partial, metonymic relation of the lock of hair to Amelia, the portrait miniature promises complete talismanic possession in its ability to fully represent her beauty. Moreover, our sense of the portrait's value to Booth is reinforced by the attention he devotes to the richness of its setting: Amelia's portrait "was set in gold, . . . had two or three little diamonds round it, [and] was worth about twenty guineas" (108).

Because of the equivalence drawn between Amelia and her portrait, the fact that it is *not* in the casket suggests that Booth is in danger of losing the original Amelia as well as her representation. The "little picture," Booth explains, was stolen a month before his departure for Gibraltar. Although he implies that Amelia is to blame for the theft, saying "she had lost [it] from her chamber" (108), the loss is clearly due to his own inattention—had he kept the miniature in his own chamber, or even worn it, as a "true" lover ought to have, he might not have had it stolen.

In fact, Booth is inattentive throughout the novel, deferring his relationship with Amelia despite her best efforts to keep him at home. This is indicated not only by his loss of the miniature and his opening fling with Miss Mathews, but also by his negligence in missing meals with Amelia. Fielding emphasizes this by describing how, while Booth has gone gambling, Amelia "employ'd herself another hour in cooking up a little supper for her husband, this being . . . his favorite meal, as indeed it was hers; and in a most pleasant and delightful manner they generally passed their time . . . though their fare was seldom of the sumptuous kind" (433). Clearly, the supper symbolizes the most healthy part of their relationship—the time they spend together as lovers, apart from their children and friends; missing this meal indicates Booth's dereliction. The failure to enjoy time with Amelia alone, the loss of the miniature, and the fling with Miss Mathews are all forms of voluntary deferral on Booth's part—a deliberate creation of absence—that stimulate an erotic tension between Amelia and Booth.

Because of Booth's inattention and his deferral of "possessing" Amelia, he becomes vulnerable to losing her to several rivals for her affection. These rivals compose a spectrum of modes of male behavior within erotic space. The first of these is Serjeant Atkinson, Amelia's foster brother, who is ultimately revealed to have been responsible for the theft of the portrait (482). Although Booth rather egotistically attributes Atkinson's attachment to him as the product of "a very strong affection for me" (107), the reader is able, retrospectively, to construct a far different motive: Atkinson wants to have a pretext to be close to Booth's wife. Even after Atkinson is married to one of Amelia's friends, Mrs. Bennet, the narrative works to perpetuate at least the appearance of an erotic tension between Atkinson and Amelia. For instance, the sergeant has a dream in which he sees Colonel James, Booth's erstwhile "friend," by Amelia's bedside, "offering to ravish her" and phallically threatening her "with a drawn sword in his hand" (379). In his dream, the sergeant leaps upon James and begins to strangle him; in reality, he nearly kills his wife, who is in bed with him. The sexual content of this dream is not to be denied: clearly, James represents a violent sexual desire for Amelia that the sergeant must repress within himself, while his real-life strangling of his wife acts out the removal of one barrier that would stand in the way of his passion.[45]

As in the case of the desire running between Booth, Miss Mathews, and Amelia, Atkinson's desire is also conveyed in tableau form. Booth bursts in on an argument between Amelia and the Atkinsons and effectively freezes the scene: "The entry of Booth turn'd all in an instant into a silent picture; in which the first figure which struck the eyes of the captain was the serjeant on his knees to his wife. Booth immediately cried—'What's the meaning of this?' " (447). Visualized here is Atkinson's attempt to mediate between his continued devotion to Amelia, figured by his kneeling position, and his obligation to his wife. Booth's momentary loss of his usual obliviousness may be due at least partially to the contrast he cannot have helped but draw between his own person and Atkinson's: Colonel James describes Booth as having "a nose like the Proboscis of an Elephant, with the Shoulders of a Porter and the Legs of a Chairman," and "not in the least the Look of a Gentleman," clearly associating his looks with the animal and with the roughness and distortions of the laboring ranks, while Atkinson, who lacks Booth's social station and military rank, has great physical charms (455). Although Atkinson's attentions to Amelia are always presented as selfless, chivalric, and completely honorable, his description as "one of the handsomest young fellows in England" (107) and his willingness to take on the kind of subterfuge involved in the theft of the portrait coalesce in the tableau to suggest that his relationship with Amelia is fraught with unexpressed sexual tensions.

In contrast to Atkinson, who represses his attraction to Amelia, the second rival, the noble lord, is portrayed as a sexual predator who feels it necessary to fulfill his every lustful urge. Booth and Amelia first encounter the noble lord through their landlady, Mrs. Ellison, who helps Booth secure a promotion to Lieutenant through the noble lord's influence. Upon this first meeting, the narrator warns that the noble lord "was so passionate an admirer of women, that he could scarce have escaped the attraction of Amelia's beauty. And few men, as I have observed, have such disinterested generosity as to serve a husband the better, because they are in love with his wife, unless she will condescend to pay a price beyond the reach of a virtuous woman" (193).

The noble lord's conspicuous consumption of sexual favors and his willingness to use his social station to satisfy his desires is, in effect, "rakish" behavior that commodifies sexuality and rejects the kind of semipermanent tie between lovers that defines erotic space. By working to reduce the deferral of his desires, the noble lord effectively short-circuits the erotic. On the most basic level, the distinction between his behavior and Atkinson's can be expressed in the difference between "love" and "lust." While Atkinson cares for Amelia enough to want her portrait, the noble lord wants her only as momentary conquest, to be discarded at the slightest hint of another passion. In this way, the noble lord's behavior toward women constitutes an antierotic practice.

The noble lord's behavior is also drawn in contrast to Atkinson's self-abasing devotion to Amelia, in that it is described largely in financial terms, further linking sexuality with commodification and the marketing of bodily beauty. Colonel James claims that if the noble lord "once fixes his eye upon a woman, he will stick at nothing to get her," including purchasing her: "I never knew any other man part with his money so very freely on these occasions" (227–28). Rather than condemning this practice, James himself adopts a financial language in speaking of women, asking Booth "Have not I shewn you . . . where you may carry your goods to market?" (228). In this way, both Colonel James and the noble lord participate in a discourse in which women are essentially fungible objects. Although this discourse is antierotic, it is still the result of miniaturization—albeit an extreme result—and can be traced to the tendency of the miniature to diminish its object's identity and sexual power.

Rather than embracing the noble lord's and James's commodifying discourse, Booth rejects its application to Amelia. As James is advising him on how to manipulate the noble lord's sexual impulses to best advantage, Booth immediately thinks of Amelia as his "goods" and his "honour" and responds violently against the suggestion of prostituting her. In fact, he worries about the noble lord stealing her from him, much as he has already been robbed of her image in miniature (228). Although Booth clearly understands the antierotic, commodifying practice urged upon him by James, and although he is implicated in its origins by his appraisal of Amelia as his "goods," he refuses it because he remains engaged with the erotic for his sense of identity. While Colonel James had intended Miss Mathews as Booth's "goods," Booth's mistaking of Amelia for those same "goods" only clarifies his fetishistic investment in her. For Booth, Amelia is not fungible because she represents more than simple sexual appeal: she is his wife and his guarantee of as stable a home life as his finances will allow. While he goes out and gambles, duels, dallies adulterously with Miss Mathews, and so on, Amelia maintains a semblance of tranquility and order in the "domestic space" of their marriage. I would suggest that this orderly domestic space is what Booth has in mind—in addition to the traditional husband's fear of being cuckolded—when he refers to Amelia as his "honour."[46] Taken by itself, Booth's injection of the rather abstract principle of honor, which can be attached to his "talismanic" view of Amelia, into James's materialistic discussion of women and sexuality signifies his difference from James and the noble lord, both of whom see her unidimensionally, as a sexual object.

As if to confirm that Booth has already made an implicit bargain with the noble lord for Amelia by requesting his aid in obtaining higher rank, the next chapter depicts her return from a visit to the noble lord, laden with gifts and ecstatically happy. Simultaneous with the apparent threat of Booth's losing her, the narrative supplies a verbal "portrait" of her beauty: "exercise had painted her face with vermilion; and the highest good humour had so sweetened every feature, and a vast flow of spirits had so lightened up her bright eyes, that she was all a blaze of beauty" (230). Indeed, Fielding digresses to quote Milton, Waller, and Suckling in further praise of her beauty, fashioning her into an aesthetic object and stressing the potential loss that Booth faces. Among the "trinkets" that Amelia and her children have received from the noble lord is a gold watch "that cost above twenty guineas" (231), a sum that may be calculated to recall the lost miniature, which Booth has valued at "about twenty guineas."[47] Here the equivalence between Amelia and her portrait is subtly extended: Booth has already lost his twenty-guinea miniature of her, now he fears that he has lost *her* as well, receiving in compensation a twenty-guinea gold watch.

The danger of Amelia's loss to the predations of the noble lord is reinforced through the story of Mrs. Bennet's "fall." The parallel between Amelia and Mrs. Bennet is similar to the equivalence drawn between Amelia and the portrait miniature, in that it is constructed upon physical resemblance: Mrs. Ellison tells Amelia that Mrs. Bennet bears "a strong resemblance . . . to yourself in the form of her person, and still more in her voice" (237). Lest we, as readers, mistrust Mrs. Ellison's opinion, the narrator confirms it: "Amelia and Mrs Atkinson [Bennet] were exactly of the same make and stature, and . . . there was likewise a very near resemblance in their voices" (421). This physical likeness is so strong that it allows them to switch places during the masquerade scene of Book 10, in which Mrs. Bennet/Atkinson is mistaken for Amelia by nearly the entire cast of *Amelia*'s characters, including Booth himself. Their strong resemblance surely accounts for Atkinson's marriage to Mrs. Bennet. Furthermore, although Amelia and Mrs. Bennet/Atkinson differ greatly in their pretensions to learning, they find themselves intellectually compatible in certain regards. For instance, in conversing, Amelia and Mrs. Bennet find themselves in agreement that beauty is the primary asset of a woman: " 'Indeed, I believe, the first wish of our whole sex is to be handsome.' Here both ladies fixed their eyes on the glass, and both smiled" (276). This scene figures not only their concurrence, but also their consciousness of their primary status as aesthetic objects. Their smiles confirm one another's meeting of the criteria of beauty, and thus of desirability.

However, when Mrs. Bennet tells her story, which occupies the entirety of Book 7, other parallels emerge as well—both Amelia and Mrs. Bennet have suffered from jealousy within their own families, and both have received special attention from the noble lord. In Mrs. Bennet's case, this attention leads to a night of pleasure at Ranelagh, ending in her being drugged and raped by the noble lord (295). In the aftermath, she discovers that she has been "polluted" by him and has also given the disease to her husband, who flies into a rage that ultimately costs him his life, leaving Mrs. Bennet a widow. Significantly, Mr. Bennet's rage results in an accident to his heart. Furthermore, venereal disease functions as a sign that is communicated between the two men through Mrs. Bennet's body, and that indicates Mr. Bennet's loss of his wife to the noble lord. This loss, and the noble lord's "ownership" of Mrs. Bennet, is marked by the annuity of 150 pounds that she accepts from him after the death of her husband (302). Such a substantial annuity confirms Colonel James's assertion that the noble lord is free with his money "on these occasions" (228), reflecting his ability to purchase any woman, and—more importantly, from Booth's perspective—potentially to "outbid" husbands. Thus, Mrs. Bennet's story not only confirms the noble lord's sexual predations and constructs a paradigm of sexual relations as commodity, it also suggests that this paradigm may well be imposed upon Amelia.[48]

If we are offered a view of clearly rakish behavior in the noble lord, Booth's third and final rival for Amelia, Colonel James, is presented as a more subtle threat because of his proximity to the Booths and the faith they have in him as a friend. As we have seen, like the noble lord, James sees women unidimensionally, as sexual commodities: having grown tired of his own wife, James first takes over Booth's discarded mistress, Miss Mathews, then covets Booth's wife. Although James's character is clearly important in rounding out Fielding's presentation of the amorality of society (in the horror of his "desiring to debauch his friend's wife" [342]), it is only significant here because it completes the spectrum of models of male behavior within the erotic. The noble lord is, of course, highly inconstant and will not be deferred in fulfilling his lusts; James is similarly inconstant and admits deferral only because his means of obtaining gratification are less powerful. In contrast to these two is Atkinson, who is the ultimate in constancy, going so far in his devotion to Amelia as to marry her look-alike, Mrs. Bennet, yet is possessed of an infinite capacity for deferral, in that he only reveals his passion to Amelia when he believes he is about to die. Between these extremes—the noble lord and James at one pole and Atkinson at the other—is Booth, who is somewhat inconstant to Amelia, as James is to his wife, but who constantly defers his relationship with Amelia, as Atkinson does. By placing Booth in the middle of this spectrum, we see that *Amelia* is focused on the problematics of male behavior in everyday erotic space rather than on the extremes of behavior exemplified in the noble lord's self-promoting rakishness and Atkinson's self-abasing sensibility.

The clustering of men around Amelia is important not only because it reflects the narrative's focus on Booth's tenuous erotic life, but also because it constitutes part of the narrative's miniaturization of Amelia as the object of a "circle of expression." Although it is used here as a narrative movement, the circle of expression derives from painterly theory and practice, where it describes a group of people whose expressions reflect different reactions to a central figure, action, or object.[49] First popularized in England through the 1701 and 1734 translations of Le Brun's *Traité sur les Passions,* the circle of expression was a form emphasized by Reynolds in his *Discourses* and used by Hogarth in his series paintings and engravings. Joseph Wright's "Academy by Lamplight" is an excellent example of the circle of expression because it depicts light seemingly emanating from the object being observed and illuminating the various expressions of the spectators (see figure 30). As evidence of the employment of the circle of expression in the novel, Ronald Paulson cites the scene in Fielding's *Joseph Andrews* where various characters react to the spectacle of Joseph's naked body after he has been robbed and stripped

30. An Academy by Lamplight (ca. 1768–69), Joseph Wright of Derby. Courtesy of Yale Center for British Art, Paul Mellon Collection.

of his clothing; epistolary novels like Richardson's *Clarissa* and Smollett's *Humphry Clinker* are particularly well adapted to the circle of expression.

For my purposes, the circle of expression is important in two regards: it shows the degree to which Amelia is the formal center of a network of erotic desires, and it reduces Amelia and those who react to her to stereotypes of behavior. In the first respect, the circle of expression furthers our appreciation of the fact that the whole of *Amelia* is structured spatio-visually in a grand tableau that locates Amelia as the focal point for interested males, including Booth, the three rivals I have just discussed, Dr. Harrison, and, in the end, Robinson the gambler. Such a structure has a precedent in Hogarth's early prints like "A Harlot's Progress" (1732), "The Distrest Poet" (1736), and "Strolling Actresses Dressing in a Barn" (1738), where he places a beautiful, virtuous, and benevolent woman at the center of his compositions as a mediator of the various difficult forces that surround her (see figure 31). The centrality of the female may have been part of a deliberate program: "Hogarth's initial notion was that civic humanism, with its image of a male aristocratic hero, seems to call for an antidote in the form of a feminized plebeian society, a bourgeois society."[50] Although by the time of the publication of *Amelia* Hogarth had abandoned his faith in the female "antidote," Fielding may very well have been influenced by it.

In the second respect, like the miniature, the circle of expression is essentially a reductive form that conventionalizes physiognomic and bodily attitudes in a "language" of response.[51] This is indicated by LeBrun's creation of "a mere spectrum or catalogue of facial responses" that referred to stereotyped emotional reactions;[52] for the theater, the resulting formulas of expression were translated, in Aaron Hill's *Essay on the Art of Acting* (1746), from the visual arts to gestures and attitudes that could be struck in acting. In correspondence with the standardization of emotions dictated by the circle of expression and its theatrical development, the characters in *Amelia* react true to type: Atkinson is the frustrated lover, the noble lord a typical rake, Colonel James the treacherous "friend," Dr. Harrison the stern father figure, and Amelia the good wife. Because, in accord with the visual limits of the circle of expression, we see only the exterior responses of these characters, they are miniaturized or reduced to conventional types of behavior.

Although I have described the circle of expression's derivation from the visual arts, it also fits the theatricality of *Amelia,* and its tendency to offer visual tableaux that could be considered either theatrical or painterly. I have already described tableaux that show Miss Mathews, Amelia,

31. Strolling Actresses Dressing in a Barn, William Hogarth.
©*The British Museum.*

and Booth meeting in prison, and Atkinson on his knees to Amelia; these are but two examples of a technique that is in evidence throughout the novel. Yet another tableau is offered when Booth misses the supper that Amelia has prepared especially for him:

> her spirits grew very low; and she was once or twice going to ring the bell to send her maid for half a pint of white-wine, but check'd her inclination in order to save the little sum of sixpence; which she did the more resolutely as she had before refused to gratify her children with tarts for their supper from the same motive. And this self-denial she was very probably practicing, to save sixpence, while her husband was paying a debt of several guineas incurred by the ace of trumps being in the hands of his adversary (439).

By giving a "picture" of Amelia's distress, loneliness, and self-sacrifice, and then contrasting it with her husband's irresponsibility, Fielding creates what amounts to a miniature view of their relationship. This points out the function of the tableaux in the novel: they sum up, in single static scenes, the status of relations between characters, making the narrative a supplement to the series of visual "takes" they offer.

Such a technique is already a form of narrative miniaturization, yet the tableaux are also often used to "miniaturize" or reduce and control the reader's perceptions. Repeatedly, even when no description of the scene is given, the narrator tells us that "a pathetic scene" (480) or "a very tender and pathetic scene" (455) ensued, encouraging us to identify emotionally with the Booths's various difficulties. As Eric Rothstein sees it, the tableaux are part of a "quasi-theatrical mode of presentation [that] denies him [Fielding] the cognitive and emotional resources that Sterne and Smollett gain from our intimate knowledge of the characters' psychology. . . . Fielding therefore must assert the values of *Amelia* through simple, emotionally striking means, which run the risk of disgusting us as "sentimental" or arbitrary."[53]

The "sentimentality" or overt attempts to manipulate the reader that Rothstein refers to here are exemplified by the scene in which Dr. Harrison returns to London to find Amelia, in the aftermath of Booth's second arrest, "in the highest agonies of grief and despair, with her two little children crying over their wretched mother" (9: 1; 364). The narrator goes on to claim that this distress was one of "the most tragical sights that human nature can furnish, and afford a juster motive to grief and tears in the beholder, than it would be to see all the heroes who have ever infested the earth, hanged all together in a string. The doctor felt this sight as he ought. He immediately endeavoured to comfort the afflicted" (IX: 1; 364). Such heavy-handed dictation of what feeling "ought" to be conjured by this "sight," or tableau, is Fielding's attempt to provide a "normative" reaction to the spectacle, and thus to control his readers' response.

All of these tableaux are ultimately directed toward defining the characters of Amelia and Booth so that we, as readers, may judge whether or not he is worthy of possessing her. Like the portrait miniatures Cosway produced, *Amelia* stylizes the beloved through the narrative techniques that I have described, reducing the inherent complexity of selfhood to a single note. Because of this stylization or reduction to "type," there is very little sense of growth or development in either Booth or Amelia; they seemed trapped in a space of financial distress and erotic deferral of their relationship. For this reason, many readers have reacted to Booth's nominal conversion to Christianity and return to Amelia as unmotivated.⁵⁴ However, there is a continuity in the ending of *Amelia* in that the resurfacing of her portrait miniature touches off the more "providential" of the narrative's two endings.⁵⁵

The other, "realistic" ending emerges first, as Dr. Harrison promises to rescue the Booths from their debts and whisk them off to the country with him. This ending seems eminently plausible and serves as a gentle rebuke to Booth's pride, in that it confirms his inability to support his family. In contrast, the providential ending depends upon highly fortuitous circumstances to reveal Amelia as an heiress and thus, ironically, to reward Booth for his irresponsibility. As John Zomchick notes, we are prepared for the providential ending by the dream that Booth describes to Amelia, in which he is released from imprisonment and poverty by a sudden transformation in Amelia's fortunes.⁵⁶ It is through Amelia's actions, not Booth's, that the denouement occurs: her recovery of the portrait miniature from Serjeant Atkinson and her subsequent pawning of it cause the revelation of her true inheritance.⁵⁷ While she is in the pawnshop, Amelia and her miniature image are recognized by Robinson, a petty gambler who had cheated Booth in prison at the beginning of the narrative and, we now learn, had also aided the lawyer Murphy in altering Amelia's mother's will so as to leave Amelia penniless.⁵⁸ Stirred to conscious guilt by the pathetic scene of the impoverished heiress pawning her own portrait miniature, Robinson confesses the whole scheme to Dr. Harrison, who soon remedies all by having Murphy arrested and Amelia restored to her rightful place as heiress.

This ending reinforces Amelia's centrality to the novel's logic, if not to its narrative concerns. Throughout *Amelia,* in contrast to Booth, Amelia is very literally "pictured" and thus reduced to a static, though central position; as Alison Conway observes, she "seems entirely passive in her efforts to achieve moral good."⁵⁹ In effect, because she is depicted as inert and reactive, she becomes the equivalent of her portrait miniature—an object of ideal beauty that Booth possesses yet neglects. In pawning her image, which she does in order to redeem Booth's debts, Amelia reenacts her original gift of herself to Booth, but this time it is done "right." Because her gift of self is performed with no possible selfish motivation, and because her performance is seen by Robinson as a pathetic scene, it has the effect of mobilizing the miniature's ability to represent her whole, original self, unscathed by the trickeries of lawyers and the irresponsibilities of Booth. In this way, as if by magic (or by providence), the talismanic image restores her fortune to her and redeems Booth.

Thus the power of the erotic—a tie so strong that it cannot be disrupted by Booth's adultery and general profligacy—asserts itself to stabilize Booth's and Amelia's identities, restoring them to the "Country House" of Booth's dream (527). Ironically, Amelia's second gift of herself closes off erotic space as it closes the narrative, because it ensures that she and Booth will be united forever, and that they will no longer need the symbols of the erotic to assert their bond. In this way they are removed from the flux of the eighteenth-century public sphere to a place of retreat where their identities will be fixed and unquestionable.

Like the other psychosocial spaces discussed in previous chapters, erotic space was created by the increased availability of media forms through which it could be articulated. These media forms—the portrait miniature, the theatrical circle of expression, and the narrative miniaturization of character—all enable the diminutive, private, yet semipublic expression of erotic ties.

While the narrative examples of *Amelia* and *Frankenstein* that I have focused on here illustrate the erotic space between husband and wife, it should also be emphasized that the desire and possession figured in the erotic is not always heterosexual. In fact, the domesticity of conventional marriage destroys the erotic, whereas more tenuous relations—secret liaisons, romantic friendships, parted siblings, or partings between any family members—cause it to flourish.

As suggested by the separations involved in each of these types of relation—whether heterosexual or not—the erotic arises most clearly in a culture dominated by circulation. After all, circulation is a social force that causes various dislocations, instabilities, and separations. Thus Amelia's gift of herself and the Booths's final elevation above circulation display the desirability of fixing identity—that is to say, escaping from the deferred, contingent identity provided by erotic ties.

Afterword

In this book I have attempted to complicate the false notion of the unified self that is often projected nostalgically upon eighteenth-century individuals. The supposed unparalleled complexity, instability, and contingency of selfhood in the twentieth century has become a commonplace assumption that leads us to downplay the problematics of constructing psychological identity in the daily life of the past.

In fact, selfhood or identity *did* need to be constructed in the eighteenth century, as it did in earlier periods of English history. In pursuing this critique of subjectivity, I am extending forward in time the work of New Historicists like Stephen Greenblatt, who have argued that Renaissance selves were not born intact but rather were produced through negotiation of an assortment of cultural factors.[1] As Greenblatt describes it, the process of fashioning the self in the English Renaissance was just as theatrical as the contemporary social interactions analyzed by Irving Goffman. If the construction of identity is similarly theatrical (and problematic) in the Renaissance, eighteenth century, and twentieth century, then we have arrived at a thread of continuity in the history of subjectivity.

What, then, accounts for our perception of historical difference in notions of selfhood? I propose that two related factors account for this historical difference: first, changes in the degree of access to the concept of constructing the self and materials that enable it; second, changes in awareness of the necessity of constructing the self. On the first count it is clear that very few individuals in the Renaissance were actively concerned with what Greenblatt calls "self-fashioning." In contrast, I have argued here that access to the psychosocial was greatly expanded in the second half of the eighteenth century due in part to an increased flow of representations and an increasing level of the literacy necessary to comprehend and manipulate them. Still, individuals most likely to be plunged into the process of identity formation were limited to those of at least lower middle class, whereas contemporary cultural critics suggest that all classes now have access to the psychosocial.

On the second count—changes in awareness of the necessity of constructing the self—it is clear that individual awareness has grown stronger and become more widespread, often resulting in alienation. Even in the eighteenth century "the present increasingly was understood as an evolving entity, a dangerously new and not quite understood formation."[2] Twentieth-century cultural critics have frequently presented the self as an oppressed amalgam, the product of internalized disciplinary discourses.

However, I would argue that cultural systems are fundamentally ambivalent in effect on the individual—they are neither exclusively oppressive nor liberating. As a whole, the readings offered in the preceding chapters are intended to suggest a modification of some of the conclusions that Michel Foucault and his interpreters have reached about the extent to which disciplinary structures control models of subjectivity and selfhood. Although each of the psychosocial spaces treated in this study is problematic for individual subjects, each is also at least potentially liberating. For instance, *Amelia*'s providential ending reflects in one sense the triumph of the erotic, in the symbolic form of Amelia's miniature portrait, over the chastisement Booth was to receive in the "realistic" denouement provided by Dr. Harrison. In fact, the "realistic" ending is heavily invested with the disciplinary discourse of Christian resignation, while the magic associated with Amelia's unselfish gift of self constitutes what John Thompson would call a secular alternative to discipline.

Of the psychosocial spaces considered here, the social, as the space of the present, is the most encompassing and disciplinary, yet the roles and positions it prescribes are vaguely defined and subject to circulative flux. This ambivalence is most visible in the pervasive theatricality of social space, in which display is not only part of a coercive "frame" designed to harness individual subjects to the social order, but also a "space" in which these subjects have some degree of choice. Thus we see Lydia Melford and Evelina reacting with delight, not terror, when they enter into the specular arena of Ranelagh's Rotunda. Moreover, display can be appropriated by individual subjects and used for the potentially antisocial purpose of internal theatricality—imaginatively representing the self to the self.

As spaces of the past and future, respectively, the historical and the erotic are "sub-versions" of the social in at least two ways: first, they are subordinate to the individual's immediate sense of self in the social space of the present; second, they can "subvert" the socially determined sense of self by offering an alternative to it. As sub-versions they can complement the social sense of self, and, by potentially subverting the social, they can nearly supplant it as a source of identity. However, historical and erotic spaces are incapable of completely replacing the social because, in the sense that they are removed from the present, they are spaces that are ultimately inaccessible to subjects.

The relative inadequacy of historical and erotic spaces in providing a stable source of identity illustrates how the psychosocial component of subjectivity is most frequently (and necessarily) a combination of spaces. Throughout the eighteenth century, those who rely on a single space for their sense of identity, like *Tristram Shandy*'s Toby, obsessively recreating the war in miniature upon the bowling green, are likely to be ridiculed as "hobby horsical." In other words, they are characterized as having devoted themselves childishly to an overly simpleminded—and thus grossly distorted—worldview. The commonly pluralized, hybrid composition of the psychosocial in practice can only complicate, and thus diffuse, the effects of disciplinary structures on identity.

Rather than being insidious, disciplinary discourses appear quite frankly in the novels and visual forms that I have considered here. For example, in *Amelia* the narrator's heavy hand is quite visible in its attempts to coerce a designated response from viewers; in representations of ruins, the "regime of tradition" dictates an air of self-resignation in drawing a lesson of mortality from the ruin; and in *Persuasion,* the influence of persuasion and the topography of social difference are thematized as part of the social grid that Anne Elliot must negotiate. The eminent visibility of discipline makes it clear that it did not creep into the consciousnesses of eighteenth-century subjects, exerting subtle control over their behavior and self-conception. Instead, disciplinary discourses were dialogized, or, more drastically, aestheticized, by their insertion into the circulating flow of representations.

AFTERWORD

The complexity of the psychosocial realm that I have described here suggests that agency is a significant factor in the relation between subject and culture. This runs counter to Foucault's *Discipline and Punish* and to John Bender's argument at the end of *Imagining the Penitentiary* that discipline controls even nominally "spontaneous" and individual responses. As Foucault later acknowledged (in *The History of Sexuality*), subjectivity is too multiform in practice, and power too dispersed, to eliminate agency. My emphasis here on forms of mass communication like the novel and visual images in circulation aims at restoring the complexity—in its assertion of norms for selfhood and its presentation of alternatives—of eighteenth- and early nineteenth-century culture in the everyday experience of individual subjects.

Notes

INTRODUCTION

1. *Ideology and Modern Culture: Critical Social Theory in the Era of Mass Communication* (Stanford, Calif.: Stanford University Press, 1990), 77.

2. Ibid., 83.

3. Neo-Marxist critics such as Althusser and Fredric Jameson have taken up the Lacanian notion of history as an inaccessible "Real" and have reformulated it as the absent cause that drives change in human culture. The effect of Lacan's model of the subject's relation to history and the use Neo-Marxists have made of it has been to erase traditional assumptions about what constitutes the proper province of history.

4. E. P. Thompson's work gives a specific example of this spatialization applied to eighteenth-century Britain. Thompson argues that, rather than being divided into competing classes, British society in the eighteenth century consisted of a "field-of-force" or a "theatre of cultural hegemony." See his "Eighteenth-Century English Society: Class Struggle without Class?" *Social History* 3, no. 2 (May 1978): 165, 162. Although hegemony, and hence domination, existed within this society, Thompson makes it clear that "hegemony, even when imposed successfully, does not impose an all-embracing view of life," and that there still was room for "a very vigorous self-activating culture of the people," which "constitutes an ever-present threat to official descriptions of reality" (164). What Thompson describes is not a hierarchy of class oppression, but rather a " 'paternalism-deference

equilibrium' " in which both parties to the equation were, in some degree, the prisoners of each other" (150).

5. Pierre Bourdieu, *Outline of a Theory of Practice,* trans. Richard Nice (New York: Cambridge University Press, 1977), 17.

6. As I have described it, social history is a positive revision of traditional historical approaches, yet it also has weaknesses. One potential difficulty with all social history is the tendency to fall back into the fallacy of assuming that one historical "truth" can be found, a transcendental signified that explains all cultural activities. The difference between the sociohistorical fallacy and that of traditional historical enterprise is that, whereas the traditional historian relies on what the social historian would consider to be only one slender strand of history for his or her "truth," the social historian can come to believe it is possible to comprehend *all* history within a sociohistorical framework, and thus to arrive at *the* truth. The phrase commonly associated with this belief is "total history"; both phrase and belief find their most common expression in the work of the French Annales school of historians, who sought to avoid the subjectivity of narrative by using grand statistical analyses of sociohistorical data. For examples of the encyclopaedic quality of Annales-school productions, see Philippe Ariés and Georges Duby's four-volume, 2,701–page *A History of Private Life*. In fact, however, although it attempts to be all-encompassing, this method necessarily excludes a host of evidence that cannot readily be expressed statistically or that diverges from what the investigator decides is the "norm." Thus, although it masquerades as an analysis carried out on the micro-level of practice and the individual subject, this method attempts to construct macro-level structural truths and to erase the subjectivities of both historical individuals and investigators.

7. In postulating that the eighteenth-century subject perceived the arts as related "spaces," I have, by default, engaged myself in the critical debate over the value of spatial approaches to literature. In fact, this debate is also at the heart of attempts to maintain boundaries between the arts since "space," as a category opposed to "time" and narration, has consistently been identified with the visual. Lessing's *Lāocoon* is the critical ancestor of the modern debate, insisting that literature is primarily a temporal medium while the visual arts are almost exclusively spatial. Despite the notable exception of Joseph Frank's *Spatial Form in Narrative,* deliberate violations of this separation between genres and between time and space categories, particularly in the modernist period, have generally been viewed as miscegenations or as attempts to impose a static, straitjacketing spatial or visual order on the verbal. See Frank Kermode, "A Reply to Joseph Frank," *Critical Inquiry* 4, no. 3 (spring 1978), and Philip Rahv's *Literature and the Sixth Sense* (Boston: Houghton Mifflin, 1969).

8. Jean Hagstrum, *The Sister Arts: The Tradition of Literary Pictorialism and English Poetry from Dryden to Gray* (Chicago: University Press of Chicago, 1958), xvi.

9. As W. J. T. Mitchell has remarked in "Going Too Far with the Sister Arts," "there is no *essential* difference between . . . [them] , no difference, that is, given for all time by the inherent natures of the media, the objects they represent, or the laws of the human mind" (2). See *Space, Time, Image, Sign,* ed. James A. W. Heffernan (New York: Peter Lang, 1987), 1–11.

10. The opposition between literature/time/maleness and visual art/space/femaleness has been articulated most powerfully by Lessing in his *Lāocoon*. Mitchell claims that, according to the traditional critical view of the arts, "Paintings, like women, are ideally silent, beautiful creatures designed for the gratification of the eye, in contrast to the sublime eloquence proper to the manly art of poetry." See his *Iconology: Image, Text, Sign* (Chicago: University of Chicago Press, 1986), 110.

NOTES TO CHAPTER 1

11. In *Iconology,* Mitchell also develops the connection between the sister arts and racial difference. Furthermore, he shows how the debate between the two most important "sisters"—literature and the visual arts—is rooted in Western culture's persistent conflict between iconophilia and iconoclasm.

12. This last version of "discourse" exemplifies Foucault's description of discourse as a spatial field within which enunciations occupy highly individualized points: "Whenever one can describe, between a number of statements, such a system of dispersion, whenever, between objects, types of statement, concepts, or thematic choices, one can define a regularity (an order, correlations, positions and functionings, transformations), we will say . . . that we are dealing with a discursive formation." See *The Archaeology of Knowledge and the Discourse on Language,* trans. A. M. Sheridan Smith (New York: Pantheon, 1972), 38.

13. Ibid., 38.

14. See *Four Fundamental Concepts of Psychoanalysis,* ed. Jacques-Alain Miller, trans. Alan Sheridan (New York: Norton, 1978).

15. Ibid., 83.

16. Ibid., 78.

17. Erving Goffman, *The Presentation of Self in Everyday Life* (New York: Doubleday, 1959), 15–16.

18. Ibid., 16.

19. Erving Goffman, *Frame Analysis: An Essay on the Organization of Experience* (Cambridge, Mass.: Harvard University Press, 1974), 10.

CHAPTER 1

1. Others have noted that the eighteenth century is particularly important in the forging of the modern notion of the "self": see John Lyons's *The Invention of the Self: The Hinge of Consciousness in the Eighteenth Century* (Carbondale, Ill.: Southern Illinois University Press, 1978) or Patricia Meyer Spacks's *Imagining a Self: Autobiography and the Novel in Eighteenth Century England* (Cambridge, Mass.: Harvard University Press, 1976), for example.

2. Several recent studies have focused on the formation of British identity in the eighteenth century, borrowing from the more broadly focused work of Benedict Anderson, *Imagined Communities: Reflections on the Origin and Spread of Nationalism,* 2d ed. (New York: Verso, 1991). These studies focus more on the concept of community and nationhood than on the individual subject. They include Linda Colley's *Britons: Forging the Nation 1707–1837* (New Haven, Conn.: Yale University Press, 1992), written from a historian's point of view, and Howard Weinbrot's *Britannia's Issue: The Rise of British Literature from Dryden to Ossian* (New York: Cambridge University Press, 1993), which clearly defines the genesis of nationalism from a literary perspective, in the formation of a recognizable canon.

3. Michael McKeon, *The Origins of the English Novel 1600–1740* (Baltimore: Johns Hopkins University Press, 1987), 167.

4. H. T. Dickinson, *Liberty and Property: Political Ideology in Eighteenth-Century Britain* (New York: Holmes and Meier, 1977), 8.

5. Frank McLynn, *Crime and Punishment in Eighteenth-Century England* (New York: Routledge, 1989), 224, 226. One study of social turmoil in a specific locale is Steve Poole's "Radicalism, Loyalism and the 'Reign of Terror' in Bath, 1792–1804," *Bath History* 3 (1990): 114–37.

6. Paul Langford, *A Polite and Commercial People: England, 1727–1783* (New York: Oxford University Press, 1989), 654.

7. T. S. Ashton shows how the period between the War of Spanish Succession (1763) and the end of the Napoleonic Wars was characterized by increases in the money supply, in government borrowing, in commercial transactions, and in the founding of provincial banks, all of which made money more available (*An Economic History of England: The 18th Century* [London: Methuen, 1955], 198–99). See Paul Langford's *A Polite and Commercial People* for details concerning the role of turnpikes in increasing eighteenth-century travel (391); the increase in inventions (655–59); and the expansion of the reading public (91–92). One example of a study devoted to a single turnpike is Brenda Buchanan's "The Great Bath Road, 1700–1830," *Bath History* 4 (1992): 71–94. Finally, by the sheer weight of the printed visual materials that she considers, M. Dorothy George shows the huge volume of images in public circulation (*Political Caricature to 1792: A Study of Opinions and Propaganda* [Oxford: Clarendon, 1959]).

8. Michel Foucault, *Discipline and Punish: The Birth of the Prison,* trans. Alan Sheridan (New York: Vintage, 1979), 26–27.

9. Ibid., 26.

10. Indeed, Foucault later retracted this insistence in *The History of Sexuality, Volume I: An Introduction,* trans. Robert Hurley (New York: Vintage, 1980).

11. Jürgen Habermas, *The Structural Transformation of the Public Sphere: An Inquiry into a Category of Bourgeois Society,* trans. Thomas Burger (Cambridge, Mass.: MIT Press, 1989), xvii.

12. See *Outline of a Theory of Practice,* trans. Richard Nice (New York: Cambridge University Press, 1977).

13. See Lawrence Stone and Jeanne C. Fawtier Stone, *An Open Elite? England 1540–1880* (New York: Oxford University Press, 1984).

14. Leonore Davidoff and Catherine Hall, *Family Fortunes: Men and Women of the English Middle Class, 1780–1850* (Chicago: University Press of Chicago, 1987), 206.

15. Roy Porter, *English Society in the Eighteenth Century* (New York: Penguin, 1982), 201.

16. Stone and Stone, *An Open Elite?,* 105.

17. Ibid., 139.

18. Ibid., 107.

19. Ibid., 137.

20. In *A Collection of Designs for Rural Retreats as Villas. Principally in the Gothic and Castle Styles of Architecture* (London: J. & T. Carpenter, 1802), James Malton argues this point

> In place then of having one or more large untenable country mansions, expending hundred of thousands of pounds to display a magnificence that can seldom be enjoyed, and requiring a large yearly revenue to keep in repair only; would it not be more consistent and more productive of happiness, to have various edifices, in various places, differing from each other in style and magnitude, as situation, society, or partial pleasure, might be the cause of their erection? (9)

21. Ian Watt's "The Reading Public and the Rise of the Novel" in *The Rise of the Novel: Studies in Defoe, Richardson, and Fielding* (Berkeley: California University Press, 1957) uses the novel's success as evidence of increasing literacy, although even Watt admits that there were limits: "there is much evidence to suggest that in the country many small farmers, their families, and the majority of labourers, were quite illiterate, while even

in the towns certain sections of the poor—especially soldiers, sailors, and the rabble of the streets—could not read" (37). Furthermore, Watt cites the exceptionally high sale of 60,000 copies of Price's *Observations on the Nature of Civil Liberty* (1776) to show that the book-buying public was "still numbered only in tens of thousands" near the end of the century (36). For other assessments of the eighteenth-century reading public, see J. Paul Hunter, *Before Novels: The Cultural Contexts of Eighteenth-Century English Fiction* (New York: W. W. Norton, 1990); R. A. Houston, *Scottish Literacy and the Scottish Identity: Illiteracy and Society in Scotland and Northern England, 1600–1800* (New York: Cambridge University Press, 1985); John Feather, *The Provincial Book Trade in Eighteenth- Century England* (New York: Cambridge University Press, 1985), ch. 3; and Thomas W. Laqueur, "The Cultural Origins of Popular Literacy in England, 1500–1850," *Oxford Review of Education* 2 (1976): 255–75. For an analysis of literacy in the seventeenth century, see David Cressy, *Literacy and the Social Order: Reading and Writing in Tudor and Stuart England* (New York: Cambridge University Press, 1980) and Margaret Spufford, *Small Books and Pleasant Histories: Popular Fiction and Its Readership in Seventeenth-century England* (Athens, Ga.: Georgia University Press, 1981).

22. Hunter, *Before Novels,* 65.

23. For the increase in book titles, see Watt, 37. According to Watt, the first such library was established in London in 1740. Although there was generally a subscription fee of "between half a guinea and a guinea a year, . . . there were often facilities for borrowing books at the rate of a penny a volume or threepence for the usual three-volume novel" (43). However, in *Judging New Wealth: Popular Publishing and Responses to Commerce in England 1750–1800* (New York: Clarendon, 1992), James Raven suggests that these libraries used subscription fees to restrict their clientele: "In the 1750s London circulating libraries were charging subscribers from between fifteen shillings and one guinea annually, and although this charge was reduced in the early 1760s, it was soon re-imposed. In 1760 two shillings could buy a stone of beef or a pair of shoes" (57). For more on the role of circulating libraries, see Hilda Hamlyn, "Eighteenth-century Circulating Libraries in England," *The Library,* 5th ser., 1 (1947): 197–222; Paul Kaufman, "The Community Library: A Chapter in English Social History," *Transactions of the American Philosophical Society* 57, no. 2 (1967): 5–67; and Lee Erickson, "The Economy of Novel Reading: Jane Austen and the Circulating Library," *Studies in English Literature, 1500–1900* 30, no. 4 (fall 1990): 573–90.

24. Terry Belanger, "Publishers and Writers in Eighteenth-Century England," pp. 5–26 in *Books and their Readers in Eighteenth-Century England,* ed. Isobel Rivers (New York: St. Martin's Press, 1982), 10.

25. See Watt, *Rise of the Novel,* 53. James Raven's *Judging New Wealth* studies the careers of eighteenth-century booksellers as representative nouveaux riches in order to determine the degree to which their financial successes led to social ascendancy.

26. See Feather, *Provincial Book Trade,* 33.

27. See Mark Rose, *Authors and Owners: The Invention of Copyright* (Cambridge, Mass.: Harvard University Press, 1993).

28. The struggle to free older texts from copyright was led by publisher/booksellers who operated outside of London. See chapter 1, "London and the Country," of Feather's *Provincial Book Trade.*

29. For Hazlitt's reading, see Richard Altick, *The English Common Reader: A Social History of the Mass Reading Public 1800–1900* (Chicago: University Press of Chicago, 1957), 55. For more on the effects of such reprint series see Richard C. Taylor, "James Harrison, *The Novelist's Magazine,* and the Early Canonizing of the English Novel," *Studies in English Literature 1500–1900* 33, no. 3 (summer 1993): 629–43.

30. Altick, *Common Reader*, 56.

31. Ibid., 57. There is considerable doubt as to Altick's claim that there were "no shops devoted exclusively to books." See Terry Belanger's "Publishers and Writers in Eighteenth-Century England," in which he notes that there were many "substantial owners of London [book]shops" (8).

32. Altick, *Common Reader*, 58. For Altick, the uniqueness of Lackington's case shows that, although reading was popular among the middle and upper classes, it was still a very "unnatural," refined habit in the eighteenth century, one that was not common among workers or peasants and farmers. In fact, the readers he describes are the ones on which I focus here, since they were likely to be able to afford miniatures and Ranelagh and Bath, as well as Gothic novels. Lackington published his autobiography as a successful bookseller under the title *Memoirs of the First Forty-five Years of the Life of James Lackington, The present Bookseller in Chiswell-street, Moorfields, London* (1791).

33. John Feather, "British Publishing in the Eighteenth Century: A Preliminary Subject Analysis," *The Library*, 6th ser., 8, no. 1 (March 1986): 32.

34. Belanger, "Publishers and Writers," 7, 19.

35. Ibid., 9, 19.

36. Roy McKeen Wiles, "The Relish for Reading in Provincial England Two Centuries Ago," in *The Widening Circle: Essays on the Circulation of Literature in Eighteenth-Century Europe*, ed. Paul J. Korshin (Philadelphia: Pennsylvania University Press, 1976), 88. See also G. A. Cranfield, *The Development of the Provincial Newspaper 1700–1760* (New York: Oxford University Press, 1962).

37. Watt, *Rise of the Novel*, 51.

38. Jon Klancher, *The Making of English Reading Audiences, 1790–1832* (Madison: Wisconsin University Press, 1989), 22. The popularity of the miscellany the *Ladies Diary* should be noted here: it was the longest-lived magazine of the time, published from 1704–1871 (J. H. Plumb, *The Pursuit of Happiness: A View of Life in Georgian England* [New Haven, Conn: Yale Center for British Art, 1997], 13).

39. Belanger, "Publishers and Writers," 5. For more on the *Gentleman's Magazine*, see W. B. Todd's "A Bibliographical Account of *The Gentleman's Magazine*, 1731–54," *Studies in Bibliography* 18(1965): 85.

40. Belanger, "Publishers and Writers," 6.

41. Altick, *Common Reader*, 65.

42. See Watt, *Rise of the Novel*, 47.

43. In "Literacy and Education in England 1640–1900," *Past and Present* 62 (1969): 69–139, Lawrence Stone has investigated eighteenth-century literacy from a broader perspective, defining literacy as the ability to write one's name. For other studies of literacy among the working and peasant classes, see Pat Rogers's "Classics and Chapbooks" in *Books and their Readers in Eighteenth-Century England*, ed. Isobel Rivers (New York: St. Martin's Press, 1982), as well as Victor E. Neuburg's *Chapbooks: Au Guide to Reference Material on English, Scottish and American Chapbook Literature of the Eighteenth and Nineteenth Centuries*. (London: Woburn Press, 2d ed., 1972) and *The Penny Histories: A Study of Chapbooks for Young Readers over Two Centuries* (New York: Harcourt, Brace and World, 1968).

44. Langford, *Polite and Commercial People*, 93.

45. Wiles, "Relish for Reading," 88.

46. Ibid., 98.

47. Ibid., 91.

48. Ibid., 104.

NOTES TO CHAPTER 1

49. Ibid., 106.
50. Ibid., 103.
51. According to Altick, "the growth of Wesleyanism was a noteworthy milestone in the spread of reading among the masses. The new sect preached the spiritual necessity of reading" (*Common Reader,* 37). Still, Altick concludes that the Wesleyan enthusiasm for reading was often viewed as fanatic by the unconverted, who were thus slowed in their own progress to literacy.
52. See Charles C. Mish, "Early Eighteenth-Century Best Sellers in English Prose Fiction," *Papers of the Bibliographical Society of America,* 413–18.
53. Feather, "British Publishing," 37.
54. Mish, "Best Sellers," 414.
55. Habermas, *Structural Transformation,* 40.
56. Ibid., 61.
57. Robert D. Mayo, *The English Novel in the Magazines, 1740–1815* (Evanston, Ill.: Northwestern University Press, 1962), 3.
58. Klancher, *The Making of English Reading Audiences* (Madison: Wisconsin University Press, 1989), 22–23.
59. Ibid., 23.
60. Ibid., 38.
61. Ibid., 39.
62. Ibid., 50.
63. Mayo, *English Novel in the Magazines,* 3.
64. Klancher, *English Reading Audiences,* 40.
65. To summarize, Klancher sees a retrenchment of social freedoms resulting from the spectre of the French Revolution.
66. Among such studies are Rensselaer Lee's *Ut Pictura Poesis: The Humanistic Theory of Painting* (New York: W. W. Norton, 1967), Jean Hagstrum's *The Sister Arts: The Tradition of Literary Pictorialism and English Poetry from Dryden to Gray* (Chicago: University Press of Chicago, 1958), and Francis Haskell's and Nicholas Penny's *Taste and the Antique* (New Haven, Conn.: Yale University Press, 1981). The Arts Council of Great Britain's book *The Age of Neoclassicism* (1972) shows that in the late eighteenth century in particular a new influx of models taken from ancient art was grafted onto the existing tradition of classical allusion and imitation. In chapter 3, on historical space, I treat the causes of the renewed interest in classical antiquity.
67. See Ronald Paulson, *Emblem and Expression: Meaning in English Art of the Eighteenth Century* (London: Thames and Hudson, 1975), 14.
68. J. H. Plumb observes that "perhaps the most remarkable feature of the surging [eighteenth-century] British art market was the relatively minor role played by noble patronage, if one excludes portraiture . . . a surprising number of artists of second and even third rank made an adequate living from the support of the public alone" (*Pursuit of Happiness,* 19).
69. See, for example, Malcolm Andrews's *The Search for the Picturesque: Landscape, Aesthetics and Tourism in Britain, 1760–1800* (Stanford, Calif.: Stanford University Press, 1989), or David Watkin, *The English Vision: The Picturesque in Architecture, Landscape and Garden Design* (New York: Harper & Row, 1982).
70. Ellis Waterhouse, *Painting in Britain 1530 to 1790. The Pelican History of Art,* 2d ed. (New York: Penguin, 1962), 75.
71. *Water-colour Painting in Britain: I. The Eighteenth Century* (London: B. T. Batsford, 1966), 49.

72. Graham Reynolds, "Introduction," in *English Drawings and Watercolors, 1550–1850, in the Collection of Mr. and Mrs. Paul Mellon,* Pierpont Morgan Library (New York: Harper & Row, 1972), xii.

73. See Elizabeth Wheeler Manwaring's *Italian Landscape in Eighteenth-Century England* (New York: Russell & Russell, 1925) and William Gaunt's *Bandits in a Landscape: A Study of Romantic Painting from Caravaggio to Delacroix* (New York: Studio Publications, 1937) for further commentary on Italian influence on English picturesque painting.

74. That Gilpin's influence is present through the early nineteenth century is shown in the fact that his tours were republished in 1808; this republication stimulated Rowlandson's response. Many artists packaged collections of prints during this period, including, for example, Paul Sandby's *Twelve Views in Aquatinta from drawings taken on the spot in South Wales* (London: P. Sandby, 1775), Edward Dayes's *The Works of the Late Edward Dayes, Containing An Excursion through the Principal Parts of Derbyshire and Yorkshire* (London: Mrs. Dayes, 1805), John Carter's *Views of Ancient Buildings in England Drawn in different Tours* (London: J. Carter, 1786–93), and William Watts's *Select Views of the Principal Buildings and Other Interesting and Picturesque Objects in the Cities of Bath and Bristol* (London: W. Watts, 1794). Like numbered novels, Watts's (and other artists') views were published in periodic installments, selling at fifteen shillings apiece.

75. John O. Lyons, *The Invention of the Self: The Hinge of Consciousness in the Eighteenth Century* (Carbondale, Ill.: Southern Illinois University Press, 1978), 174.

76. Hardie, *Water-colour Painting in Britain,* 86.

77. See also Jean-Claude Lebensztejn's essay on Cozens's method, "In Black and White," in Norman Bryson's *Calligram: Essays in New Art History From France* (New York: Cambridge University Press, 1988) and Kim Sloan's *Alexander and John Robert Cozens* (New Haven, Conn.: Yale University Press, 1986).

78. John H. Hammond, *The Camera Obscura: A Chronicle* (Bristol, U.K.: Adam Hilger, 1981), 82.

79. Ibid., 82–84.

80. Ibid., 82.

81. Ralph Cohen, *The Art of Discrimination: Thomson's "The Seasons" and the Language of Criticism* (New York: Routledge & Kegan Paul, 1964), 133.

82. In fact, the camera obscura was an imperfect instrument that often had a poor "depth of field" in focusing and sometimes distorted natural colors. In this way, it clearly undermined its intended purpose—the capturing of reality in its natural, objective state.

83. Hammond, *Camera Obscura,* 82.

84. Peter Bicknell, "Introduction," in *Beauty, Horror, and Immensity: Picturesque Landscape in Britain, 1750–1850* (New York: Cambridge University Press, 1981), xii.

85. Hardie, *Water-colour Painting in Britain,* 23–24.

86. See David H. Solkin, *Painting for Money: The Visual Arts and the Public Sphere in Eighteenth-Century England* (New Haven, Conn.: Yale University Press, 1993).

87. Richard D. Altick, *The Shows of London* (Cambridge, Mass.: Harvard University Press, 1978), 101.

88. Ibid., 102.

89. For the history of these professional societies, see Algernon Graves's *The Society of Artists of Great Britain 1760–91, and The Free Society of Artists, 1761–83* (Bath, U.K. [Somerset]: Kingsmead Reprints, 1969); Derek Hudson and Kenneth Luckhurst's *The Royal Society of Arts, 1754–1954* (London: Murray, 1954); and Sidney C. Hutchinson's *The History of the Royal Academy, 1768–1968* (London: Chapman and Hill, 1968).

90. Hudson and Luckhurst, *Royal Society of Arts,* 16–17.

NOTES TO CHAPTER 1

91. I refer to the professional artist with masculine pronouns because, other than Maria Cosway, Mary Moser, and Angelica Kauffman, artists and exhibitors were invariably male.

92. Hardie, *Water-colour Painting in Britain*, 102.

93. This act originally offered a fourteen-year protection of the artist's copyrighted design; in 1767, this protection was extended to twenty-eight years.

94. In his biography of Hogarth, Ronald Paulson shows how Hogarth's control of all profits—from both subscriptions and later publication—was unequalled even by such literary predecessors as Dryden and Pope (*Hogarth: His Life, His Art, and Times* [New Haven, Conn: Yale University Press, 1971], 1:281).

95. Reynolds, "Introduction," xii.

96. Altick, *Shows*, 110.

97. Ibid.

98. The bow windows and display cabinets that are now standard features of retail sales shops of all sorts were developed in the eighteenth century. In contrast to the hutches, chests, and booths that early eighteenth-century merchants were forced to work in, by the 1790s George Dance was designing shops of "spacious elegance" that were "the true precursors of their commercial descendents which serve our present society of mass consumption" (Neil McKendrick, John Brewer, and J. H. Plumb, *The Birth of a Consumer Society: The Commercialization of Eighteeth-Century England* [Bloomington: Indiana University Press, 1982], 85). According to J. H. Plumb, the term "bow window" was first used in 1753 (Ibid., 274). For more on shop displays, see H. Kalman, "The Architecture of Mercantilism," in *The Triumph of Culture; Eighteenth Century Perspectives*, ed. Paul Fritz and David Williams (Toronto: A. M. Hakkert, 1972), 69–83.

99. *Political Caricature to 1792: A Study of Opinions and Propaganda* (Oxford: Clarendon, 1959), 111

100. Altick, *Shows*, 117. As reproduced by Hardie, Paul Sandby's watercolor "The Magic Lantern" pictures a family in a darkened room, watching images projected from the lantern to a sheet. As reproduced by Altick, C. Williams's 1822 engraving, again entitled "The Magic Lantern," shows a small audience, again probably a family, enjoying a projection of George IV caricatured as a mandarin.

101. Ibid., 121–22.

102. All details regarding Barker's panorama, which closed in 1863, are derived from Altick's *The Shows of London*.

103. For more on the late eighteenth- and early nineteenth-century enthusiasm for the panorama see Ralph Hyde's *Panoramania!:The Art and Entertainment of the 'All-Embracing' View* (London: Trefoil, 1988). This is the textual accompaniment to an exhibition held at the Barbican Art Gallery, 3 November 1988–15 January 1989.

104. Altick, *Shows*, 136.

105. Ibid., 105.

106. Although my discussion of *Evelina* here removes the text from the biographical and feminist optics through which it has typically been viewed, I certainly do not wish thereby to discount the quite formidable body of recent critical work on Burney or *Evelina*, which includes Margaret Anne Doody, *Frances Burney: The Life in the Works* (New Brunswick, N.J.: Rutgers University Press, 1988); Julia Epstein, *The Iron Pen* (Madison: Wisconsin University Press, 1989); Katharine M. Rogers, *Frances Burney: The World of Female Difficulties* (Hemel Hempstead: Harvester Wheatsheaf, 1990); and Kristina Straub, *Divided Fictions: Fanny Burney and the Feminine Strategy* (Athens, Ga.: Georgia University Press, 1987).

107. Susan Staves's "*Evelina*, or Female Difficulties," *Modern Philology* 73 (May 1976): 368–81 discusses the threatening aspects of Evelina's debut in detail.

108. Langford, *Polite and Commercial People*, 576.

109. Fanny Burney, *Evelina; or, the History of a Young Lady's Entrance into the World*, ed. Edward and Lillian Bloom (New York: Oxford University Press, 1968), 26. All subsequent references to *Evelina* will be taken from this edition and will be noted parenthetically in my text.

110. A full discussion of this subject would lead me into an analysis of the social thematics of *Evelina* that I must avoid here. Suffice it to say that performance includes not only physical behavior but proper deployment of etiquette. Evelina fails to "perform" properly at the private ball (letter xi), where she laughs at the fop Lovel, or at the ridotto (letter xiii), where she claims to be engaged to dance in order to avoid him. Because of her violations of etiquette—which do not correspond to either her beauty or her apparent social station—she becomes the object of conversation aimed at determining who she is, both literally, in terms of her name and origins, and figuratively, in terms of her character and reasons for her behavior.

111. E. Beresford Chancellor, *The Eighteenth Century in London: An Account of Its Social Life and Arts* (London: B. T. Batsford, 1920), 103.

112. Warwick Wroth, *The London Pleasure Gardens of the Eighteenth Century* (New York: MacMillan, 1896), 213.

113. See Thompson, "Eighteenth-Century English Society: Class Struggle without Class?" *Social History* 3, no. 2 (May 1978): 133–65.

114. The original Pantheon burned down in 1792 and was rebuilt in 1795. In 1810, this second version was demolished and rebuilt in a third version, which was ultimately converted into a warehouse in 1862. Before this time, in all its incarnations, it served as a place of social gathering. For more on the Pantheon, see Chancellor, *Eighteenth Century in London*, 115–19.

115. Ibid., 115.

116. Langford, *Polite and Commercial People*, 578.

117. The Pantheon's middle-rank to elite audience is clarified by the fact that there existed another "Pantheon" in Spa Fields, often called the Little Pantheon, whose clientele was far more common: "the place was principally resorted to by apprentices and small tradesmen. . . . A nearer examination of this crowded assembly showed that it consisted of journeymen tailors, hairdressers, milliners and servant maids" (Wroth, *London Pleasure Gardens*, 25–26). This Little Pantheon was not as successful as its downtown counterpart—opened in 1770, it was closed by 1776. The Oxford Street location of *the* Pantheon was important in attracting its more fashionable crowd: Oxford Street, with over 153 shops, "was the commercial shop window of England. Here fashion reached its apotheosis in splendour and variety" (See McKendrick, Brewer, and Plumb, *Birth of a Consumer Society*, 78).

118. Brian Allen, "The Landscape," in *Vauxhall Gardens*, ed. T. J. Edelstein (New Haven, Conn.: Yale Center for British Art, 1983), 11. For more on this garden tradition, see Ronald Paulson's "The Pictorial Circuit and Related Structures in 18th-Century England," in *The Varied Pattern: Studies in the 18th Century*, ed. Peter Hughes and David Williams (Toronto: A. M. Hakkert, 1971), David Watkin's *The English Vision: The Picturesque in Architecture, Landscape, and Garden Design* (New York: Harper & Row, 1982), or John Dixon Hunt's *The Figure in the Landscape* (Baltimore: Johns Hopkins University Press, 1976).

119. My discussion of Vauxhall owes a great deal to the work of Brian Allen and

NOTES TO CHAPTER 1

T. J. Edelstein in *Vauxhall Gardens* (ed. T. J. Edelstein [New Haven, Conn.: Yale Center for British Art, 1983]), which was designed to accompany the Yale Center for British Art's exhibition of prints, engravings, and other materials connected with Vauxhall.

120. Edelstein, *Vauxhall Gardens*, 20.
121. Ibid., 20.
122. Ibid., 22.
123. Ibid., 13.
124. Ibid., 25. As in the decoration of the Rotunda's chandelier with the rape of Semele, the sexual content of the paintings is not only quite explicit, but places the male in the aggressive posture. This is indicated by titles such as "A shepherd playing on his pipe and decoying a shepherdess into a wood" and "The kiss stolen."
125. Ibid., 25.
126. Ibid., 30. Edelstein argues that many of Hayman's original designs were derived from earlier emblem books. Paulson's concept of "bifocal" reading of visual designs, implying both popular/naive and polite/literate levels of reading, corresponds to Edelstein's conclusion that the Vauxhall dinner-box paintings may be seen in two ways: "the first way to experience them is obviously and directly, as delightful representations of innocent games. On another level they warn of the vanity of all such pursuits" (30).
127. Ibid., 14.
128. Vauxhall was accessible to provincial audiences in its local incarnations: "every market town had its 'Vauxhall'. . . . In the provinces these pleasure gardens were less ambitious but equally popular: they provided usually a small collection of animals and birds, a teashop, winding walks, a bowling green, and from time to time a special feature—a set piece of fireworks, a slackwire artist, or, after Lunardi, a balloonist" (Plumb, *Pursuit of Happiness*, 16).
129. Wroth, *London Pleasure Gardens*, 205.
130. For more on the rise of the museum, see Olive Impey and Arthur MacGregor, eds., *The Origins of Museums: The Cabinet of Curiosities in Sixteenth and Seventeenth Century Europe* (New York: Oxford University Press, 1985) and Tony Bennett, *The Birth of the Museum: History, Theory, Politics* (New York: Routledge, 1995), which focuses more on the nineteenth and twentieth centuries.
131. For more on the impulse to collect, see Douglas and Elizabeth Rigby, *Lock, Stock and Barrel: The Story of Collecting* (New York: Lippincott, 1944) and James Clifford, "On Collecting Art and Culture," in *The Predicament of Culture: Twentieth-Century Ethnography, Literature, and Art* (Cambridge, Mass.: Harvard University Press, 1988). For more on the museum's institutional relation to the public, see Michael S. Shapiro, "The Public and the Museum," in *The Museum: A Reference Guide*, ed. M. S. Shapiro (New York: Greenwood, 1990).
132. Altick, *Shows*, 18.
133. Altick, *Shows*, 26. See also Edward Miller, *That Noble Cabinet: A History of the British Museum* (Athens, Ohio: Ohio University Press, 1974). Arthur MacGregor offers a series of essays on the origin of the Ashmolean Museum in *Tradescant's Rarities: Essays on the Foundation of the Ashmolean Museum, 1683* (New York: Clarendon, 1983).
134. Kenneth Hudson, *A Social History of Museums: What the Visitors Thought* (Atlantic Highlands, N.J.: Humanities Press, 1975), 9.
135. Watkin, *The English Vision*, vii.
136. Ibid., vii.
137. For more on the rise of the great house tour in England, see Adrian Tinniswood, *A History of Country House Visiting: Five Centuries of Tourism and Taste* (London: Blackwell and The National Trust, 1989)

138. In one notorious instance, the Cherokee chiefs were taken to Vauxhall, where over ten thousand visitors flocked to see them get drunk. When proprietors of taverns, gardens, or other sights had advance notice that the Cherokees were coming, they "ran newspaper advertisements announcing that fact and raised their prices" (Altick, *Shows*, 47).

139. For more on the visits of American Indians to England, see Richmond P. Bond's *Queen Anne's American Kings* (New York: Oxford University Press, 1952) and Carolyn Thomas Foreman's *Indians Abroad, 1493–1938* (Norman: Oklahoma University Press, 1943) 65–81. For more on Omai, see Thomas Blake Clark, *Omai: First Polynesian Ambassador to England* (Honolulu: Hawaii University Press, 1941).

140. Gerald Reitlinger, *The Economics of Taste, Volume 2: The Rise and Fall of Objets d'Art Prices Since 1750* (London: Barrie and Rockliff, 1963), 58.

141. Langford, *Polite and Commercial People,* 514.

142. Linda Colley, *Britons: Forging the Nation 1707–1837* (New Haven, Conn.: Yale University Press, 1992), 6.

Chapter 2

1. The *Oxford English Dictionary* cites this 1676 usage of "speculum" to mean diagram: "A Speculum of the Geniture, or a Table of the Radiations of the Planets."

2. See Bender's *Imagining the Penitentiary: Fiction and the Architecture of Mind in Eighteenth-Century England* (Chicago: University of Chicago Press, 1987).

3. Although I see *Roderick Random* as a picaresque novel, there has been critical controversy on this point. Most notably, G. S. Rousseau has argued that Smollett is not a writer of picaresque novels in "Smollett and the Picaresque: Some Questions about a Label," *Studies in Burke and His Time* 12 (1970–71). Critics who see Smollett related more closely to the picaresque include Robert Alter, "The Picaroon as Fortune's Plaything," pp. 131–53 in *Essays on the Eighteenth-Century Novel,* ed. R. D. Spector (Bloomington: Indiana University Press, 1965) and A. G. Fredman, "The Picaresque in Decline," pp. 189–208 in *English Writers of the Eighteenth Century,* ed. John Middendorf (New York: Columbia University Press, 1971). Perhaps most commentators might agree that Smollett's career as a writer shows a growing divergence from the picaresque, culminating in *Humphry Clinker.*

4. *Satire and the Novel in Eighteenth-Century England* (New Haven, Conn.: Yale University Press, 1967), 198. In "The Public Sphere and the Eighteenth-Century Novel: Social Criticism and Narrative Enactment," *Eighteenth-Century Life* 16 (November 1992): 114–29, John Richetti expands on Paulson's comments: "Matt Bramble offers a searching satiric critique of modern British life but is himself put under novelistic examination by the epistolary format, the observations of his fellow travelers, and by the series of events and movements around the island of Great Britain that is the novel's plot" (122–23). Reading *Humphry Clinker* in the context of eighteenth-century critiques of luxury, Aileen Douglas recognizes that "Bramble is implicated in luxury in ways that undermine his social analysis" (*Uneasy Sensations: Smollett and the Body* [Chicago: University Press of Chicago, 1995]), 177. To read *Humphry Clinker* as a novel in which Bramble's voice is dominant is thus inaccurate. I must disagree on this point with Susan Jacobsen, who claims that the "views [of Lydia and Jery] are presented as those of the naïve young," while "Bramble's censorious observations dominate the scene" (76). Bramble is himself the object of satire, and the other travelers' views provide the reader with a useful counterpoise to his often skewed perspective.

5. Tobias Smollett, *The Expedition of Humphry Clinker* (New York: Penguin, 1978),

110. All subsequent references to *Humphry Clinker* will be taken from this text and will be noted parenthetically in my text.

6. Much critical attention has been devoted to discussion of Bramble's illness. John Sekora, in *Luxury: The Concept in Western Thought* (Baltimore: Johns Hopkins University Press, 1977), uses Bramble as an example of how luxury is connected with disease in eighteenth-century cultural discourse. Aileen Douglas, working from Sekora's premise, further connects women with luxury and thus, women with disease: "Under Bramble's guidance the reader begins to identify illness with women . . . the 'cure' of Matthew Bramble requires the containment of female sexuality" (*Uneasy Sensations,* 169–70). Bramble's illness, or rather his progress toward health, has also been used to describe the structure of the entire novel, as exhibited in the work of William A. West, "Matt Bramble's Journey to Health," *Texas Studies in Literature and Language* 11 (1969), and B. L. Reid, "Smollett's Healing Journey," *Virginia Quarterly Review* 41 (1965).

7. Susan Jacobsen argues that these marriages carry little comedic power because they occur in winter and because they involve minor characters. This leads her to conclude that "the novel's ending is ultimately pessimistic and nostalgic" ("Tinsel of the Times," 88). While her argument is interesting, it fails to account for the fact that the novel makes those "minor" characters—especially Clinker—responsible for Bramble's rejuvenation. Moreover, the narrative does not need to dispel all of the problems of Great Britain to be positive; as Richetti points out, the ending is positive in the sense that Bramble ultimately sees that he must drop his alienated stance and accept the necessity of his involvement in the community and nation: "personal discovery involves the establishment of patriarchal links and the assuming of a long-neglected authority at the head of a reinvigorated rural network, a family that now includes and resolves in the marriages of Humphry/Winifred, Lismahago/Tabitha, and Lydia/Dennison most of the social problems and inequities the novel has encountered"(*The Public Sphere,* 128).

8. By 1750, Bath received as many as 12,000 visitors each season. In addition, the city's resident population swelled from "less than 3000 in 1700 to nearly 35,000 a century later" (Paul Langford, *A Polite and Commercial People: England, 1727–1783* [New York: Oxford University Press, 1989], 106).

9. In 1771, John Wood the Younger finished construction of a building that was soon called the New or Upper Assembly Rooms to distinguish it from the Old or Lower Assembly Rooms. Upon the opening of the Upper Rooms, there were actually two "Kings" of Bath—one for each Assembly—although the office of Master of Ceremonies of the Upper Rooms was regarded as more prestigious.

10. Thomas Hinde, *Tales from the Pump Room* (London: Victor Gollancz, 1988), 36. Goldsmith's *Life of Richard Nash* can be found in a collection of essays, *The Bee and Other Essays,* ed. Humphrey Milford (New York: Oxford Universtiy Press, 1914).

11. See Terry Castle, *Masquerade and Civilization: The Carnivalesque in Eighteenth-Century English Culture and Fiction* (Stanford, Calif.: Stanford University Press, 1986).

12. In "Consumptive Communities: Commodifying Nature in Spa Society," *The Eighteenth Century: Theory and Interpretation* 36, no. 3 (1995): 203–19, Barbara M. Benedict argues that the carnival spirit of festive misrule in early spa culture was co-opted in the course of the eighteenth century: "During Queen Anne's reign, indeed, the outlandish spa dress was replaced as Beau Nash established a fashionable uniform at Bath, so that visitors could masquerade properly. This commercialization of social role-playing subsumes carnival into tourist discourse" (205).

13. Ernest S. Turner, *Taking the Cure* (London: Michael Joseph, 1967), 60.

14. Ibid., 61.

15. Other factors contribute to the impression that circulation was increasingly subjected to monitoring attention. For instance, due to its reputation as a place where social distinctions were at least eased if not erased, Bath had become a haven for beggars. By 1805, however, there was a "Society for the Suppression of Vagrants" that intended, "by a firm resolution on the part of the inhabitants and visitors to withold casual alms," that "the nuisance of street-beggars, so long its reproach, may by degrees be banished from Bath" (*Improved Bath Guide,* 50–51).

16. See chapter 9, "Terraces, Squares, and Crescents," of Mark Girouard's *The English Town: A History of Urban Life* (New Haven, Conn.: Yale University Press, 1990) for a full account of the crescent's evolution. See also Jean Starobinski, *The Invention of Liberty, 1700–1789* (New York: Rizzoli, 1987), especially "Public Squares and Public Houses," 43–49.

17. Thomas Malton's *Royal Crescent, General view from south-east* and John Robert Cozens's *Royal Crescent, General view from south-west* are reproduced in Walter Ison's *The Georgian Buildings of Bath from 1700–1830* (London: Faber, 1948).

18. The architectural implications of the square are quite different from those of the circle or crescent: as John Bender has pointed out in *Imagining the Penitentiary: Fiction and the Architecture of Mind in Eighteenth-Century England* (Chicago: University Press of Chicago, 1987), the square plan is based on an ideal of rectilinear articulation and regularization of space. See Felix Barker and Ralph Hyde's *London As It Might Have Been* (London: John Murphy, 1982) for a survey of the numerous plans for the reconstruction of London after the Great Fire of 1666 that were based on this ideal. As late as 1766, the architect John Gwynn continued to urge that London adopt a unified, rectilinear program of expansion and reconstruction. That this model of development was motivated by the desire for centralized control is illustrated by Gwynn's belief in "the necessity of a general plan of the whole capital, improved and divided into proper districts" (v).

19. See Mark Girouard, *The English Town,* 161.

20. R. S. Neale, *Bath 1680–1850: A Social History* (Boston: Routledge & Kegan Paul, 1981), 199.

21. Girouard, *English Town,* 163.

22. Neale, *Bath 1680–1850,* 207.

23. Ibid., 207.

24. Patricia Brückmann, "Sir Walter Elliot's Bath Address," *Modern Philology* 80 (August 1982): 58.

25. Douglas Murray, "Gazing and Avoiding the Gaze," in *Jane Austen's Business: Her World and Her Profession,* ed. Juliet McMaster and Bruce Stovel (New York: St. Martin's Press, 1996), 47.

26. This theater-like design may not have been completely without precedent: in Rome, "the Piazza di Sant'Ignazio [is] a Rococo jewel whose carved facades were designed to imitate a theater set" (Paula Butturini, "What's Doing in Rome," *New York Times* 6 October 1996, travel section: 10).

27. Summerson, *Heavenly Mansions, and Other Essays on Architecture* (New York: Norton, 1963), 101.

28. Eric Rothstein, *Systems of Order and Inquiry in Later Eighteenth-Century Fiction* (Berkeley: California University Press, 1975), 245.

29. "The Rise of the Promenade: The Social and Cultural Use of Space in the English Provincial Town c. 1660–1800," *British Journal for Eighteenth-Century Studies* (1986): 130.

30. Cited in Warwick Wroth, *The London Pleasure Gardens of the Eighteenth Century* (New York: MacMillan, 1896), 205.

NOTES TO CHAPTER 2

31. Ibid., 202.

32. E. Beresford Chancellor, *The Eighteenth Century in London: An Account of Its Social Life and Arts* (London: B. T. Batsford, 1920), 98.

33. Ibid., 102.

34. Wroth, *Pleasure Gardens*, 206.

35. Ibid., 203.

36. Jeremy Bentham's *Plan of the Panopticon* was originally published in *The Works of Jeremy Bentham,* ed. Bowring, vol. 4, 1843. A photo of this plan is found in Michel Foucault, *Discipline and Punish: The Birth of the Prison,* trans. Alan Sheridan (New York: Vintage, 1979).

37. Paulson has described a similar dispersal in the earlier, circulative structure of pictorial circuits in the gardens at Stowe and Stourhead:

> Movement through a garden like that at Stourhead depends on the transition from one part—one temple or statue—to another, although the visitor may also try to divine a sense of the overall pattern. The fixed perspective point has been replaced by a roving one, extremely inferential, and requiring the materializing of relationships rather than a total plan (*Popular* 112).

The difference between this structure and that of the Rotunda is that the gardens lack any socially specular dimension; thus, they direct the visitors' attention toward introspection rather than toward display.

38. Jon Klancher, *The Making of English Reading Audiences, 1790–1832* (Madison: Wisconsin University Press, 1989), 32.

39. See my discussion of fictive direct lineage in chapter 1, pp. 000.

40. Peter Borsay, "The Rise of the Promenade: The Social and Cultural Use of Space in the English Provinical Town c. 1660–1800," *British Journal for Eighteenth-Century Studies* (1986): 130.

41. See Borsay, "Rise of the Promenade," for an examination of York, Bath, and Preston's promenade facilities. As indicated in Barbara Benedict's "Consumptive Communities," each provincial social site tended to cater to a specific clientele. The decentralization of the social to the domestic level probably had an ambivalent effect on the involvement of the lower classes. This is because the incursion of the social field into the domestic realm was something experienced only by the servants of those who could afford to live in one of the fashionable crescents. In *Heavenly Mansions,* Sir John Summerson makes the exclusivity of Bath's prime residential complexes clear in his description of the reduction of the Colosseum idea to circus size: "The Colosseum was built for an audience of perhaps 45,000 people; the Bath Circus for the residence of thirty-three gentlemen and their families" (100). Meanwhile, the pleasure gardens, especially Vauxhall, were accessible to a truly *popular* crowd.

42. Jane Austin, *Persuasion,* ed. and intro. D. W. Harding (New York: Penguin, 1987), 161. All subsequent references to *Persuasion* will be taken from this text and will be noted parenthetically in my text.

43. There may be more than a hint of irony in Sir Walter's preference for Camden Crescent. Charles Pratt, Lord Chancellor Camden (1714–94), was indeed a man of lofty, dignified stature in the public realm, but he was also of humble origin, a parvenu lawyer whose nobility was earned by service, not inherited. As such, he is emblematic of the class of nobility that Sir Walter rejects as a debasement of the "true" aristocracy (35). Patricia Brückmann adds to the irony by noting that, because of its precarious position on high, yet unstable, ground, Camden crescent was never finished ("Sir Walter Elliot's Bath Address," 60).

44. "The Architectural Setting of Jane Austen's Novels," *Journal of the Warburg and Courtauld Institutes* 32 (1968): 416.

45. *Jane Austen and the War of Ideas* (New York: Oxford University Press, 1975), 282.

46. *Narrative and Its Discontents: Problems of Closure in the Traditional Novel* (Princeton, N.J.: Princeton University Press, 1981), 100.

47. This activity approximates the realm of practice described by Pierre Bourdieu in his *Outline of a Theory of Practice* (New York: Cambridge University Press, 1977). As I have described it, the Bath social field involved submitting one's self to an extensive code of regulations that prescribed dress, provided a timed regimen of activities, and, to some degree, preserved the precedence of the aristocracy. Among its other directives, this code effectively divided the population of the Assembly Rooms into three classes: Dress Ball subscribers, walking subscribers, and those admitted by a one-night ticket. Within the classes and conduct mandated by these rules, an individual subject was free to shape his or her identity through slight, "practical" deviations from them.

48. For more on Sir Walter's "scopophilia"—his love of being seen—see Murray, "Gazing," especially 48–49.

49. This despite the fact that Wentworth and Anne share a "satiric amusement" that marks their inherent affinity. See Isobel Grundy, "*Persuasion,* or The Triumph of Cheerfulness," in *Jane Austen's Business: Her World and Her Profession,* ed. Juliet McMaster and Bruce Stovel (New York: St. Martin's Press, 1996), 3–16.

50. For a discussion of this passage in the context of Anna Laetitia Barbauld's comments on gender difference, see Grundy, "Triumph of Cheerfulness," especially 5–9.

51. *Romantic Vision and the Novel* (New York: Cambridge University Press, 1987), 79.

52. D. A. Miller, *Narrative and Its Discontents: Problems of Closure in the Traditional Novel* (Princeton, N.J.: Princeton University Press, 1981), 101.

Chapter 3

1. See *The Ordering of the Arts in Eighteenth-Century England* (Princeton, N.J.: Princeton University Press, 1970).

2. Frank Palmeri, "History as Monument: Gibbon's *Decline and Fall,*" *Studies in Eighteenth-Century Culture* 18 (1989): 226.

3. In *Totem and Taboo* Freud collapses both of these desires into a single image, that of the sons of the primal horde cannibalizing their father. He claims that "in the act of devouring him they accomplished their identification with him" (*Standard Edition* [London: Hogarth Press, 1953–74], 13:142). In this way, they both celebrated the father's death and reconstituted his being as a part of their own flesh.

4. Rose Macauley, *Pleasure of Ruins* (London: Weidenfeld and Nicolson, 1953), 23.

5. See Jean Starobinski, *The Invention of Liberty, 1700–1789* (New York: Rizzoli, 1987). Regarding ruins, Starobinski claims that "The ancient monument had originally been a memorial, a 'monition,' perpetuating a memory. . . . Its melancholy resides in the fact that it has become a monument of lost significance. . . . But awareness of this oblivion implied awareness of the necessity of remembering" (180).

6. "Ruin" describes only palaces, sumptuous tombs or public edifices. One would never use the word "ruin" in speaking of a private home, whether that of peasants or of bourgeois; one would then say "ruined buildings." From "La Poétique des ruines," *Word and Image* 4, no. 1 (January–March 1980): 232.

7. *La poétique des ruins en France* (Geneva: Librairie Droz, 1974), 9; the ruin belongs

most frequently to the high style (palaces, monuments), sometimes to the middle style, and never to the low style.

8. Ibid., 10; already in the seventeenth and eighteenth centuries, the presence of the ruin in paintings corresponded to a desire to integrate Time into the visual arts in symbolic terms.

9. Ibid., 10–11; liberating the viewer from spatio-temporal contingencies, the ruin permits the imagination to plunge into the flow of time without hindrance, to dream one's self outside of the present, in a hallowed past or in a mysteriously divined future.

10. *The Unfinished Manner: Essays on the Fragment in the Later Eighteenth Century* (Charlottesville: Virginia University Press, 1994), 148.

11. Ibid., 149.

12. Thomas McFarland, *Romanticism and the Forms of Ruin: Wordsworth, Coleridge, and Modalities of Fragmentation* (Princeton N.J.: Princeton University Press, 1981), 7.

13. Anne Janowitz, *England's Ruins: Poetic Purpose and the National Landscape* (Cambridge, Mass.: Basil Blackwell, 1990), 4.

14. McFarland, *Romanticism*, 31.

15. Janowitz, *England's Ruins*, 4. For more documentation of the relation between the eighteenth-century lyric and the ruin, see Robert Arnold Aubin, *Topographical Poetry in XVIII-Century England* (New York: Modern Language Association, 1936), especially chapter 4.

16. Similarly, Patrick Wright's *On Living in an Old Country: The National Past in Contemporary Britain* (London: Verso, 1985) considers the modern country house and general preservation movements in England as symptoms of the nationalist agenda.

17. Gerald Reitlinger, *The Economics of Taste, Volume 2: The Rise and Fall of Objets d'Art Prices Since 1750* (London: Barrie and Rockliff, 1963), 77.

18. For more on the rise of British antiquarianism, see Graham Parry, *The Trophies of Time: English Antiquarians of the Seventeenth Century* (New York: Oxford University Press, 1995) and Stuart Piggott, *Ruins in a Landscape: Essays in Antiquarianism* (Edinburgh: Edinburgh University Press, 1976).

19. The first secretary of the Society of Antiquaries was William Stukeley, who was later the author of one of the first tour books of native ruins, *Itinerarium Curiosum* (London: W. Stukeley, 1724).

20. For more on the often highly emblematic and usually aristocratic tradition of landscape gardening established in England during the eighteenth century, see Ronald Paulson, *Emblem and Expression: Meaning in English Art of the Eighteenth Century* (Cambridge, Mass.: Harvard University Press, 1975) and David Watkin, *The English Vision: The Picturesque in Architecture, Landscape, and Garden Design* (New York: Harper & Row, 1982). Maynard Mack's *The Garden and the City* (Toronto: Toronto University Press, 1969) deals specifically with the ideal of retreat from the values of the city as it is reflected in the construction of hermitages and grottoes.

21. A photograph of Edgehill is available in Watkin (*English Vision*, 50), who also reproduces Miller's watercolor design for Wimpole (51). Miller's work is also discussed in Stuart Barton, *Monumental Follies: An Exposition on the Eccentric Edifices of Britain* (Worthing, Sussex: Lyle Publications, 1972); and the National Trust's *Follies and Pleasure Pavilions* (London: Pavilion, 1989).

22. This tally is David Watkin's in *The English Vision*, 52.

23. The Netley Abbey transept at Cranbury Park is pictured in Watkin, *The English Vision*, 49.

24. Barbara Mildred Jones, *Follies and Grottoes* (Toronto: Longmans, Green, 1953), 3.

25. Barton, *Monumental Follies,* 35–36.

26. This plan is reproduced in Dora Wiebenson's "Documents of Social Change: Publications about the Small House," in *Studies in Eighteenth-Century British Art and Aesthetics,* ed. Ralph Cohen (Berkeley: California University Press, 1985), 82–127.

27. Richard D. Altick, *The Shows of London* (Cambridge, Mass.: Harvard University Press, 1978), 95.

28. Ibid., 19. The 1752 date attribution of this originally undated pamphlet is determined by Brian Allen in "The Landscape," in *Vauxhall Gardens,* ed. T. J. Edelstein (New Haven, Conn.: Yale Center for British Art, 1983), 17.

29. Quoted in Barton, *Monumental Follies,* 36.

30. In attempting to distinguish a poetics of ruins, Roland Mortier goes so far as to deny that Hubert Robert is a true painter of ruins because of his indulgence in ahistorical fantasy; Mortier believes that, for a ruin, "Son origine, son histoire, son lieu ne sont jamais indifferent: la poésie ne se satisfait pas des ruines imaginaires, interchangeables d'un Poussin, d'un Pannini, ou d'un Robert, fixation suffisante pour l'oeil, mais non pour la pensée. Lorsqu'elle cesse d'être un «mémorial», la poésie cesse aussi bientôt d'exister" (13).

(Its origin, its history, its location are never unimportant: the poetics of ruins is not satisfied by the imaginary and interchangeable ruins of a Poussin, a Pannini, or a Robert, ruins which offer sufficient interest for the eye, but not for the mind. When a ruin ceases to be a "memorial," the poetics of ruins likewise ceases to exist).

The "ahistoricism" that Mortier rejects in the capricci is parallel to the dehistoricizing tendency that Janowitz sees in late eighteenth-century British writers on ruins.

31. Martin Hardie, *Water-colour Painting in Britain: I, The Eighteenth Century* (London: B. T. Batsford, 1966), 113; 89.

32. Kenneth Hudson, *A Social History of Museums: What the Visitors Thought* (Atlantic Highlands, N.J.: Humanities Press, 1975), 22.

33. For more on the Society of Dilettanti, see Sir Lionel Henry Cust's *History of the Society of Dilettanti* (New York: Macmillan, 1898) and Paulson's account of their attempts to control the proposed academy of artists in *Hogarth: His Life, His Art, and Times* (New Haven, Conn.: Yale University Press, 1971).

34. One exception to this rule is the "Temple of Augustus" erected for George IV at Virginia Water in 1826–27. This temple was part of the remains of a Roman settlement at Lepcis Magna in North Africa; as such it was one of the only "real" Classic ruins to be transported to England. For more on Virginia Water, see Watkin, *The English Vision,* 63.

35. Paulson likens the emblematic use of Classic architecture in English gardens to the construction of a sentence: "the temples drew on a vocabulary of Roman buildings . . . these known elements were used like words to make new sentences" (*Emblem and Expression,* 21).

36. For more on the Prix de Rome, see Philippe Grunchec, *The Grand Prix de Rome: Paintings from the École des Beaux Arts, 1797–1863* (Washington, D.C.: International Exhibitions Foundation, 1984).

37. This tendency to use the visual arts for nationalist purposes was extended by Napoleon and Alexandre Lenoir, the director of the Musée des Monuments Français, who revolutionized the concept of the museum by welcoming the public to view its patriotic collections. See Reitlinger, *Economics of Taste,* 91–93.

38. Martin Price, "The Picturesque Moment," in *From Sensibility to Romanticism,* ed. Frederick W. Hilles and Harold Bloom (New York: Oxford University Press, 1965), 285.

39. Although these "regimes" may be seen as corresponding roughly to the critical constructs of "Neoclassicism" and "Romanticism," it would be incorrect to assume their

equivalence. By using the term "regime" I have tried to displace traditional academic nomenclature so as to distinguish between two different ways of perceiving history, neither of which is bound to those entities called Neoclassicism and Romanticism. In this way, the interests of my project coincide with those of Robert Rosenblum, Howard Weinbrot, and others who have worked to show the inadequacy of these labels in describing specific instances of artistic production and audience reception in the eighteenth century. Thus the importance of the notion of overlap between the regimes: although patterns or tendencies toward one regime or the other may be evident in an artwork, in general the regimes are found in mixed proportion.

40. I have resisted defining this opposition between "regimes" in terms of politics and religion because I hope to retain my focus on the individual's relation to historical space, rather than offering what could only be a superficial treatment of elements that are treated thoroughly in traditional histories of the eighteenth century. See Paul Monod's "Painters and Party Politics in England, 1714–1760," *Eighteenth-Century Studies* 26, no. 3 (spring 1993): 367–98, for a discussion of how the regime of tradition might be associated with High Church/Catholic/Tory ideology, while the regime of change might be roughly matched to Low Church/Whig ideology. A similar opposition is articulated in Nigel Everett's *The Tory View of Landscape* (New Haven, Conn.: Yale University Press, 1994).

41. *Reading in Detail: Aesthetics and the Feminine* (New York: Methuen, 1987), 15.

42. Christopher Flint, " 'The Family Piece': Oliver Goldsmith and the Politics of the Everyday in Eighteenth-Century Domestic Portraiture," *Eighteenth-Century Studies* 29, no. 2 (winter 1995–96): 127–52.

43. Naomi Schor contends further that the campaign against the detail reflects a form of misogyny: "The matching up of sexual and aesthetic hierarchies is apparent in Reynolds's association of the sublime style with virility, [sic] it is for him 'the more manly, noble dignified manner . . .' ([Discourse] VIII, 153)" (*Reading in Detail*, 20). Because of the conventional association of the detail with the feminine, it has a "tendency to subvert an internal hierarchic ordering of the work of art which clearly subordinates the periphery to the center, the accessory to the principal, the foreground to the background" (Schor, *Reading in Detail*, 20).

44. Quoted in Macaulay, *Pleasure of Ruins*, 25.

45. N. M. Penzer, "The Warwick Vase," *Apollo* 62, no. 570 (December 1955): 183.

46. See Reitlinger, *Economics of Taste*, 62. The Warwick Vase was acquired in 1978 by the Glasgow Art Museum; a replica presently graces Warwick Castle.

47. Quoted in Palmeri, "History as Monument," 245.

48. *Transformations in Late Eighteenth-Century Art* (Princeton, N.J.: Princeton University Press, 1967), 40–46.

49. However, this is as far as Rosenblum's analysis goes; he neglects to pursue the widow image, for instance, as an expression of male anxiety concerning the fact that, in dying, they must leave "their" women to others. The chief "virtue" of the grieving widow surely lies in her status as a figure of wish-fulfillment for male viewers, promising that their control over their wives will extend beyond death.

50. Quoted by Devendra P. Varma, "Introduction," in *The Recess* (New York: Arno Press, 1972), xxiv.

51. William Gilpin, *Observations on the Western Parts of England* (Richmond, England: Richmond Publishing, 1973), 138–39.

52. Writing in 1750, the Reverend Dr. Pococke anticipates Gilpin's assessment of the monastic past. Moreover, as an example of its harmful effect on the British people, he claims to discern a persisting negative influence in the area surrounding the ruins of

ancient Glastonbury abbey: "The people here seem to have learned by tradition to lament the loss of the support they had from this abbey. . . . But it is much better the poor should earn their bread by labour than be maintained in idleness" (see Macaulay, *Pleasure of Ruins,* 347). The association made by both Pococke and Gilpin between monasticism and "idleness" reflects, on the one hand, a typically Protestant emphasis on the value of works in obtaining salvation, as opposed to the Catholic belief that faith alone is sufficient. On the other hand, it also reflects the advent of capitalism and its inherent antagonism to the Christian communism embodied in the monastic order.

53. Michael Levey, *Rococo to Revolution: Major Trends in Eighteenth-Century Painting* (London: Thames and Hudson, 1966), 166

54. Diana Ketcham, *Le Désert de Retz: A Late Eighteenth- Century Folly Garden, The Artful Landscape of Monsieur de Monville* (Cambridge, Mass.: MIT Press, 1994), 4. The Broken Column is one of twenty follies at the Désert, most of which have now been restored.

55. Although the language used here may imply that the regime of change was progressivist—and it was, at least in the discourses of imperialism and positivism—it was not so in practice, where it suggested more the possibility of *alternatives* to the status quo. For example, Hogarth's series "Industry and Idleness," while overtly bowing to disciplinary discourse in showing the good apprentice rewarded and the idle one destroyed, goes beyond presenting a simple polarity of choice to show how the parameters of the individual's "choice" are culturally restricted. By exposing this as an artificial reduction of alternatives, Hogarth shows his awareness of the fact "that his age has inherited and moulded itself on a system of cultural formulae . . . that simplify and create order" (see Paulson, *Emblem and Expression,* 73).

56. For more on Gandy, see Sir John Summerson's "The Vision of J. M. Gandy" in his *Heavenly Mansions, and Other Essays on Architecture* (New York: Norton, 1963).

57. Gandy's painting operates this way for viewers, but probably did not for Sir John Soane, Gandy's patron and architect of the Bank of England. In commissioning this painting of the destruction of his own work, Soane seems, on the one hand, to be indulging in masochism, while, on the other, narcissistically associating himself and England with the fallen grandeur of Rome. In this way, "The Bank of England in Ruins" had a private meaning for Soane that reflects the regime of tradition's mourning complex. For more on Soane, see Sir John Summerson, "Sir John Soane and the Furniture of Death," *Art Review* 163 (March 1978): 147–55.

58. Michael Fried, *Absorption and Theatricality: Painting and the Beholder in the Age of Diderot* (Berkeley: California University Press, 1980), 108–9.

59. Eric Rothstein, " 'Ideal Presence' and the 'Non Finito' in Eighteenth-Century Aesthetics," *Eighteenth-Century Studies* 9, no. 3 (spring 1976): 323.

60. Constable's first sketch of this subject was made in July of 1814; the image reproduced here was completed in 1828 and exhibited at the 1829 Royal Academy exhibition. Basil Taylor's *Constable: Paintings, Drawings and Watercolours* (New York: Phaidon, 1973) reproduces several versions of Hadleigh Castle in plates 120–23. The exhibition title of the painting is "Hadleigh Castle. The Mouth of the Thames—morning, after a stormy night."

61. For two different views of "Hadleigh Castle," see Paulson, *Literary Landscape: Turner and Constable* (New Haven, Conn.: Yale University Press, 1982) and James A. W. Heffernan, *The Re-Creation of Landscape: A Study of Wordsworth, Constable, and Turner* (Hanover, N.H.: University Press of New England, 1984). In brief, Paulson sees the primary castle tower as a blocking agent that prevents the viewer from access to the serene

landscape in the background (126–33). While this interpretation roughly coincides with mine, Heffernan argues for a more autobiographical approach: "The historic authority of the dark ruin, which is charged with all the anguish of Constable's recent personal history, is ultimately overpowered by the sublime magnificence of the sunlit sky, which here becomes a symbol of renewal" (78).

62. Galard, "La Poétique des ruines," 233. Ruins are the ideal site for love; modesty is less forbidding there, and desire is more ambitious. To enter into a painting of ruins is to return to a purer state of being (the state of nature?), to penetrate the world of myth.

63. More on the eighteenth-century British love of Italian landscape can be found in William Gaunt's *Bandits in a Landscape: A Study of Romantic Painting from Caravaggio to Delacroix* (New York: Studio Publications, 1937).

64. Michel Serres has pointed out that the painting—"tableau" in French—is a "tabulation" of sorts. Walmsley appears to be giving the viewer this kind of diagrammatic summation. For more on the painting as tabulation, see Serres's "Turner Translates Carnot," in *Calligram: Essays in New Art History From France*, ed. Norman Bryson, 154–64 (New York: Cambridge University Press, 1988).

65. Anne Janowitz's *England's Ruins* treats this particular aspect of the ruin's significance in detail.

66. Ronald Paulson, *Breaking and Remaking: Aesthetic Practice in England, 1700–1820* (New Brunswick, N.J.: Rutgers University Press, 1989), 15. Jeremy Gregory cites a 1773 incident in which the dean of St. Paul's requested that members of the Royal Academy furnish religious paintings for his church. However, the Bishop of London cancelled this plan and quashed the eager Academy painters—who were ready to donate their work—out of fear that such images in St. Paul's would be considered "an artful introduction of popery." See "Anglicanism and the Arts: Religion, Culture, and Politics in the Eighteenth Century" in *Culture, Politics and Society in Britain, 1660–1800*, ed. Jeremy Black and Jeremy Gregory (New York: Manchester University Press, 1991), 82–109.

67. Reitlinger, *Economics of Taste*, 99. See also Margaret Aston, "English Ruins and English History: The Dissolution and the Sense of the Past," *Journal of the Warburg and Courtauld Institutes* 36 (1973): 231–55; Martin S. Briggs, *Goths and Vandals: A Study of the Destruction, Neglect and Preservation of Historical Buildings in England* (London: Constable, 1952); and Eamon Duffy, *The Stripping of the Altars: Traditional Religion in England c. 1400–c. 1580* (New Haven, Conn.: Yale University Press, 1992).

68. These dangerous, somehow unlawful forms of utterance are described as "the unspeakable" by Eve K. Sedgwick in her study of the literary Gothic, *The Coherence of Gothic Conventions* (New York: Methuen, 1986).

69. Roy Porter, *English Society in the Eighteenth Century* (New York: Penguin, 1990), 101.

70. Quoted in Macaulay, *Pleasure of Ruins*, 341. Keate (1729–97) was also a painter of ruins (see Hardie, *Water-colour Painting in Britain*, 112).

71. Quoted in Macaulay, *Pleasure of Ruins*, 342.

72. This split is literalized to this day in the existence of "divided churches" such as the parish church of St. Nicholas in Arundel (Sussex), which has for centuries featured separate Anglican and Roman Catholic worship areas in a single fourteenth- and fifteenth-century building. In the case of St. Nicholas, the Catholic Fitzalan Chapel within it was maintained by the powerful Catholic Dukes of Norfolk, one of whom is the father of the heroines of *The Recess*. See Thomas Zaniello's unpublished paper, "Services for the Dead and the Divided Victorian Church," presented at the Interdisciplinary Conference on Nineteenth-Century Studies, April 4–5, 1997, at The University of California, Berkeley.

73. *The Recess* went through "four editions as of 1792, a fifth in 1804, an Irish edition in 1791, and various printings and abridgements in 1800, 1802, 1824, 1827, and 1840. Its French translation appeared in 1787 and it had a Portuguese version in 1806" (Varma, "Introduction," xxv). One 1802 abridgement noted by Ralph Mayo in *The English Novel in the Magazines, 1740–1815* was nearly one fifth of the length of the original, and was published in the *Marvellous Magazine,* which had a reputation for presenting drastically cut versions of Gothic novels (Evanston, Ill.: Northwestern University Press, 1962, 368–69, 577).

74. J. M. S. Tompkins, "Foreword," in *The Recess,* ed. Devendra P. Varma (New York: Arno Press, 1972), i; quoted in Varma's "Introduction" to *The Recess,* xxv.

75. Although Thomas Leland's *Longsword, Earl of Salisbury* (1762) is most often credited as being the first historical novel in English, *The Recess* may, as Varma argues, have been more influential in creating a "historical" trend in novels. Varma cites other historical novels that were published soon after *The Recess,* including Anne Fuller's *Alan Fitz-Osborne, an Historical Tale* (1787); *William of Normandy, An Historical Novel* (1787); Rosetta Ballin's *The Statue Room* (1790), set in Elizabeth's reign; Mrs. Harley's *The Castle of Mowbray* (1788), set in the reign of Edward I; Henry Siddon's *William Wallace, or the Highland Hero* (1791); and the anonymous *Edward de Courcy* (1794), set during the Wars of the Roses ("Introduction," xxvii–xxx).

76. Interest in Lee has been sporadic in the twentieth century; recent critical attention will culminate in a new edition of *The Recess* scheduled for publication by University of Kentucky Press. For various critical views on *The Recess,* see J. M. S. Tompkins, *The Popular Novel in England 1770–1800* (1932; reprint, Lincoln, Neb.: Nebraska University Press, 1962); Montague Summers, *The Gothic Quest: A History of the Gothic Novel* (1938; reprint, New York: Russell & Russell, 1964); Jane Spencer, *The Rise of the Woman Novelist: From Aphra Behn to Jane Austen* (Oxford: Blackwell, 1986); Bette B. Roberts, "Sophia Lee's *The Recess* (1785): The Ambivalence of Female Gothicism" *Massachusetts Studies in English* 6, nos. 3 & 4 (1979): 68–82; Jayne Lewis, " 'Ev'ry Lost Relation': Historical Fictions and Sentimental Incidents in Sophia Lee's *The Recess,*" *Eighteenth-Century Fiction* 7, no. 2 (January 1995): 166–84; and Megan Lynn Isaac, "Sophia Lee and the Gothic of Female Community," *Studies in the Novel* 28, no. 2 (summer 1996): 200–18. See also April Alliston's unpublished dissertation, "Epistles from the Ladies; or, *Genre,* and the Transmission of Narrative" (New Haven, Conn.: Yale University, 1988) and the related "The Value of a Literary Legacy: Retracing the Transmission of Value through Female Lines," *Yale Journal of Criticism* 4 (1990): 109–27. Treating *The Recess* in the context of French and English epistolary novels, Alliston explores how the patterns of narrative transmission in these novels reflect on the cultural position of women and their distinctive strategies of inheritance within patriarchal society.

77. Quoted in Varma, "Introduction," xvii.

78. Sophia Lee, *The Recess* (New York: Arno Press, 1972), 1:42. All subsequent references to *The Recess* will be taken from this edition and will be noted parenthetically in my text.

79. Lee's choice of saint names for both convent and estate may be designed to contribute to the themes of her novel: St. Winifred was a Welsh virgin who, rather than be defiled by a savage suitor, was decapitated; St. Vincent of Saragossa was a leader of the early Christian church who, rather than abandon his faith, was roasted on a gridiron by the Romans. See David Farmer, *The Oxford Dictionary of Saints* (Oxford: Clarendon, 1978).

80. Among Matilda's various trials, she is forced to conceal her identity, not only as Mary's daughter, but as Leicester's wife (because of Elizabeth's jealousy); is betrayed by

her aunt, Lady Mortimer (2: 66–67, 70–71); falls into madness upon the murder of Leicester (2: 72); is kidnapped by her amorous, yet treacherous cousin, Lord Mortimer (2: 89–111); gives birth to a daughter while in Mortimer's power (2: 97); helplessly witnesses the rape and suicide of her best friend, Rose Cecil (2: 100–102); is transported to Jamaica, imprisoned, and lamed by rheumatic fever (2: 113–46); returns to England to find her sister mad; and, in the third volume of *The Recess,* is imprisoned again, in which setting her daughter is poisoned (3: 339–41).

81. Although I examine *The Recess* here through the Gothic lens, critics in general have been troubled by its apparent generic indeterminacy. Montague Summers considered it to be an example of the blending of historical and gothic concerns, whereas Robert D. Hume argues that in spite of its "use of historical personages, [it] is in reality a sentimental-domestic novel transposed into a supposedly historical situation with Gothic trimmings added for savor" ("Gothic Versus Romantic: A Revaluation of the Gothic Novel," *Publications of the Modern Language Association* 84, no. 2 (March 1969): 283). Taking the kernel of Hume's somewhat derisive classification, Jayne Lewis contends that *The Recess* combines the techniques of both historiography and the sentimental novel in order to critique both forms: "Collaborating critically as much with Georgian historians as with her fellow sentimental novelist, Lee uses the figure of an injured queen to investigate the secretly twinned structures of historiography and sensibility" (" 'Ev'ry Lost Relation,' " 168).

82. Claire Kahane, "Gothic Mirrors and Feminine Identity," *Centennial Review* 24, no. 1 (winter 1980): 45–46.

83. This leads to another key difference between Kahane's definition and *The Recess* that I have no space to pursue: there is no "powerful male figure" to authorize threats of violence—the violence stems from a female, Elizabeth. In fact, men in *The Recess* are fated to die pitifully as pawns in power games between Elizabeth, Mary, Ellinor, and Matilda. For instance, Leicester, Matilda's first love, continually overestimates his own abilities and is hence overcome by Elizabeth's cunning: thinking himself safely escaped to France, he is murdered in his bed by Elizabeth's emissaries. The dominance of women in Lee's novel may be connected to one of Kahane's further observations about the Gothic: "[W]hat I see repeatedly locked into the forbidden center of the Gothic . . . is the spectral presence of a dead-undead mother, archaic and all-encompassing, a ghost signifying the problematics of female identity which the heroine must confront" ("Gothic Mirrors," 47–48).

Indeed, Elizabeth may be read, on one level, as the evil, monstrous half of the absent mother that Matilda and Ellinor both seek and fear; on the other hand, they idealize their biological mother, Mary (who is also Elizabeth's cousin), whom neither of them ever meet. Especially given the diminution of the male role in *The Recess,* it is more than plausible to read this novel in terms of the struggle to define female identity and lineage through the mother. Mary's absence and her imprisonment dictate, to a large extent, the actions of her two daughters. Moreover, what may be viewed as the split in the mother figure between Elizabeth and Mary is a phenomenon of ambivalence that has been explored by many, including C. G. Jung; Dorothy Dinnerstein, in *The Mermaid and the Minotaur: Sexual Arrangements and Human Malaise* (New York: Harper & Row, 1976), and Nancy Chodorow, in *The Reproduction of Mothering:Psychoanalysis and the Sociology of Gender* (Berkeley: California University Press, 1978).

84. For a recent study of the supernatural in British drama and fiction of the eighteenth century, see Emma J. Clery, *The Rise of Supernatural Fiction, 1762–1800* (New York: Cambridge University Press, 1995).

85. The fact that *The Recess* defines these lineages in female terms and places women in the historical limelight leads Jane Spencer to argue that Lee believes romantic love to

be "an illusion standing in the way of women's access to the romance of mother-daughter reconciliation and female power" (*Rise of the Woman Novelist,* 200).

86. " 'Ev'ry Lost Relation,' " 183.

87. *Simulations,* trans. Paul Foss, Paul Patton, and Philip Beitchman (New York: Semiotext(e), 1983), 19.

Chapter 4

1. Janis P. Stout, "Jane Austen's Proposal Scenes and the Limitations of Language," *Studies in the Novel* 14, no. 3 (fall 1982): 320–21.

2. This narcissism is seen in Leicester's use of portrait miniatures in *The Recess*: before attaching himself to Matilda, Leicester tries both Mary and Queen Elizabeth, obtaining miniatures of both. Rather than confess his attraction to Mary (and the fact that he has sent a marriage proposal to her), he flamboyantly throws her portrait into the Thames (1: 122). Later, when he is being hunted down by his treacherous domestics, he gives Elizabeth's miniature to Matilda, saying, "Look but at that picture, and you will find an indubitable evidence of my rank" (1: 94). Leicester's portrait miniatures are thus signs of his interest in playing one Queen against the other, and in entertaining romantic liaisons primarily for his own sense of worth.

3. Mary Shelley, *Frankenstein; or, the Modern Prometheus* (New York: Signet, 1965), 136. All subsequent references to *Frankenstein* will be taken from this edition and will be indicated parenthetically within the text.

4. The ideal aspects of their mother's love are illustrated symbolically in her name: she was both "beau" and "fort," beautiful and strong.

5. Norman Bryson, *Calligram: Essays in New Art History From France* (New York: Cambridge University Press, 1988), xv.

6. For more on the social function of the portrait, see Marcia Pointon, *Hanging the Head: Portraiture and Social Formation in Eighteenth-Century England* (New Haven, Conn.: Yale University Press, 1993).

7. John Berger, et al., *Ways of Seeing* (New York: Penguin, 1972), 52.

8. Although it might be argued that the nude is a "special case" that must be studied apart from "normal" portraiture, I would contend that such a separation cannot be made, for both historical and theoretical reasons. First, in historical practice, the nude was considered to be appropriate artistic subject matter. The painter of Nell Gwyn, Sir Peter Lely (1618–80), was one of the most prolific portraitists of the seventeenth century, and was not particularly noted for his nudes. From Lely's example, it can be concluded that, at least from the perspective of the painter, nudes and clothed portraits were viewed as a presenting a single common difficulty—the representation of the human figure. Furthermore, nude and "normal" portraiture share a fascination with the human body as the principal site of beauty and erotic stimulus.

9. Adam Smith, *Essays on Philosophical Subjects: The Glasgow Edition of the Works and Correspondence of Adam Smith,* ed. W. P. D. Wightman and J. C. Bryce (New York: Oxford University Press, 1980), 3:182.

10. Ibid., 181.

11. Richard Wendorf, *The Elements of Life: Biography and Portrait Painting in Stuart and Georgian England* (Oxford: Clarendon, 1990), 132–33.

12. George C. Williamson and Henry L. D. Engleheart, *George Engleheart 1750–1829, Miniature Painter to George III* (London: George Bell, 1902) 38.

13. M. Kirby Talley Jr., " 'All Good Pictures Crack': Sir Joshua Reynolds's Practice and Studio," in *Reynolds,* ed. Nicholas Penny (New York: Abrams, 1986), 59. For a broader

survey of portrait prices among the London painters, see Marcia Pointon, "Portrait Painting as a Business Enterprise in London in the 1780s," *Art History* 7, no. 2 (June 1984): 187–205.

14. Patricia Fumerton, "'Secret' Arts: Elizabethan Miniatures and Sonnets," *Representations* 15 (summer 1986): 97.

15. Patrick Noon, "Miniatures on the Market," in *The English Miniature,* John Murdoch et al. (New Haven, Conn.: Yale University Press, 1981), 192.

16. This number is counted as one of Cosway's boasts by George Williamson, who suggests that Cosway was probably referring not to finished miniatures, but rather to first sittings (See Williamson's *Richard Cosway* [London: George Bell, 1897], 102). Certainly Cosway's output was greater than that of the majority of his fellow artists, such as William Wood, whose records show that he still painted over sixty miniatures per year: "As he was in no more favorable position than many of his competitors, these figures are another index of the extraordinary bulk of miniature paintings of this period" (Graham Reynolds, *English Portrait Miniatures,* rev. ed. (New York: Cambridge University Press, 1988), 154–55.

17. Noon, "Miniatures on the Market," 197.

18. See Sue McKechnie, *British Silhouette Artists and Their Work, 1760–1860* (Totowa, N.J.: Sotheby, Parke Bernet, 1978), 3. The term "silhouette" was not used in England until 1835, when the French artist Augustin Edouart published a book of "silhouette likenesses" in English.

19. McKechnie, *British Silhouette Artists,* 41. The pairing of watch and miniature was a fashion rage in the 1770s and 1780s: "source after source tells us that two watches, or one watch and one miniature, suspended from ribbons or watch chains, were the prevailing mode. 'Two watches *were universal* unless a picture was substituted for one of them' said the *Ipswich Journal* of 1788. But by 1792 the *Lady's Magazine* firmly pronounced their death knell: 'watches, trinkets, etc. quite mauvais ton'" (See Neil McKendrick, John Brewer, and J. H. Plumb, *The Birth of a Consumer Society: The Commercialization of Eighteenth-Century Enlgand* [Bloomington: Indiana University Press, 1982], 75).

20. Williamson, *Cosway,* 115.

21. Susan Stewart, *On Longing: Narratives of the Miniature, the Gigantic, the Souvenir, the Collection* (Baltimore: Johns Hopkins University Press, 1984), 126.

22. George C. Williamson's biography of Cosway, entitled *Richard Cosway* (London: George Bell, 1897), has been surpassed by Stephen Lloyd's *Richard and Maria Cosway: Regency Artists of Taste and Fashion* (Edinburgh: Scottish National Portrait Gallery, 1995).

23. Frank Davis, "New Interest in Eighteenth Century Miniatures," *Country Life* (1958): 457.

24. Williamson, *Cosway,* 100.

25. For a different view of the representational qualities of both miniature and standard oil portraits, see Shearer West, who contends that "miniature painting allowed artists to move away from the idealism of power portraiture. Although at times miniatures were virtually smaller versions of grand manner portraits, in most instances, they were meant to be seen only by a loved one or close relation, rendering idealisation unnecessary" ("Patronage and Power: The Role of the Portrait in Eighteenth-Century England," in *Culture, Politics and Society in Britain, 1660–1800,* ed. Jeremy Black and Jeremy Gregory [New York: Manchester University Press, 1991], 146).

26. Williamson, *Cosway,* 100–101.

27. Ibid., 107.

28. Along with many of his contemporaries, Cosway "had early trained himself upon

49. For a more thorough treatment of the circle of expression than I can afford here, see Ronald Paulson's "The Pictorial Circuit and Related Structures in 18th-Century England" in *The Varied Pattern: Studies in the 18th Century,* ed. Peter Hughes and David Williams (Toronto: A. M. Hakkert, 1971), 165–87.

50. Paulson, *Breaking and Remaking: Aesthetic Practice in England, 1700–1820* (New Brunswick, N.J.: Rutgers University Press, 1989), 200–201.

51. For more on the stereotypic effect of expression, see Brewster Rogerson's "The Art of Painting the Passions," *Journal of the History of Ideas* 14 (1953): 68–94. See also Alastair Smart's "Dramatic Gesture and Expression in the Age of Hogarth and Reynolds," *Apollo* 82 (1965): 90–97.

52. Paulson, "Pictorial Circuit," 171.

53. Eric Rothstein, *Systems of Order and Inquiry,* 204–5.

54. For example, in "Man Not Providence: Fielding's *Amelia* as a Novel of Social Criticism" (*Forum for Modern Language Studies* 20 [1984]), Mona Scheuermann argues that "Booth, who could be expected to learn from his various follies . . . , shows no basic change" (107). Similarly, in *Fielding and the Nature of the Novel* (Cambridge, Mass.: Harvard University Press, 1968), Robert Alter considers *Amelia* to be a "problem novel" partially because of Booth's surprise conversion.

55. In my discussion of Amelia's double ending I am indebted to both Sheldon Sacks's *Fiction and the Shape of Belief* (Berkeley: California University Press, 1964) and Eric Rothstein's *Systems of Order and Inquiry in Later Eighteenth- Century Fiction* (Berkeley: California University Press, 1975).

56. John Zomchick, *Family and the Law in Eighteenth-Century Fiction: The Public Conscience in the Private Sphere* (New York: Cambridge University Press, 1993), 151.

57. In "The Two Amelias: Henry Fielding and Elizabeth Justice," *English Literary History* 62, no. 2 (1995), Elizabeth Kraft emphasizes the commercial nature of the transaction that triggers Amelia's transformation into heiress: "[I]t is significant that while Amelia refuses to 'sell herself' for money, she does not hesitate to pawn her portrait. . . . When Booth sees his wife for the first time after he has learned of this recovery [of her fortune], Amelia appears transformed. She is the aesthetic embodiment of wifeliness, her pawned portrait come to life" (320). Although I consider Amelia's action more in the light of a gift of self that redeems Booth from his error, I acknowledge that she is also sacrificing herself by stooping to sell her own image, and is thus inevitably—if only momentarily and only to a slight degree—involved in the same commodified vision of the erotic that Col. James and the Noble Lord embody.

58. For more on Robinson's role in the narrative, see Zomchick, who suggests that "Robinson is Booth's double" (*Family and the Law,* 153).

59. Conway, "Fielding's *Amelia,*" 45. For a contrasting view, see Angela Smallwood's *Fielding and the Woman Question* (New York: St. Martin's Press, 1989), in which Smallwood argues that the ending show how Booth "is notoriously passive and inert and . . . stands still to contemplate his passions and his problems," while "Amelia has the training to translate her tenderness and concern into action" (171).

AFTERWORD

1. See Greenblatt, *Renaissance Self-Fashioning: From More to Shakespeare* (Chicago: University of Chicago Press, 1980).

2. John Ricchetti, "The Public Sphere and the Eighteenth-Century Novel: Social Criticism and Narrative Enactment," *Eighteenth-Century Life* 16 (November 1992): 117.

Works Cited

Ackermann, Rudolf. *The Microcosm of London; or, London in Miniature.* London: T. Bensley, 1808–11.
Adam, Robert. *The Ruins of the Palace of the Emperor Diocletian at Spalatro in Dalmatia.* London: Robert Adam, 1764.
Allen, Brian. "The Landscape." In *Vauxhall Gardens,* by T. J. Edelstein, 17–24. New Haven, Conn.: Yale Center for British Art, 1983.
Alliston, April. "Epistles from the Ladies; or *Genre,* and the Transmission of Narrative." Dissertation. New Haven, Conn.: Yale University, 1988.
———. "The Value of a Literary Legacy: Retracing the Transmission of Value through Female Lines." *Yale Journal of Criticism* 4 (1990): 109–27.
Alter, Robert. *Fielding and the Nature of the Novel.* Cambridge, Mass.: Harvard University Press, 1968.
———. "The Picaroon as Fortune's Plaything." In *Essays on the Eighteenth-Century Novel,* edited by R. D. Spector, 131–53. Bloomington: Indiana University Press, 1965.
Altick, Richard D. *The English Common Reader: A Social History of the Mass Reading Public 1800–1900.* Chicago: University Press of Chicago, 1957.
———. *The Shows of London.* Cambridge, Mass.: Harvard University Press, 1978.
Anderson, Benedict. *Imagined Communities: Reflections on the Origin and Spread of Nationalism.* 2d. ed. New York: Verso, 1991.
Andrews, Malcolm. *The Search for the Picturesque: Landscape Aesthetics and Tourism in Britain, 1760–1800.* Stanford, Calif.: Stanford University Press, 1989.

Ariés, Philippe, and Georges Duby, eds. *A History of Private Life*. 4 vols. Cambridge, Mass.: Belknap Press, 1987–1991.
Art of Drawing, and Painting in Water-Colours. London: J. Peele, 1732.
Arts Council of Great Britain. *The Age of Neoclassicism*. London: Arts Council, 1972.
Ashton, T. S. *An Economic History of England: The 18th Century*. London: Methuen, 1955.
Aston, Margaret. "English Ruins and English History: The Dissolution and the Sense of the Past." *Journal of the Warburg and Courtauld Institutes* 36 (1973): 231–55.
Aubin, Robert Arnold. *Topographical Poetry in XVIII-Century England*. New York: Modern Language Association, 1936.
Austen, Jane. *Persuasion*. Edited and introduction by D. W. Harding. New York: Penguin, 1987.
Bakhtin, Mikhail. *The Dialogic Imagination: Four Essays*. Edited by Michael Holquist. Translated by Caryl Emerson and Michael Holquist. Austin: Texas University Press, 1981.
Ballin, Rosetta. *The Statue Room*. London: H. D. Symonds, 1790.
Bardo, Pamela Pierrepont. *English and Continental Portrait Miniatures: The Latter-Schlesinger Collection*. Preface by Graham Reynolds. New Orleans: New Orleans Museum of Art, 1978.
Barker, Felix, and Ralph Hyde. *London As It Might Have Been*. London: John Murphy, 1982.
Barton, Stuart. *Monumental Follies: An Exposition on the Eccentric Edifices of Britain*. Worthing, Sussex: Lyle Publications, 1972.
Battestin, Martin C., and Ruth R. Battestin. *Henry Fielding: A Life*. New York: Routledge, 1989.
Baudrillard, Jean. *Simulations*. Translated by Paul Foss, Paul Patton, and Philip Beitchman. New York: Semiotext(e), 1983.
Bayne-Powell, Robert. *Catalogue of Portrait Miniatures in the Fitzwilliam Museum, Cambridge*. New York: Cambridge University Press, 1985.
Belanger, Terry. "Publishers and Writers in Eighteenth-Century England." In *Books and Their Readers in Eighteenth-Century England,* edited by Isobel Rivers, 5–26. New York: St. Martin's Press, 1982.
Bender, John. *Imagining the Penitentiary: Fiction and the Architecture of Mind in Eighteenth-Century England*. Chicago: University of Chicago Press, 1987.
Benedict, Barbara M. "Consumptive Communities: Commodifying Nature in Spa Society." *The Eighteenth Century: Theory and Interpretation* 36, no. 3 (1995): 203–19.
Benjamin, Walter. *Illuminations*. Edited and introduction by Hannah Arendt. New York: Harcourt, Brace and World, 1968.
Bennett, Tony. *The Birth of the Museum: History, Theory, Politics*. New York: Routledge, 1995.
Berger, John, Sven Blomberg, Chris Fox, Michael Dibb, and Richard Hollis. *Ways of Seeing*. New York: Penguin, 1972.
Bicknell, Peter. Introduction to *Beauty, Horror, and Immensity: Picturesque Landscape in Britain, 1750–1850,* ix–xvi. New York: Cambridge University Press, 1981.
Black, Jeremy. "Ideology, History, Xenophobia and the World of Print in Eighteenth-Century England." In *Culture, Politics and Society in Britain, 1660–1800,* edited by Jeremy Black and Jeremy Gregory, 184–216. New York: Manchester University Press, 1991.
Black, Jeremy, and Jeremy Gregory, eds. *Culture, Politics and Society in Britain, 1660–1800*. New York: Manchester University Press, 1991.
Bond, Richmond P. *Queen Anne's American Kings*. New York: Oxford University Press, 1952.
Borsay, Peter. " 'All the town's a stage': Urban Ritual and Ceremony 1660–1800." In *The*

Works Cited

Transformation of English Provincial Towns 1600–1800, edited by Peter Clark. London: Hutchinson, 1984.

———. "The Rise of the Promenade: The Social and Cultural Use of Space in the English Provincial Town c. 1660–1800." *British Journal for Eighteenth-Century Studies* (1986): 125–48.

Boucé, Paul-Gabriel. *The Novels of Tobias Smollett.* Translated by Antonia White. New York: Longman, 1976.

Bourdieu, Pierre. *La Noblesse d'état: grandes écoles et esprit de corps.* Paris: Les Éditions de minuit, 1989.

———. *Outline of a Theory of Practice.* Translated by Richard Nice. New York: Cambridge University Press, 1977.

Briggs, Martin S. *Goths and Vandals: A Study of the Destruction, Neglect and Preservation of Historical Buildings in England.* London: Constable, 1952.

Brückmann, Patricia. "Sir Walter Elliot's Bath Address." *Modern Philology* 80 (August 1982): 56–60.

Bryson, Norman, ed. *Calligram: Essays in New Art History From France.* New York: Cambridge University Press, 1988.

Bryson, Norman. *Word and Image: French Painting of the Ancien Régime.* New York: Cambridge University Press, 1983

Buchanan, Brenda. "The Great Bath Road, 1700–1830." *Bath History* 4 (1992): 71–94.

Burney, Fanny. *Evelina; or the History of a Young Lady's Entrance into the World.* Edited by Edward and Lillian Bloom. New York: Oxford University Press, 1968.

Butler, Marilyn. *Jane Austen and the War of Ideas.* New York: Oxford University Press, 1975.

Butturini, Paula. "What's Doing in Rome." *New York Times* 6 October 1996, travel section: 10.

Campbell, Jill. *Natural Masques: Gender and Identity in Fielding's Plays and Novels.* Stanford, Calif.: Stanford University Press, 1994.

Carter, John. *Views of Ancient Buildings in England Drawn in different Tours.* London: John Carter, 1786–93.

Castle, Terry. *Clarissa's Ciphers: Meaning and Disruption in Richardson's Clarissa.* Ithaca, N.Y.: Cornell University Press, 1982.

———. *Masquerade and Civilization: The Carnivalesque in Eighteenth-Century English Culture and Fiction.* Stanford, Calif.: Stanford University Press, 1986.

Chancellor, E. Beresford. *The Eighteenth Century in London: An Account of Its Social Life and Arts.* London: B. T. Batsford, 1920.

Charlesworth, Michael. "The Ruined Abbey: Picturesque and Gothic Values." In *The Politics of the Picturesque: Literature, Landscape, and Aesthetics since 1770,* edited by Stephen Copley and Peter Garside, 62–80. New York: Cambridge University Press, 1994.

Chodorow, Nancy. *The Reproduction of Mothering: Psychoanalysis and the Sociology of Gender.* Berkeley: California University Press, 1978.

Clark, Thomas Blake. *Omai: First Polynesian Ambassador to England.* Honolulu: Hawaii University Press, 1969.

Clayton, Jay. *Romantic Vision and the Novel.* New York: Cambridge University Press, 1987.

Clery, Emma J. *The Rise of Supernatural Fiction, 1762–1800.* New York: Cambridge University Press, 1995.

Clifford, James. "On Collecting Art and Culture." In *The Predicament of Culture: Twentieth-Century Ethnography, Literature, and Art.* Cambridge, Mass.: Harvard University Press, 1988.

Cohen, Ralph. *The Art of Discrimination: Thomson's "The Seasons" and the Language of Criticism.* New York: Routledge & Kegan Paul, 1964.

Colley, Linda. *Britons: Forging the Nation 1707–1837.* New Haven, Conn.: Yale University Press, 1992.

Combe, William. *The Three Tours of Doctor Syntax.* London: G. Routledge, 1800.

Conway, Alison. "Fielding's *Amelia* and the Aesthetics of Virtue." *Eighteenth-Century Fiction* 8, no. 1 (October 1995): 35–50.

Cozens, Alexander. *A New Method of Assisting the Invention in Drawing Original Compositions of Landscape.* London: A. Cozens, 1785.

Cranfield, G. A. *The Development of the Provincial Newspaper 1700–1760.* New York: Oxford University Press, 1962.

Cressy, David. *Literacy and the Social Order: Reading and Writing in Tudor and Stuart England.* New York: Cambridge University Press, 1980.

Cust, Sir Lionel Henry. *History of the Society of Dilettanti.* New York: Macmillan, 1898.

Davidoff, Leonore, and Catherine Hall. *Family Fortunes: Men and Women of the English Middle Class, 1780–1850.* Chicago: University Press of Chicago, 1987.

Davis, Frank. "New Interest in Eighteenth Century Miniatures." *Country Life* (1958): 456–57.

Dayes, Edward. *The Works of the Late Edward Dayes, Containing An Excursion through the Principal Parts of Derbyshire and Yorkshire.* London: Mrs. Dayes, 1805.

Dickinson, H. T. *Liberty and Property: Political Ideology in Eighteenth-Century Britain.* New York: Holmes and Meier, 1977.

Dinnerstein, Dorothy. *The Mermaid and the Minotaur: Sexual Arrangements and Human Malaise.* New York: Harper & Row, 1976.

Doody, Margaret Anne. *Frances Burney: The Life in the Works.* New Brunswick, N.J.: Rutgers University Press, 1988.

Douglas, Aileen. *Uneasy Sensations: Smollett and the Body.* Chicago: University Press of Chicago, 1995.

Duffy, Eamon. *The Stripping of the Altars: Traditional Religion in England c.1400–c.1580.* New Haven, Conn.: Yale University Press, 1992.

Edelstein, T. J. *Vauxhall Gardens.* New Haven, Conn.: Yale Center for British Art, 1983.

Edward de Courcy. London: 1794.

Epstein, Julia. *The Iron Pen.* Madison: Wisconsin University Press, 1989.

Erickson, Lee. "The Economy of Novel Reading: Jane Austen and the Circulating Library." *Studies in English Literature, 1500–1900* 30, no. 4 (fall 1990): 573–90.

Everett, Nigel. *The Tory View of Landscape.* New Haven, Conn.: Yale University Press, 1994.

Farmer, David. *The Oxford Dictionary of Saints.* Oxford: Clarendon, 1978.

Feather, John. "British Publishing in the Eighteenth Century: A Preliminary Subject Analysis." *The Library,* 6th ser., 8, no. 1 (March 1986): 32–46.

———. *A History of British Publishing.* New York: Croom Helm, 1988.

———. *The Provincial Book Trade in Eighteenth-Century England.* New York: Cambridge University Press, 1985.

Fielding, Henry. *Amelia.* Edited by Martin C. Battestin. Oxford: Clarendon, 1983.

Flint, Christopher. "'The Family Piece': Oliver Goldsmith and the Politics of the Everyday in Eighteenth-Century Domestic Portraiture." *Eighteenth-Century Studies* 29, no. 2 (winter 1995–96): 127–52.

Foreman, Carolyn Thomas. *Indians Abroad, 1493–1938.* Norman: Oklahoma University Press, 1943.

Works Cited

Foucault, Michel. *The Archaeology of Knowledge and The Discourse on Language.* Translated by A. M. Sheridan Smith. New York: Pantheon, 1972.

———. *Discipline and Punish: The Birth of the Prison.* Translated by Alan Sheridan. New York: Vintage, 1979.

———. *The History of Sexuality, Volume I: An Introduction.* Translated by Robert Hurley. New York: Vintage, 1980.

Frank, Joseph. *The Idea of Spatial Form.* New Brunswick, N.J.: Rutgers University Press, 1991.

Fredman, A. G. "The Picaresque in Decline." In *English Writers of the Eighteenth Century,* edited by John Middendorf, 189–208. New York: Columbia University Press, 1971.

Freud, Sigmund. *The Standard Edition of the Complete Psychological Works of Sigmund Freud.* Vols. 1–24. Translated and edited by James Strachey, Anna Freud, Alix Strachey, and Alan Tyson. London: Hogarth Press, 1953–74.

Fried, Michael. *Absorption and Theatricality: Painting and the Beholder in the Age of Diderot.* Berkeley: California University Press, 1980.

Fuller, Anne. *Alan Fitz-Osborne, An Historical Tale.* London: T. Wilkins, 1787.

Fumerton, Patricia. "'Secret' Arts: Elizabethan Miniatures and Sonnets." *Representations* 15 (summer 1986): 57–97.

Galard, Jean. "La poétique des ruines." *Word and Image* 4, no. 1 (January–March 1988): 231–37.

Gaunt, William. *Bandits in a Landscape: A Study of Romantic Painting from Caravaggio to Delacroix.* New York: Studio Publications, 1937.

George, M. Dorothy. *Political Caricature to 1792: A Study of Opinions and Propaganda.* Oxford: Clarendon, 1959.

Gilpin, William. *Observations on the Western Parts of England.* Introduction by Sutherland Lyall. Richmond, England: Richmond Publishing, 1973.

Girouard, Mark. *Cities and People: A Social and Architectural History.* New Haven, Conn.: Yale University Press, 1981.

———. *The English Country House: A Social and Architectural History.* New Haven, Conn.: Yale University Press, 1978.

———. *The English Town: A History of Urban Life.* New Haven, Conn.: Yale University Press, 1990.

Goffman, Erving. *Frame Analysis: An Essay on the Organization of Experience.* Cambridge, Mass.: Harvard University Press, 1974.

———. *The Presentation of Self in Everyday Life.* New York: Doubleday, 1959.

Goldsmith, Oliver. *The Bee and Other Essays.* Edited by Humphrey Milford. New York: Oxford University Press, 1914.

Goldstein, Laurence. *Ruins and Empire: The Evolution of a Theme in Augustan and Romantic Literature.* Pittsburgh: Pittsburgh University Press, 1977.

Graves, Algernon. *The Society of Artists of Great Britain, 1760–91, and the Free Society of Artists, 1761–83.* Bath, UK (Somerset): Kingsmead Reprints, 1969.

Greenblatt, Stephen. *Renaissance Self-Fashioning: From More to Shakespeare.* Chicago: University of Chicago Press, 1980.

Gregory, Jeremy. "Anglicanism and the Arts: Religion, Culture, and Politics in the Eighteenth Century." In *Culture, Politics and Society in Britain, 1660–1800,* edited by Jeremy Black and Jeremy Gregory, 82–109. New York: Manchester University Press, 1991.

Grunchec, Philippe. *The Grand Prix de Rome: Paintings from the École des Beaux Arts, 1797–1863.* Washington, D.C.: International Exhibitions Foundation, 1984.

Grundy, Isobel. "*Persuasion,* or The Triumph of Cheerfulness." In *Jane Austen's Business:*

Her World and Her Profession, edited by Juliet McMaster and Bruce Stovel, 3–16. New York: St. Martin's Press, 1996.

Gwynn, John. *London and Westminster Improved, Illustrated by Plans.* London: Dodsley, 1766.

Habermas, Jürgen. *The Structural Transformation of the Public Sphere: An Inquiry into a Category of Bourgeois Society.* Translated by Thomas Burger. Cambridge, Mass.: MIT Press, 1989.

Haggerty, George E. "Fielding's Novel of Atonement: Confessional Form in *Amelia.*" *Eighteenth-Century Fiction* 8, no. 3 (April 1996): 383–400.

Hagstrum, Jean. *The Sister Arts: the Tradition of Literary Pictorialism and English Poetry from Dryden to Gray.* Chicago: University Press of Chicago, 1958.

Hamlyn, Hilda. "Eighteenth-Century Circulating Libraries in England." *The Library,* 5th ser., 1 (1947): 197–222.

Hammond, John H. *The Camera Obscura: A Chronicle.* Bristol, U.K.: Adam Hilger, 1981.

Hardie, Martin. *Water-colour Painting in Britain: I, The Eighteenth Century.* London: B. T. Batsford, 1966.

Harley, Mrs. M. *The Castle of Mowbray.* London: C. Stalker and H. Setchell, 1788.

Harries, Elizabeth. *The Unfinished Manner: Essays on the Fragment in the Later Eighteenth Century.* Charlottesville, Va.: Virginia University Press, 1994.

Harris, Joseph. *Treatise of Optics.* London: B. White, 1775.

Haskell, Francis, and Nicholas Penny. *Taste and the Antique.* New Haven, Conn.: Yale University Press, 1981.

Heffernan, James A. W. *The Re-Creation of Landscape: A Study of Wordsworth, Constable, and Turner.* Hanover, N.H.: University Press of New England, 1984.

Heffernan, James A. W., ed. *Space, Time, Image, Sign.* New York: Peter Lang, 1987.

Hill, Aaron. *The Art of Acting.* London: J. Osborn, 1746.

Hinde, Thomas. *Tales from the Pump Room.* London: Victor Gollancz, 1988.

Houston, R. A. *Scottish Literacy and the Scottish Identity: Illiteracy and Society in Scotland and Northern England, 1600–1800.* New York: Cambridge University Press, 1985.

Hudson, Derek, and Kenneth Luckhurst. *The Royal Society of Arts, 1754–1954.* London: Murray, 1954.

Hudson, Kenneth. *A Social History of Museums: What the Visitors Thought.* Atlantic Highlands, N.J.: Humanities Press, 1975

Hume, Robert D. "Gothic Versus Romantic: A Revaluation of the Gothic Novel." *Publications of the Modern Language Association* 84, no. 2 (March 1969): 282–90.

Hunt, John Dixon. *The Figure in the Landscape.* Baltimore: Johns Hopkins University Press, 1976.

Hunter, J. Paul. *Before Novels: The Cultural Contexts of Eighteenth-Century English Fiction.* New York: W. W. Norton, 1990.

Hutchison, Sidney C. *The History of the Royal Academy, 1768–1968.* London: Chapman and Hill, 1968.

Hyde, Ralph. *Panoramania!:The Art and Entertainment of the 'All-Embracing' View.* Introduction by Scott B. Wilcox. An exhibition at the Barbican Art Gallery, 3 November 1988–15 January 1989. London: Trefoil, 1988.

Impey, Olive, and Arthur MacGregor, eds. *The Origins of Museums: The Cabinet of Curiosities in Sixteenth and Seventeenth Century Europe.* New York: Oxford University Press, 1985.

The Improved Bath Guide. Bath, England: Wood and Cunningham, 1809.

Irigaray, Luce. *Speculum of the Other Woman.* Translated by Gillian C. Gill. Ithaca, N.Y.: Cornell University Press, 1985.

Works Cited

Isaac, Megan Lynn. "Sophia Lee and the Gothic of Female Community." *Studies in the Novel* 28, no. 2 (summer 1996): 200–18.

Ison, Walter. *The Georgian Buildings of Bath from 1700 to 1830.* London: Faber, 1948.

The Iveagh Bequest. *Pompeo Batoni and his British Patrons.* Introduction by Edgar Peters Bowron. London: Greater London Council, 1982.

Jacobsen, Susan L. " 'The Tinsel of the Times': Smollett's Argument against Conspicuous Consumption in *Humphry Clinker.*" *Eighteenth-Century Fiction* 9, no. 1 (October 1996): 71–88.

Janowitz, Anne. *England's Ruins: Poetic Purpose and the National Landscape.* Cambridge, Mass.: Basil Blackwell, 1990.

Jones, Barbara Mildred. *Follies and Grottoes.* Toronto: Longmans, Green, 1953.

Jung, Carl Gustav. *Psychological Types; or, the Psychology of Individuation.* Translated by H. Godwin Baynes. London: Routledge & Kegan Paul, 1959.

Kahane, Claire. "Gothic Mirrors and Feminine Identity." *Centennial Review* 24, no. 1 (winter 1980): 43–64.

Kalman, H. "The Architecture of Mercantilism." In *The Triumph of Culture; Eighteenth Century Perspectives,* edited by Paul Fritz and David Williams, 69–83. Toronto: A. M. Hakkert, 1972.

Kaufman, Paul. "The Community Library: A Chapter in English Social History." *Transactions of the American Philosophical Society* 57, no. 2 (1967): 3–67.

Kermode, Frank. "A Reply to Joseph Frank." *Critical Inquiry* 4, no. 3 (spring 1978):

Ketcham, Diana. *Le Désert de Retz: A Late Eighteenth-Century Folly Garden, The Artful Landscape of Monsieur de Monville.* Cambridge, Mass.: MIT Press, 1994.

Klancher, Jon. *The Making of English Reading Audiences, 1790–1832.* Madison: Wisconsin University Press, 1989.

Kraft, Elizabeth. "The Two Amelias: Henry Fielding and Elizabeth Justice." *English Literary History* 62, no. 2 (1995): 313–28.

Lacan, Jacques. *The Archaeology of Knowledge and the Discourse on Language.* Translated by A. M. Sheridan Smith. New York: Pantheon, 1972.

———. *Écrits: A Selection.* Translated by Alan Sheridan. New York: W. W. Norton, 1977.

———. *Four Fundamental Concepts of Psychoanalysis.* Edited by Jacques-Alain Miller. Translated by Alan Sheridan. New York: Norton, 1978.

Lackington, James. *Memoirs of the First Forty-five Years of the Life of James Lackington, The present Bookseller in Chiswell-street, Moorfields, London.* London: J. Lackington, 1791.

Langford, Paul. *A Polite and Commercial People: England, 1727–1783.* New York: Oxford University Press, 1989.

Laqueur, Thomas W. "The Cultural Origins of Popular Literacy in England 1500–1850." *Oxford Review of Education* 2 (1976): 255–75.

———. "Toward a Cultural Ecology of Literacy in England, 1660–1850." In *Literacy in Historical Perspective,* edited by Daniel P. Resnick, 43–57. Washington, D.C.: Library of Congress, 1983.

Lebensztejn, Jean-Claude. "In Black and White." In *Calligram: Essays in New Art History From France,* edited by Norman Bryson 131–53. New York: Cambridge University Press, 1988.

LeBrun, Charles. *A Method to Learn to Design the Passions Proposed in a Conference on their General and Particular Expression.* Introduction by Alan T. McKenzie. Los Angeles: William Andrews Clark Library, 1980.

Lee, Rensselaer. *Ut Pictura Poesis: The Humanistic Theory of Painting.* New York: W. W. Norton, 1967.

Lee, Sophia. *The Recess: A Tale of Other Times.* Vols. 1–3. Edited by Devendra P. Varma. New York: Arno Press, 1972.

Lees-Milne, James, and David Ford. *Images of Bath.* Richmond-University Presson-Thames, England: St. Helena Press, 1982.

Leland, Thomas. *Longsword, Earl of Salisbury.* London: W. Johnston, 1762.

Levey, Michael. *Rococo to Revolution: Major Trends in Eighteenth-Century Painting.* London: Thames and Hudson, 1966.

Lewis, Jayne. " 'Ev'ry Lost Relation': Historical Fictions and Sentimental Incidents in Sophia Lee's The Recess." *Eighteenth-Century Fiction* 7, no. 2 (January 1995): 166–84.

Lipking, Lawrence. *The Ordering of the Arts in Eighteenth-Century England.* Princeton, N.J.: Princeton University Press, 1970.

Lloyd, Stephen. *Richard and Maria Cosway: Regency Artists of Taste and Fashion.* Includes essays by Roy Porter and Aileen Ribeiro. Edinburgh: Scottish National Portrait Gallery, 1995.

Lockman, J. *A Sketch of Spring Gardens, Vauxhall.* London: G. Woodfall, 1750.

Lovell, Terry. *Consuming Fiction.* New York: Verso, 1987.

Lyons, John O. *The Invention of the Self: The Hinge of Consciousness in the Eighteenth Century.* Carbondale, Ill.: Southern Illinois University Press, 1978.

Macaulay, Rose. *Pleasure of Ruins.* London: Weidenfeld and Nicolson, 1953.

MacCannell, Dean. *The Tourist: A New Theory of the Leisure Class.* New York: Schocken, 1976.

Macfarlane, Alan. *The Culture of Capitalism.* New York: Blackwell, 1987.

MacGregor, Arthur, ed. *Tradescant's Rarities: Essays on the Foundation of the Ashmolean Museum, 1683.* New York: Clarendon, 1983.

Mack, Maynard. *The Garden and the City.* Toronto: University of Toronto Press, 1969.

Malton, James. *A Collection of Designs for Rural Retreats as Villas. Principally in the Gothic and Castle Styles of Architecture.* London: J. & T. Carpenter, 1802.

Manwaring, Elizabeth Wheeler. *Italian Landscape in Eighteenth Century England.* New York: Russell & Russell, 1925.

Martin, Benjamin. *A New and Compendious System of Optics.* London: James Hodges, 1740.

Masters, Brian. *Georgiana, Duchess of Devonshire.* London: Hamish Hamilton, 1981.

Mayo, Robert D. *The English Novel in the Magazines, 1740–1815.* Evanston, Ill.: Northwestern University Press, 1962.

McFarland, Thomas. *Romanticism and the Forms of Ruin: Wordsworth, Coleridge, and Modalities of Fragmentation.* Princeton, N.J.: Princeton University Press, 1981.

McKechnie, Sue. *British Silhouette Artists and their Work, 1760–1860.* Totowa, N.J.: Sotheby, Parke Bernet, 1978.

McKendrick, Neil, John Brewer, and J. H. Plumb. *The Birth of a Consumer Society: The Commercialization of Eighteenth-Century England.* Bloomington: Indiana University Press, 1982.

McKeon, Michael. *The Origins of the English Novel 1600–1740.* Baltimore: Johns Hopkins University Press, 1987.

McLynn, Frank. *Crime and Punishment in Eighteenth-Century England.* New York: Routledge, 1989.

McMaster, Juliet, and Bruce Stovel, eds. *Jane Austen's Business: Her World and Her Profession.* New York: St. Martin's Press, 1996.

Miller, D. A. *Narrative and Its Discontents: Problems of Closure in the Traditional Novel.* Princeton, N.J.: Princeton University Press, 1981.

Miller, Edward. *That Noble Cabinet: A History of the British Museum.* Athens, Ohio: Ohio University Press, 1974.

Works Cited

Mish, Charles C. "Early Eighteenth-Century Best Sellers in English Prose Fiction." *Papers of the Bibliographical Society of America* 413–18.

Mitchell, W. J. T. *Iconology: Image, Text, Sign.* Chicago: University of Chicago Press, 1988.

Monod, Paul. "Painters and Party Politics in England, 1714–1760." *Eighteenth-Century Studies* 26, no. 3 (spring 1993): 367–98.

Morris, Desmond. *Manwatching: A Field Guide to Human Behavior.* New York: Harry Abrams, 1977.

Mortier, Roland. *La poétique des ruins en France: Ses origines, ses variations de la Renaissance à Victor Hugo.* Geneva: Librairie Droz, 1974.

Mott, George, and Sally Sample Aall. *Follies and Pleasure Pavilions.* London: Pavilion (The National Trust), 1989.

Murdoch, John, Jim Murrell, and Patrick Noon. *The English Miniature.* New Haven, Conn.: Yale University Press, 1981.

Murphy, Peter. *Poetry as an Occupation and an Art in Britain, 1760–1830.* New York: Cambridge University Press, 1993.

Murray, Douglas. "Gazing and Avoiding the Gaze." In *Jane Austen's Business: Her World and Her Profession,* edited by Juliet McMaster and Bruce Stovel, 42–53. New York: St. Martin's Press, 1996.

Murrell, Jim. "The Craft of the Miniaturist." In *The English Miniature,* by John Murdoch, Jim Murrell, and Patrick Noon, chap. 1. New Haven, Conn.: Yale University Press, 1981.

The National Trust. *Follies and Pleasure Pavilions.* London: Pavilion, 1989.

Neale, R. S. *Bath 1680–1850: A Social History.* Boston: Routledge & Kegan Paul, 1981.

Neuburg, Victor E. *Chapbooks: A Guide to Reference Material on English, Scottish and American Chapbook Literature of the Eighteenth and Nineteenth Centuries.* 2d ed. London: Woburn Press, 1972.

———. *The Penny Histories: A Study of Chapbooks for Young Readers over Two Centuries.* New York: Harcourt, Brace and World, 1968.

Noon, Patrick. "Miniatures on the Market." In *The English Miniature,* by John Murdoch, Jim Murrell, and Patrick Noon, chap. 4. New Haven, Conn.: Yale University Press, 1981.

The Novelist's Magazine. Vol. 1. London: Harrison, 1781.

Ousby, Ian. *The Englishman's England: Taste, Travel, and the Rise of Tourism.* New York: Cambridge University Press, 1990.

Palmeri, Frank. "History as Monument: Gibbon's *Decline and Fall.*" *Studies in Eighteenth-Century Culture* 18 (1989): 225–45.

Parry, Graham. *The Trophies of Time: English Antiquarians of the Seventeenth Century.* New York: Oxford University Press, 1995.

Paulson, Ronald. *Book and Painting: Shakespeare, Milton, and the Bible; Literary Texts and the Emergence of English Painting.* Knoxville: Tennessee University Press, 1982.

———. *Breaking and Remaking: Aesthetic Practice in England, 1700–1820.* New Brunswick, N.J.: Rutgers University Press, 1989.

———. *Emblem and Expression: Meaning in English Art of the Eighteenth Century.* Cambridge, Mass.: Harvard University Press, 1975.

———. *Hogarth: His Life, His Art, and Times.* New Haven, Conn.: Yale University Press, 1971.

———. *Literary Landscape: Turner and Constable.* New Haven, Conn.: Yale University Press, 1982.

———. "The Pictorial Circuit and Related Structures in 18th-Century England." In *The*

Varied Pattern: Studies in the 18th Century, edited by Peter Hughes and David Williams, 165–87. Toronto: A. M. Hakkert, 1.971.
———. *Popular and Polite Art in the Age of Hogarth and Fielding.* Notre Dame, Ind.: University of Notre Dame Press, 1979.
———. *Satire and the Novel in Eighteenth-Century England.* New Haven, Conn.: Yale University Press, 1967.
Peach, R. E. M. *Bath, Old and New.* London: Simpkin, Marshall; Bath: G. Mundy, 1891.
Pears, Iain. *The Discovery of Painting: The Growth of Interest in the Arts in England, 1680–1768.* New Haven, Conn.: Yale University Press, 1988.
Penzer, N. M. "The Warwick Vase." *Apollo* 62, no. 370 (December 1955): 183–88.
Pevsner, Nikolaus. "The Architectural Setting of Jane Austen's Novels." *Journal of the Warburg and Courtauld Institutes* 32 (1968): 404–22.
Pierpont Morgan Library. *English Drawings and Watercolors, 1550–1850, in the Collection of Mr. and Mrs Paul Mellon.* New York: Harper & Row, 1972.
Piggott, Stuart. *Ruins in a Landscape: Essays in Antiquarianism.* Edinburgh: Edinburgh University Press, 1976.
Plumb, J. H. *The Pursuit of Happiness: A View of Life in Georgian England.* New Haven, Conn.: Yale Center for British Art, 1977.
Pointon, Marcia. *Hanging the Head: Portraiture and Social Formation in Eighteenth-Century England.* New Haven, Conn.: Yale University Press, 1993.
———. "Portrait-Painting as a Business Enterprise in London in the 1780s." *Art History* 7, no. 2 (June 1984): 187–205.
Poole, Steve. "Radicalism, Loyalism and the 'Reign of Terror' in Bath, 1792–1804." *Bath History* 3 (1990): 114–37.
Porter, Roy. *English Society in the Eighteenth Century.* New York: Penguin, 1990.
Price, Martin. "The Picturesque Moment." In *From Sensibility to Romanticism,* edited by Frederick W. Hilles and Harold Bloom, 259–92. New York: Oxford University Press, 1965.
Priestley, Joseph. *History and Present State of Discoveries Relating to Vision, Light and Colours.* London: J. Johnson, 1772.
Rahv, Philip. *Literature and the Sixth Sense.* Boston: Houghton Miflin, 1969.
Raven, James. *Judging New Wealth: Popular Publishing and Responses to Commerce in England 1750–1800.* New York: Clarendon, 1992.
Reid, B. L. "Smollett's Healing Journey." *Virginia Quarterly Review* 41 (1965): 549–70.
Reitlinger, Gerald. *The Economics of Taste, Volume 2: The Rise and Fall of Objets d'Art Prices Since 1750.* London: Barrie and Rockliff, 1963.
Reynolds, Graham. Introduction to *English Drawings and Watercolors, 1550–1850, in the Collection of Mr. and Mrs. Paul Mellon,* edited by Pierpont Morgan Library, xi–xvi. New York: Harper & Row, 1972.
———. *English Portrait Miniatures.* 1953. Rev. ed., New York: Cambridge University Press, 1988.
Reynolds, Sir Joshua. *Discourses. The Works of Sir Joshua Reynolds.* Vol. 2. London: Cadell and Davies, 1797.
Ricchetti, John. "The Public Sphere in the Eighteenth-Century Novel: Social Criticism and Narrative Enactment." *Eighteenth-Century Life* 16 (November 1992): 114–29.
Rigby, Douglas, and Elizabeth Rigby. *Lock, Stock and Barrel: The Story of Collecting.* New York: Lippincott, 1944.
Rivers, Isobel, ed. *Books and their Readers in Eighteenth-Century England.* New York: St. Martin's Press, 1982.

Works Cited

Roberts, Bette B. "Sophia Lee's *The Recess* (1785): The Ambivalence of Female Gothicism." *Massachusetts Studies in English* 6, nos. 3 & 4 (1979): 166–84.

Rogers, Katharine M. *Frances Burney: The World of Female Difficulties.* Hemel Hempstead: Harvester Wheatsheaf, 1990.

Rogers, Pat. "Classics and Chapbooks." In *Books and Their Readers in Eighteenth-Century England,* edited by Isobel Rivers, 27–46. New York: St. Martin's Press, 1982.

Rogerson, Brewster. "The Art of Painting the Passions." *Journal of the History of Ideas* 14 (1953): 68–94.

Rose, Mark. *Authors and Owners: The Invention of Copyright.* Cambridge, Mass.: Harvard University Press, 1993.

Rosenblum, Robert. *Transformations in Late Eighteenth Century Art.* Princeton, N.J.: Princeton University Press, 1967.

Rothstein, Eric. " 'Ideal Presence' and the 'Non Finito' in Eighteenth-Century Aesthetics." *Eighteenth-Century Studies* 9, no. 3 (spring 1976): 307–32.

———. *Systems of Order and Inquiry in Later Eighteenth-Century Fiction.* Berkeley: California University Press, 1975.

Rousseau, G. S. "Smollett and the Picaresque: Some Questions about a Label." *Studies in Burke and His Time* 12 (1970–1971):

Sacks, Sheldon. *Fiction and the Shape of Belief.* Berkeley: California University Press, 1964.

Sandby, Paul. *Twelve Views in Aquatinta from drawings taken on the spot in South Wales.* London: P. Sandby, 1775.

Sanderson, Michael. "Literacy and Social Mobility in the Industrial Revolution in England." *Past and Present* 56 (1972): 75–104.

Scheuermann, Mona. "Man Not Providence: Fielding's *Amelia* as a Novel of Social Criticism." *Forum for Modern Language Studies* 20 (1984): 106–23.

Schofield, R. S. "Dimensions of Illiteracy, 1750–1850." *Explorations in Economic History* 10 (1973): 437–54.

Schofield, R. S., and E. A. Wrigley. *The Population History of England, 1541–1871: A Reconstruction.* Cambridge, Mass.: Harvard University Press, 1981.

Schor, Naomi. *Reading in Detail: Aesthetics and the Feminine.* New York: Methuen, 1987.

Schwarzschild, Edward. "I Will Take the Whole upon My Own Shoulders: Collections and Corporeality in *Humphry Clinker*." *Criticism* 36 (fall 1994): 541–68.

Sedgwick, Eve K. *The Coherence of Gothic Conventions.* New York: Methuen, 1986.

Sekora, John. *Luxury: The Concept in Western Thought.* Baltimore: Johns Hopkins University Press, 1977.

Sena, John. "Smollett's Matthew Bramble and the Tradition of the Physician-Satirist." *Papers on Language and Literature* 11 (1975): 380–96.

Serres, Michel. "Turner Translates Carnot." In *Calligram: Essays in New Art History From France,* edited by Norman Bryson, 154–64. New York: Cambridge University Press, 1988.

Shaffer, Julie. "Non-Canonical Women's Novels of the Romantic Era: Romantic Ideologies and the Problematics of Gender and Genre." *Studies in the Novel* 28, no. 4 (winter 1996): 469–92.

Shapiro, Michael S. "The Public and the Museum." In *The Museum: A Reference Guide,* edited by M. S. Shapiro. New York: Greenwood, 1990.

Shelley, Mary. *Frankenstein; or, the Modern Prometheus.* Afterword by Harold Bloom. New York: Signet, 1965.

Siddons, Henry. *William Wallace, or the Highland Hero.* London: G. & T. Wilkie, 1791.

Smallwood, Angela. *Fielding and the Woman Question.* New York: St. Martin's Press, 1989.

Smart, Alastair. "Dramatic Gesture and Expression in the Age of Hogarth and Reynolds." *Apollo* 82 (1965): 90–97.

Smith, Adam. *Essays on Philosophical Subjects. The Glasgow Edition of the Works and Correspondence of Adam Smith.* Vol. 3. Edited by W. P. D. Wightman and J. C. Bryce. New York: Oxford University Press, 1980.

Smith, Robert. *Compleat System of Optics.* 1738.

Smollett, Tobias. *The Expedition of Humphry Clinker.* New York: Penguin, 1978.

Snow, Edward. "Theorizing the Male Gaze: Some Problems." *Representations* 25 (winter 1987): 30–41.

Solkin, David H. *Painting for Money: The Visual Arts and the Public Sphere in Eighteenth-Century England.* New Haven, Conn.: Yale University Press, 1993.

Spacks, Patricia Meyer. *Imagining a Self: Autobiography and the Novel in Eighteenth-Century England.* Cambridge, Mass.: Harvard University Press, 1976.

Spencer, Jane. *The Rise of the Woman Novelist: From Aphra Behn to Jane Austen.* Oxford: Blackwell, 1986.

Spufford, Margaret. *Small Books and Pleasant Histories: Popular Fiction and Its Readership in Seventeenth-Century England.* Athens, Ga.: Georgia University Press, 1981.

Starobinski, Jean. *The Invention of Liberty, 1700–1789.* New York: Rizzoli, 1987.

Staves, Susan. "*Evelina,* or Female Difficulties." *Modern Philology* 73 (May 1976): 368–81.

Stuart, James, and Nicholas Revett. *The Antiquities of Athens.* 5 vols. London: J. Haberkorn, 1762–1800.

Stewart, Susan. *On Longing: Narratives of the Miniature, the Gigantic, the Souvenir, the Collection.* Baltimore: Johns Hopkins University Press, 1984.

Stone, Lawrence. "Literacy and Education in England 1640–1900." *Past and Present* 62 (1969): 69–139.

Stone, Lawrence, and Jeanne C. Fawtier Stone. *An Open Elite? England 1540–1880.* New York: Oxford University Press, 1984.

Stout, Janis P. "Jane Austen's Proposal Scenes and the Limitations of Language." *Studies in the Novel* 14, no. 3 (fall 1982): 316–26.

Straub, Kristina. *Divided Fictions: Fanny Burney and the Feminine Strategy.* Athens, Ga.: Georgia University Press, 1987.

Stukeley, William. *Itinerarium Curiosum.* London: W. Stukeley, 1724.

Summers, Montague. *The Gothic Quest: A History of the Gothic Novel.* New York: Russell & Russell, 1964.

Summerson, Sir John Newenham. *Heavenly Mansions, and Other Essays on Architecture.* New York: Norton, 1963.

———. "John Wood and the English Town-Planning Tradition." In *Heavenly Mansions, and Other Essays on Architecture,* edited by Sir John Newenham Summerson, 87–110. New York: Norton, 1963.

———. "Sir John Soane and the Furniture of Death." *Art Review* 163 (March 1978): 147–55.

Talley Jr., M. Kirby. " 'All Good Pictures Crack': Sir Joshua Reynolds' Practice and Studio." In *Reynolds,* edited by Nicholas Penny, 55–70. New York: Harry Abrams, 1986.

Taylor, Basil. *Constable: Paintings, Drawings and Watercolours.* New York: Phaidon, 1973.

Taylor, Richard C. "James Harrison, *The Novelist's Magazine,* and the Early Canonizing of the English Novel." *Studies in English Literature 1500–1900* 33, no. 3 (summer 1993): 629–43.

Thompson, E. P. "Eighteenth-Century English Society: Class Struggle without Class?" *Social History* 3, no. 2 (May 1978): 133–65.

Works Cited

Thompson, John B. *Ideology and Modern Culture: Critical Social Theory in the Era of Mass Communication.* Stanford, Calif.: Stanford University Press, 1990.

Tinniswood, Adrian. *A History of Country House Visiting: Five Centuries of Tourism and Taste.* London: Blackwell and The National Trust, 1989.

Tompkins, J. M. S. Foreword to *The Recess,* by Sophia Lee, edited by Devendra P. Varma, 1: i–v. New York: Arno Press, 1972.

———. *The Popular Novel in England 1770–1800.* Lincoln, Neb.: University of Nebraska Press, 1962.

Tristram, Philippa. *Living Space in Fact and Fiction.* New York: Routledge & Kegan Paul, 1989.

Turner, Ernest S. *Taking the Cure.* London: Michael Joseph, 1967.

Varma, Devendra P. Introduction to *The Recess,* by Sophia Lee, 1: vii–xlviii. New York: Arno Press, 1972.

von Boehn, Max. *Miniatures and Silhouettes.* Translated by E. K. Walker. New York: Benjamin Blom, 1928.

Waterhouse, Ellis. *Painting in Britain 1530 to 1790.* The Pelican History of Art. 2d ed. New York: Penguin, 1962.

Watkin, David. *The English Vision: The Picturesque in Architecture, Landscape, and Garden Design.* New York: Harper & Row, 1982.

Watt, Ian. *The Rise of the Novel: Studies in Defoe, Richardson, and Fielding.* Berkeley: California University Press, 1957.

Watts, William. *Select Views of the Principal Buildings and Other Interesting and Picturesque Objects in the Cities of Bath and Bristol.* London: W. Watts, 1794.

Weinbrot, Howard D. *Augustus Caesar in "Augustan" England: The Decline of a Classical Norm.* Princeton, N.J.: Princeton University Press, 1978.

Weinbrot, Howard. *Britannia's Issue: The Rise of British Literature from Dryden to Ossian.* New York: Cambridge University Press, 1993.

Wendorf, Richard. *The Elements of Life: Biography and Portrait Painting in Stuart and Georgian England.* Oxford: Clarendon, 1990.

West, Shearer. "Patronage and Power: The Role of the Portrait in Eighteenth-Century England." In *Culture, Politics and Society in Britain, 1660–1800,* edited by Jeremy Black and Jeremy Gregory. New York: Manchester University Press, 1991.

West, William A. "Matt Bramble's Journey to Health." *Texas Studies in Literature and Language* 11 (1969): 1197–1208.

Wiebenson, Dora. "Documents of Social Change: Publications about the Small House." In *Studies in Eighteenth-Century British Art and Aesthetics,* edited by Ralph Cohen, 82–127. Berkeley: California University Press, 1985.

Wiles, Roy McKeen. "The Relish for Reading in Provincial England Two Centuries Ago." In *The Widening Circle: Essays on the Circulation of Literature in Eighteenth-Century Europe,* edited by Paul J. Korshin. Philadelphia: Pennsylvania University Press, 1976.

Wilkinson, Robert. *Londina Illustrata.* 2 vols. London: Wilkinson, 1819.

William of Normandy, An Historical Novel. London: 1787.

Williams, Anne Patricia. "Description and Tableau in the Eighteenth-Century British Sentimental Novel." *Eighteenth- Century Fiction* 8, no. 4 (July 1996): 465–84.

Williamson, George C. *Richard Cosway.* London: George Bell and Sons, 1897.

Williamson, George C., and Henry L. D. Engleheart. *George Engleheart 1750–1829, Miniature Painter to George III.* London: George Bell, 1902.

Wright, Patrick. *On Living in an Old Country: The National Past in Contemporary Britain.* London: Verso, 1985.

Wroth, Warwick. *The London Pleasure Gardens of the Eighteenth Century.* New York: MacMillan, 1896.

Zaniello, Thomas. "Services for the Dead and the Divided Victorian Church." Interdisciplinary Conference on Nineteenth-Century Studies, University of California, Berkeley, April 4–5, 1997.

Zomchick, John. *Family and the Law in Eighteenth-Century Fiction: The Public Conscience in the Private Sphere,* 130–53. New York: Cambridge University Press, 1993.

Index

Page numbers referring to illustrations are in italics

Altick, Richard, 29, 31, 44, 45
Amelia (Fielding), 142, 157–73; allusions to Greek and Latin texts, 158–59, 205 n. 41; circle of expression in, 167–69; doubling in, 165–66; modes of male behavior in, 162–67; tableaux in, 159, 163, 169–71
Antiquarianism, 101, 103–5. *See also* Dilettanti, Society of
Architecture, 77. *See also* Bath: crescents, King's Circus; Panopticon
Art exhibitions, 42–43
Austen, Jane. See *Persuasion*

Bakhtin, Mikhail, 18
Barker, Robert. *See* Panorama
Bath: Assembly Rooms, 71–72, 84, *86*, 194 n. 47; crescents, 73–76; in *Humphry Clinker,* 69–70; King's Circus, 72–73; social topography, 82–84; treatment of beggars, 192 n. 15
Batoni, Pompeo, 147–48, *149, 150*
Baudrillard, Jean, 138
Bender, John, 66, 178
Benjamin, Walter, 156

Bentham, Jeremy. *See* Panopticon
Berger, John, 144
Blot art. *See* Cozens, Alexander
Borsay, Peter, 76
Bourdieu, Pierre, 14–15
British museum. *See* Museums
Burney, Frances (Mme. d'Arblay). See *Evelina*

Camera obscura, 40–41
Catholicism, 100, 123–26, 199 n. 72. *See also* Ruins
Cavendish, Georgiana (Duchess of Devonshire), 151, *152, 153*
Circulation, 20, 21, 24, 69, 80–81; and decentralization of power, 89–90, 91; and increasing literacy, 28–39; and social instability, 23–24, 27–28; and visual arts, 36–45
Claude glasses, 41
Constable, John. See *Hadleigh Castle*
Conway, Alison, 172
Copley, John Singleton, 48–49
Copyright Act, 29
Cosway, Richard, 146, 148, 151, *152, 153;* and classicism, 203–4 n. 28

INDEX

Cox's museum. *See* Museums
Cozens, Alexander, 39–40
Cruikshank, Isaac, 57

Davidoff, Leonore, 26
Désert de Retz, 114
Dilettanti, Society of, 105
Don Saltero's coffeehouse. *See* Museums

Eidophusikon. *See* Loutherbourg, Philippe de
Engleheart, George, 146, 154
Engravers Act, 43
Erotic space, 22, 141–42, 173; and narcissism, 142, 151–52
Evelina (Burney), 49–51, 53, 58, 63–64
exoticism: foregn visitors in England, 62–63; oriental taste, 63

Fielding, Henry. See *Amelia*
Flint, Christopher, 109
Follies. *See* Ruins
Foucault, Michel, 15–16, 18, 25, 178
Frankenstein (Shelley), 143–44
Freud, Sigmund, 96–97
Fried, Michael, 117–18

Galard, Jean, 97–98, 121
Gandy, Joseph, 115–16
George, M. Dorothy, 45
Gibbon, Edward, 111
Gillray, James, 44–45, 47
Gilpin, William, 37, 38, 109, 113–15
Goffman, Erving, 20–21, 50, 175
Goldstein, Laurence, 98–99
Gordon Riots, 24, 124
Greenblatt, Stephen, 175

Habermas, Jürgen, 33, 34
Hadleigh Castle (Constable), 118, *119*
Haggerty, George, 205 n. 48
Hall, Catherine, 26
Harries, Elizabeth, 98
Hayman, Francis, 56
Hill, Aaron, 169
Historical space, 21, 95; and genealogy, 96, 131–33; and *The Recess*, 130–31, 139
History, attitudes toward: didacticism, 113; fatalism, 136; regime of change, 108, 115–16; regime of tradition, 108–15

Hogarth, William, 42, 43–44, 56–57, 109, 169, *170*, 198 n. 55
Humphry Clinker (Smollett), 67–70, 76, 77–78, 80–81, 92; and disease, 191 n. 6
Hunter, J. Paul, 28

Iconoclasm, 122–23, 199 n. 66
Identity. *See* Self

Jacobsen, Susan, 191 n. 7
Janowitz, Anne, 99–100
Jones, Barbara, 102

Kahane, Claire, 134
Kames, Lord, 110, 138
Klancher, John, 43–45, 80
Kraft, Elizabeth, 206 n. 57

Lacan, Jacques, 14, 19, 66, 100
Lackington, James, 29, 184 n. 32
Lee, Sophia. See *The Recess*
Leverian museum. *See* Museums
Licensing Act, 30
Lipking, Lawrence, 95
Literacy. *See* Circulation
Loutherbourg, Philippe de, 46, 48–49
Lyons, John, 38

Macaulay, Rose, 97
McFarland, Thomas, 99
McKeon, Michael, 23
Magazines, 30–31, 33–35
Mayon, Robert, 33, 35
Miller, Sanderson, 101–2
Miniaturization, 147. *See also Amelia;* Portrait miniatures
Mortier, Roland, 98
Mourning, 96–97, 110, 111
Museums: British Museum, 61; Cox's museum, 59–60; Don Saltero's coffeehouse, 60; Leverian museum, 61–62

Nash, Richard "Beau," 71–72
Nudes, 144, 202 n. 8

Oil painting, 37; history painting, 107; portraiture, 144–46. *See also* Shows

Panopticon, 79–80
Panoramas, 48. *See also* Shows

222

Index

Pantheon, 52–53, 188 n. 117
Pars, William, 104, *105*
Paulson, Ronald, 123, 167
Persuasion (Austen), 81–83; and decentralized authority, 89–90, 91; and erotic space, 142; and social instability or decline, 90–91
Picaresque, 67
Pictorial circuits, 193 n. 37
Picturesque, 37–38, 107, 115, 116; in *The Recess,* 129
Piranesi, Giovanni Battista, 104, 111
Portrait miniatures, 142; affordability of, 145–46; in *Amelia,* 161–62, 172; anonymization of sitters, 153; eye miniatures, 154; in *Frankenstein,* 143–44, 154–55; as jewelry, 146–47, 154–55; and mimetic standards, 145; in *The Recess,* 202 n. 2; and stylization, 148; as talisman, 152, 161;
Practice, 15–16
Price, Martin, 108
Prints, 43–45
Psychosocial space, 13–14, 176–78

Ranelagh, 51–52, 76–80 (*77*)
The Recess (Lee), 113, 126–37; and genealogy, 131–33; and the Gothic, 133–34, 201 n. 81; mother figures in, 201 n. 83; ruins in, 128, 129
Reduction. *See* Miniaturization
Reynolds, Sir Joshua, 44, 107, 109, 146
Robert, Hubert, 104, 115, *117*
Rooker, Michael, 118–19, *120*
Rosenblum, Robert, 113
Roslin Castle, 39, 41
Rothstein, Eric, 171
Rowlandson, Thomas, 37, 44
Ruins: and antiquarianism, 101; and Catholicism, 123–26; classic, 103–7; as cultural figures, 97–100, 122, 137–39; and love, 121–22, 129; pastoralism and domestication of, 118–19; and secrecy, 128; shams or follies, 101–3

Sandby, Paul, 37, *39,* 41, 44
Schor, Naomi, 109
Self: as construction, 19, 20, 175–76; as discriminator, 33, 58–59, 64; and the gaze, 19; and literacy, 32–33; and psychosocial space, 13–14; and traditional rank, 64, 66. *See also* Theatricality
Shelley, Mary. *See Frankenstein*
Shows, 45–49; country house touring, 62; Eidophusikon, 46–49; event painting, 48–49; magic lanterns, 46; panoramas, 48. *See also* Exoticism; Art exhibitions
Shop displays, 187 n. 98
Silhouettes, 146
Sister arts, 16–18
Smith, Adam, 145
Smith, John "Warwick," 104
Smollett, Tobias, 70. *See also Humphry Clinker*
Soane, Sir John, 198 n. 57
Social space, 65, 82–84, 92. *See also* Circulation
Specularity, 65, 70, 78, 87
Sterne, Laurence. *See Tristram Shandy*
Stewart, Susan, 148
Stone, Lawrence, 26, 27
Stone, Jeanne C. Fawtier, 26, 27
Subject. *See* Self

Theatricality, 20–21, 34, 77, 169–71; in *Evelina,* 50, 55, 56; and sham ruins, 102–3
Thompson, E. P., 52, 179 n.4
Tompkins, J. M. S., 133
Towne, Francis, 104, *106*
Towneley, Charles, 105
Tristram Shandy (Sterne), 177

Varma, Devendra, 133
Vauxhall, 53–57 (*55*)

Walmsley, Thomas, 120–*21*
Walpole, Horace, 53, 79
Warwick Vase, 110–11, *112*
Water colors, 44
Wendorf, Richard, 145, 204 n. 29
West, Benjamin, 48, 49, 107
Williamson, George, 151
Wood, John (the elder), 73, 75
Wood, John (the younger), 75, 191 n. 9
Wright, Joseph, 167, *168*

223